Microsoft® Works for Educators on the IBM® PC and Compatibles

Microsoft® Works for Educators on the IBM® PC and Compatibles

John F. Beaver

State University of New York College at Buffalo

Brooks/Cole Publishing Company
Pacific Grove, California

Brooks/Cole Publishing Company
A Division of Wadsworth, Inc.

Printed in the United States of America

10 9 8 7 6 5 4 3 2 1

Library of Congress Cataloging-in-Publication Data

Beaver. John F.
    Microsoft Works for educators on the IBM PC and compatibles / John
F. Beaver.
        p.   cm.
    Includes index.
    ISBN 0-534-16356-4
    1. Education—United States—Data processing. 2. Microsoft Works
(Computer program) 3. Computer-assisted instruction—United States.
I. Title.
LB1028.43.B42   1991
370'.285—dc20   91-32926
                                                          CIP

Trademarks
Apple and **Macintosh** are registered trademarks of Apple Computer, Inc. **CompuServe** is a registered trademark of CompuServe, Inc. **DIALOG** is the Servicemark of Dialog Information Services. **HyperCard** is a registered trademark of Apple Computer, Inc., licensed to Claris Corporation. **HyperStudio** is a registered trademark of Roger Wagner Publishing, Inc. **IBM PC** and **LinkWay** are registered trademarks of International Business Machines Corporation. **In the Holy Lands** is a trademark of Optical Data Corporation. **Microsoft** is a registered trademark of Microsoft Corporation. **Prodigy** is a registered trademark of Prodigy Services Company. All other product names are trademarks or registered trademarks of their respective companies.

Sponsoring Editor: *Michael J. Sugarman*
Editorial Assistants: *Lainie Giuliano* and *Carol Ann Benedict*
Production Coordinator: *Marlene Thom*
Production: *Scratchgravel Publishing Services*
Manuscript Editor: *Lisa Sanders*
Permissions Editor: *Carline Haga*
Interior and Cover Design: *Katherine Minerva*
Photo Editor: *Ruth Minerva*
Typesetting: *Scratchgravel Publishing Services*
Printing and Binding: *R.R. Donnelley & Sons Company*

Preface

This book is written to help educators master the use of computers in enhancing their professional and personal productivity. It is also specifically designed to help *education* majors develop competence in the instructional use of technology. *Microsoft® Works for Educators* differs from other texts in its focus on computer applications that relate directly to the needs of teachers and administrators.

Intended for use in an introductory course in educational computing, the text contains practical exercises that also allow it to serve as a self-paced, independent study guide. Detailed instructions throughout the book will guide even novice computer users through the steps required to produce educationally appropriate products. At the same time, easy-to-follow directions allow students to master the applications independently, thus leaving valuable class time for the important task of reinforcing conceptual understanding. In addition, students can proceed at rates appropriate to their own technological backgrounds.

The organization of the book is the result of insights developed during a decade of introducing educators to instructional technology, as a classroom teacher, a computer coordinator, and a college of education faculty member. Chapters in the text discuss how to use the major components of Microsoft® Works—word processing, database managing, spreadsheet manipulating, charting, communicating, and data integrating—to complete tasks that are relevant to educational practitioners.

Each chapter begins with a simple scenario portraying the use of one component of Microsoft Works in an educational setting to motivate the reader to explore the application. This section is followed by an explanation of important terminology and the presentation of a conceptual framework for understanding the application.

The major portion of each chapter consists of hands-on activities designed to develop mastery of the application once students are motivated to learn and adequately oriented. Each chapter concludes with suggestions for integrating the use of the application into classroom instruction. These activities can be modified for use in educational settings ranging from elementary to college classrooms.

Acknowledgments

This project could never have been completed without the support and assistance of a number of individuals. I first wish to acknowledge the help provided by my editor, Dr. Nancy Deal. Her suggestions and revisions helped me improve the text tremendously. In addition, I want to thank the many graduate students at SUNY College at Buffalo who worked through the exercises in the hands-on sections and provided suggestions for clarifying and simplifying the instructions.

The comments and suggestions of the following reviewers were useful in helping me develop the manuscript: Louis H. Berry, University of Pittsburgh; Les Blackwell, Western Washington University; Phyllis Broughton, East Carolina University; Bill Corbin, Vanderbilt University; Joseph Frasca, Sonoma State University; Gail Grejda, Clarion University; Peggy Kelly, California Technology Project; Gaylen Kelley, Boston University; Stephen Weissmann, Plymouth State College; and James A. White, University of South Florida. In addition, a special note of thanks is due to Margaret Niess, of Oregon State University, who class-tested a version of the manuscript.

John F. Beaver

Contents

6   Focusing on Database Managers   89

9   Focusing on Charting   175

10   Focusing on Spreadsheets, Charts, and Word Processing— A Second Look at Data Integration   201

Introduction

Why Should Educators Learn to Use Computers?

Microcomputer systems have permeated business environments and are becoming increasingly common in homes. Our schools, where technological change often comes slowly, have also witnessed a substantial influx of microcomputers—in administrators' offices, computer laboratories, and individual classrooms. Business people will readily adopt computers or any other technological advancement that is likely to give them an efficiency advantage over their competitors. Schools, on the other hand, are not yet uniformly equipped to embrace technological change.

Aside from the fact that computer use is a "hot" educational topic, what incentive is there for educators to spend the time necessary to master the machine? Educators, like other professionals, are very busy performing the tasks associated with their jobs. Many people feel their professional lives are already so filled that they have no time to accept another commitment, such as becoming a competent computer user. Nonetheless, educators who have become computer competent marvel that they ever performed efficiently without them.

Computers can help you improve your productivity and increase both the quality and quantity of your work. Your standard for acceptable work will increase along with the scope of the projects you will undertake. Rough, handwritten notices will be replaced by polished, word-processed signs that include illustrations. Your manual information management system will be replaced by a powerful and flexible electronic database. Your time-consuming grading, budget, and inventory systems will be replaced by an electronic spreadsheet that will remove the calculation drudgery from these necessary chores. And, in addition to improving the quality of your professional products, you will spend less time completing them than before you began using a computer!

As educators, we can help lead the changes developing in our schools and our society by understanding new technologies and assuming leadership roles in

Many educators are using computers to handle their professional tasks and to enrich their students' learning experiences. *(Courtesy of International Business Machines Corporation)*

shaping and guiding this revolution. By learning to use computers to enhance productivity in the many professional tasks they are called on to perform, educators can take the first important step toward understanding and mastering these new technologies. They can then enhance their students' learning experiences by using computers instructionally in classroom activities that fit within the existing curriculum. After seeing their successes, their colleagues will come to them with questions about how to use computers.

In the long term, by broadening and deepening your understanding of technology, you will be helping yourself prepare for a future that is certain to rely on extensive use of technology. The mission of this text is to help educators, like you, establish the technology-enriched classrooms of tomorrow.

Why Use This Text to Learn about Computers?

Some individuals try to master computers or a particular software package with their own trial-and-error method or with only the reference materials that ac-

Computers are widely used in business and industry to enhance productivity. *(Courtesy of International Business Machines Corporation)*

company the software. If you are already experienced with computers, these approaches are likely to succeed. For new or inexperienced users, though, a text like this one can alleviate confusions and establish a framework for understanding the computer's capabilities. In addition, a text can provide the external motivation some individuals need to "take the plunge" and master the powers of computer technology.

This text is written specifically to address the needs and interests of educators. It explores the role of computers in education, not business or science. Using Microsoft® Works, the exercises in the text will help educators master the productivity powers available from a computer. In addition, each chapter includes suggestions for integrating the computer capabilities into instructional situations.

Computer novices will find that the simple, straightforward explanations and exercises will help them quickly master the computer's powers. More experienced users will discover that the discussions and examples will increase their mastery and deepen their understanding of the different educational applications available.

1   Components of the Computer System

The microcomputer you will use with this text is more accurately labeled a **computer system**. Computer systems are made up of physical components—keyboards, monitors, and disk drives—connected together so that they operate as one unit (Figure 1.1). These physical devices are referred to as computer **hardware**. **Software** is the set of instructions that tells the computer what to do. Computer programmers create sets of instructions, called **programs,** to control the computer's operations. Most people using computers use these programs. Widely used computer programs include word processors, database managers, and electronic spreadsheets. The following sections provide a more thorough description of the elements in a computer system.

Hardware

Generally speaking, hardware refers to the computer equipment itself:

- monitor
- printer

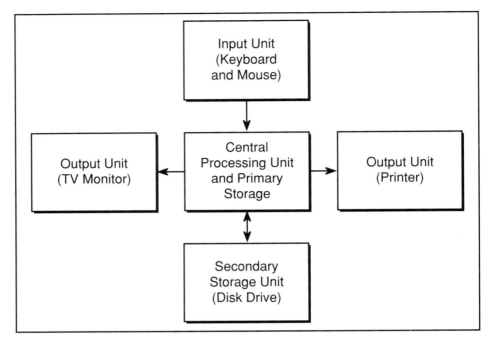

Figure 1.1 Components of a computer system

- plotter
- keyboard
- disk drive
- mouse
- joystick
- graphics tablet
- modem
- memory and processing chips

Computer hardware can be further categorized according to its function—either input, processing, output, or storage. **Input** devices accept information into the computer system from the user or another source. Common input devices include the keyboard, mouse, joystick, graphics tablet, disk drive, and modem. **Output** devices send information from the computer system to a user or another device. Common output devices include the monitor, printer, speaker, plotter, disk drive, and modem. Note that the last devices—disk drive and modem—occurred on both lists. Both are input and output devices; that is, they are capable of both sending information out from and accepting information into a computer.

All the silicon chips that process and control the information flow are inside the main computer system housing. These chips store data internally for use by the system. The single most important chip in the computer is known as the

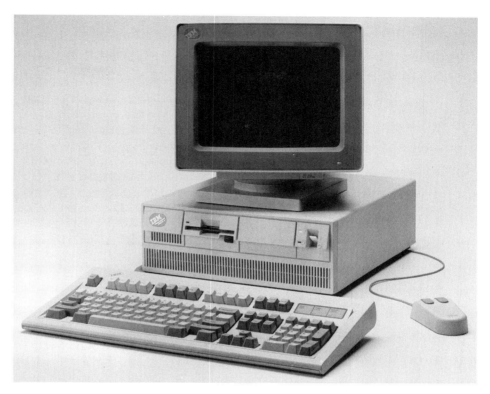

An IBM PS/2 Model 30 computer with a mouse attached. *(Courtesy of International Business Machines Corporation)*

central processing unit, or **CPU**. The CPU is often called the "brain of the computer" because it is responsible for managing the computer system. The CPU controls the flow of information between the input and output devices and stores data in the computer's primary memory.

Input Devices

Computer users must have devices connected to their machines that allow them to enter information into the system. These devices are called **input devices** because they permit users to "input" data into the computer system. Common input devices include:

- keyboard
- mouse
- joystick
- graphics tablet
- disk drive
- modem

Although all these devices are input devices, each serves a different function. The most widely used input device is the keyboard. Another common input device is the mouse. A mouse is a small device—roughly the size of a pack of playing cards—with a roller ball on its bottom. The user controls the location of the cursor (an electronic point of light on the computer screen that indicates the current position in a document) by sliding the mouse around on the desktop. Buttons on the mouse are used to activate commands.

Two somewhat less common input devices are the joystick and the graphics tablet. A joystick is a hand-operated device with a lever that permits left–right or up–down movement of the cursor on the screen. Joysticks are primarily used for computer games. A graphics tablet is an input device used for drawing or creating computer graphics. Graphics tablets, which are generally the size of a textbook, usually include a stylus for drawing on the tablet's surface. Whatever is drawn on the tablet is also displayed on the monitor and is available for manipulating by computer commands.

The last two input devices in the list function as both input and output devices. The first of these input/output devices, the disk drive, is very important to all microcomputer users. The disk drive reads the programs (such as Microsoft® Works) that you will copy into your computer system. Disk drives can hold either "floppy" or hard disks. Since disk drives are so important, they will be discussed in greater detail in the **Secondary Storage** section of this chapter. Finally, the modem is also both an input and an output device. Modems connect computers to telephone lines so that users can interact with other computers in distant locations. Modems will be discussed thoroughly in Chapter 12.

Processing and Computer Memory

Once data are entered into the computer, they are transformed, or processed, into usable information. For example, test scores can be input as data and then manipulated to formulate a class curve. The CPU is the series of electronic circuits that process the data into organized information. In addition to the CPU, many other silicon chips serve vital roles in the computer's operation. All the instructions the computer uses must be stored where they can be accessed by the CPU. These instructions are stored internally in memory chips of two distinct types—**ROM** and **RAM**—commonly referred to as **primary memory.**

ROM is an abbreviation for **Read Only Memory**. ROM chips hold permanent instructions placed there by the manufacturer when the machine was built. These chips execute such basic operations as recognizing which keystroke represents which character and displaying that information on the monitor for the user. Regardless of the computer program you are using, the information held in the ROM chips remains the same; it can only be "read" or accessed by the computer or user, but not "written on" or changed. The instructions in the ROM chips stay the same every time you turn the computer on and off.

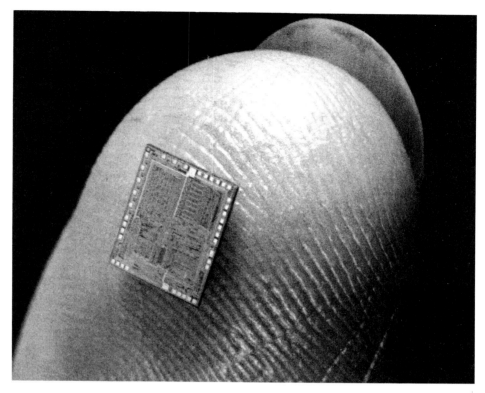

A computer chip shown on a fingertip to illustrate its tiny size. *(Brooks/Cole)*

On the other hand, **RAM** chips hold information only temporarily. RAM stands for **Random Access Memory**. The random-access capability means that information can be retrieved in any sequence, not simply the order in which it has been stored (or entered) in the computer. This capability is different from the "serial access" that characterizes audiocassette or videotape players. A tape player works in a sequential series; when you want to view the middle part of a videotape, you must first advance through the first half of the tape. To reach the middle of the tape without having to view the first half, your only alternative is to play the tape at fast-forward speed. By contrast, the random-access capability of a computer's memory allows you to instantly retrieve information from any part of RAM (the computer's temporary memory).

Unlike ROM, information stored in RAM is dynamic, modifying with each change the user makes. Another name for RAM is **Read/Write** memory because the RAM chips can store information that can be read or accessed as well as written on or changed. Information remains in the RAM chips only as long as the computer is left on. When the system is turned off, the information stored in RAM is lost unless you have already saved it on a more permanent medium, such as a hard disk or floppy disk.

■ Measuring Computer Memory

The amount of memory a computer can hold indicates its storage capacity and, in large measure, determines its power. (The speed with which it can process instructions is the other major factor determining power.) Memory is measured in terms of storage capacity—the number of characters that a computer can hold in RAM at one time. You'll need to learn several terms associated with memory capacity.

The computer's memory is based on the binary or base two system. The binary system contains only two digits, 0 and 1, which correspond to the only two states that a computer knows: on or off. Combinations of 0s and 1s—or on and off electronic signals—make up the computer's memory. By contrast, our standard number system, the decimal or base ten system, uses ten digits—0, 1, 2, 3, 4, 5, 6, 7, 8, and 9. The simple table below illustrates the difference between the two systems.

Decimal System (base 10)	Binary System (base 2)
0	0_2
1	1_2
2	10_2
3	11_2
4	100_2
5	101_2
6	110_2
7	111_2
8	1000_2
9	1001_2
10	1010_2
11	1011_2
12	1100_2
•	•
•	•
100	1100100_2
101	1100101_2
102	1100110_2
103	1100111_2
104	1101000_2

A **bit**—short for a **bi**nary digit—is either a 0 or a 1. Computers use bits to process information. Internally, a computer represents everything—command, character, numeral—as either a 0 (electronically, the switch is off) or a 1 (electronically, the switch is on).

Computers group bits together to represent characters. Originally, eight bits were grouped together to form a **byte**, or character. On recent computers, the number of bits that a computer uses to represent a character can be sixteen or even thirty-two bits, but the principle remains the same: a byte represents a character to the computer. When we talk of memory capacity, we speak in terms of **kilobytes, megabytes**, and, **gigabytes**. A kilobyte is 1024 bytes (kilo equals one thousand), a megabyte is 1,048,576 bytes (mega equals one million), and a gigabyte is approximately one billion bytes.

We use gigabytes to discuss the storage capacities of large mainframe computers, the systems used by universities, large businesses, and government agencies. The memory capacities of microcomputers, such as the machine you will use with this text, are measured in kilobytes (abbreviated as **K**) and megabytes (abbreviated as **meg**). When you ask about a microcomputer's memory capacity, you generally want to ask, "How many K or meg of memory does this computer have?"

Early microcomputers had low memory capacity, often as little as eight or sixteen kilobytes. Many computers today have 512 kilobytes or one megabyte of memory, and the trend for increased memory sizes continues steadily. Your computer's memory capacity determines which computer programs you can use. For instance, you must have at least 512 K of memory to use the software program Microsoft Works on an IBM®-compatible computer. Many programs require one megabyte or more of memory.

Output Devices

Computer users must also connect to their computers devices that show the results of the system's processing of the entered data. These devices, called **output devices,** include:

- monitor
- speaker
- printer
- plotter
- disk drive
- modem

The most common output device is the computer monitor. Monochrome monitors can display only one color, whereas color monitors can display up to several hundred thousand colors but are usually considerably more expensive. The speaker is another common output device. Most computers include built-in speakers that allow the system to communicate with the user via beeps, music, or voice—depending on the software being used.

Printers are devices used to display the computer's output on paper instead of on a monitor. Printers can be dot matrix, daisy wheel, ink-jet, or laser. Dot matrix printers, which are generally the least expensive type of printers, can print both text and graphics. However, dot matrix printouts are often not very high quality. Daisy wheel printers are more expensive than most dot matrix printers, but they do produce letter quality printouts. However, daisy wheel printers can print only text, not graphics. Ink-jet printers can produce good quality printouts including both text and graphics. The cost of ink-jet printers is generally somewhere between the cost of dot matrix printers and the cost of daisy wheel printers. Laser printers are the top-of-the-line printers for microcomputers. The most expensive, laser printers also produce the highest quality text and graphics printouts. Finally, plotters are similar to printers, but they use a series of pens to produce

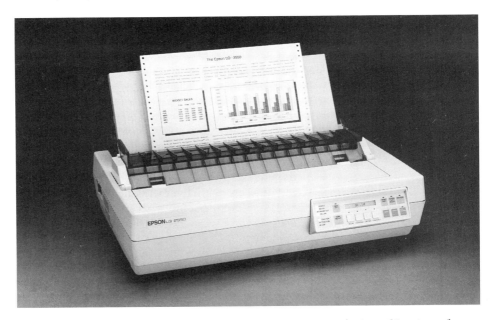

A printer is one of the most common computer system output devices. *(Courtesy of Epson America, Inc.)*

their output. Plotters are essential to architects and computer-assisted design professionals who create precise, intricate drawings.

The last two output devices in the list are the combined input/output devices—disk drives and modems. Disk drives are used as output devices when you copy information that you have created (such as a word-processed letter) from the computer system to a disk in the drive. Modems are output devices when you send information from your computer through the telephone lines to a computer in another location. Disk drives are discussed more fully in the next section, and modems are discussed in Chapter 12.

Secondary Storage Devices

Even though large memory capacities permit computers to operate larger, more complex programs, the memory is still volatile and temporary. Because of the impermanent nature of the internal storage capacities of RAM chips, computer systems also need to have external storage capabilities. These external storage devices, commonly called **secondary memory**, allow for the long-term storage of data on magnetic media outside of the computer. Common external storage devices include floppy disk drives, hard disk drives, and tape drives. Each of these devices serves to store computer data—computer programs and user data—outside the computer's temporary memory chips.

Floppy disk drives are so named because the small, removable disks on which they store data are very pliable, or "floppy." (Although the casing on the 3.5 inch disk is hard, the disk inside the casing is still pliable.) Disk drives are designed to use either a 3.5 inch or a 5.25 inch disk, the most common sizes for IBM-compatible computers.

The floppy disk drive functions in much the same way as a stereo turntable. It rapidly spins the disk while information is accessed or stored onto the surface of the disk by the drive's read/write head. However, unlike the spiral tracks on stereo albums, computer disks have tracks in concentric circles where data are stored and accessed.

A hard disk drive is the other common type of secondary storage device. Hard disk drives function in much the same manner as floppy disk drives except the magnetizable surface is hard, not pliable, and is generally not removable from its housing. (There are some hard disk drives that feature removable and replaceable hard disks.) The hard disk drive spins the disk surface while the read/write head passes the magnetic instructions back and forth between the computer and the disk surface.

The major differences between hard and floppy disk drives are their speed and storage capacities. Hard disk drives can access and store data much faster than floppy disk drives. In addition, while floppy disks generally hold less than one megabyte of data (often much less), the smallest hard disks today store twenty megabytes of data. Today, 40, 80, and even 120 megabyte hard disks are quite common.

Because of their high memory requirements an increasing number of programs now require a hard disk drive to operate them efficiently. As you might expect, hard disk drives are considerably more expensive than floppy disk drives. Most people who have a hard disk drive, however, soon decide that the increased performance a hard disk drive provides justifies the extra cost. Hard disks are generally much more reliable than floppy disks, but because they are very fast and reliable, their owners often get careless and forget routine safeguards such as backing up their data on a regular basis. Like all other equipment, hard disk drives sometimes fail. Whether you use a floppy or a hard disk drive system for storing your data, plan a routine schedule for making back-up copies of your work on more than one type of external storage device—and stick to it!

Types of Software

Software refers to the instructions that tell the computer what to do: the operating system, application programs (for example, word processors or database managers), games, and individual user data (for example, word-processed letters or student record databases). Software can be categorized according to the function that it serves. **Operating-system commands** are the first set of software instructions entered into a computer when it is built. In the IBM PC-compatible world, the operating system programs are called "MS-DOS" or "PC DOS"; with the Macintosh®, they are simply called "the System"; for Apple® II computers, they are known as "ProDOS" or "DOS 3.3." The operating system programs are referred to as **low level programs** because they are written in "low level" languages such as machine language or assembler. These programs include the basic commands needed to control the computer system.

Application software includes programs that run in computers once operating system software is installed. These higher level programs fall into three general categories: **programming languages, instructional programs,** and **productivity programs.** Programming languages are computer software designed to generate other computer programs. Every application program has been written in some language by a computer programmer. Typical programming languages are FORTRAN, Pascal, BASIC, COBOL, and Logo, each written with a set of commands and syntax (or rules governing the manner in which commands must be used) specifically designed for a particular application. COBOL, for instance, is designed for business applications, and FORTRAN is used for mathematical and scientific programs. As the name implies, instructional programs, written to teach and reinforce skills or concepts in a number of subjects, include drill and practice software, tutorials, educational games, and simulations.

Productivity programs are designed to increase the efficiency and productivity of the user. The most widely used programs in the business world, they are rapidly becoming popular in schools as well. Productivity programs include word processors, database managers, spreadsheets, charting programs, drawing programs, and communications programs. This text will concentrate on using one particularly effective productivity program, Microsoft Works, to improve the quality and quantity of the professional products of educators.

2   A General Introduction to Educational Computing

Historical Trends in Educational Computing

Computers have been used educationally for nearly fifty years, even though computer use was very limited until the last decade. During the 1940s and 1950s, computers were very expensive to purchase, operate, and maintain. As a result, only a few large universities (such as Harvard, the University of Pennsylvania, and the Massachusetts Institute of Technology) used computers in an educational setting. These institutions used **mainframes**, large computer systems that supported multiple users through dedicated terminals. These systems used vacuum tubes to control their electronic operations; they were huge but not especially reliable. During this early period, students used computers primarily to study for mathematics or computer science courses. Computer programming and data analysis were two common activities at this time. Individual users would *log-on*, that is, follow the necessary procedures to begin using the computer, such as giving an appropriate password or a correct user account

The ENIAC was one of the first mainframe computers. Its huge size accommodated thousands of vacuum tubes. *(Brooks/Cole)*

number. They would then use the computer to perform mathematical computations, to execute a computer program, or to analyze some statistical data.

Mainframes were the only computers available for many years and, although prices continued to drop steadily through the 1950s and 1960s, the educational use of computers was limited to institutions of higher education and a few high schools. When tiny transistors replaced vacuum tubes in the early 1960s, computers became much smaller, more reliable, and much faster than the earlier machines.

During these intermediate years, computer science activities such as programming continued to be the most common use of computers in educational environments. However, some tutorial software (such as the **PLATO** Project—**P**rogrammed **L**ogic for **A**utomatic **T**eaching **O**perations) was being developed to facilitate learning by programming the computer to function as a teacher. The early tutorial software was very primitive compared with today's software standards, and computers continued to be large and expensive; therefore, educational computer use remained limited. Concurrently, **minicomputers** were being produced that were smaller, less powerful, and less expensive than the mainframes. Even so, these computers were created mainly for the middle-size business market.

The production of **silicon chips** in the late 1960s and early 1970s marked the real beginning of the computer revolution that is sweeping schools today. A silicon chip is a piece of silicon (a material found in quartz and sand) with electronic circuits etched on it that conduct electronic impulses. Throughout the 1970s and 1980s, engineers produced smaller and more powerful silicon chips that contained integrated circuits. Eventually computer scientists developed the **microprocessor**, basically a computer on a silicon chip and the "brain" of the microcomputers that you see in schools and businesses today.

Starting in 1977 with Tandy corporation's TRS-80 and, later that same year, with the first microcomputers from Apple Computer, Inc., and Commodore, the production of powerful and relatively inexpensive microcomputers finally made them affordable for many schools. During the 1980s, microcomputers continued to decrease in price and increase in power. The software industry has produced a wide variety of programs for educators, facilitating an increase in computer use in schools.

During most of the 1980s, tutorial (or teaching) programs gradually replaced computer programming as the predominant computer application in schools. Many of the early versions of tutorial programs were merely drill and practice games and "electronic flashcard" screens, designed to reinforce learning in the

The Commodore PET was one of the first microcomputers. *(Courtesy of Commodore Business Machines, Inc.)*

same way as traditional cardboard flashcards. As the decade progressed, software developers worked more closely with educators to create powerful programs designed to help students build problem-solving and other higher-order thinking skills.

By the late 1980s, the role of productivity programs such as word processors and database managers also became increasingly important for schools. Today, although tutorial software is still an essential learning tool, especially in elementary and middle schools, productivity programs have become the most widely supported application of computers in education. Computer science activities such as programming are now more common in secondary schools and institutions of higher education. One exception to that trend is the popularity of the programming language Logo. Known primarily for its graphic capabilities and triangular-shaped "turtle," Logo provides elementary students with a highly motivating, problem-solving experience.

Thanks to the significant and consistent trends in the computer technology industry described in this section, computer software has evolved from programs suitable only for mathematical and scientific applications to those that enhance learning in all disciplines and at all grade levels. During the last four decades:

- Computers have become less expensive.
- Computers have become smaller.
- Computers have become more powerful.
- Computer memory has become larger (and less expensive).
- Computer operations have become faster.
- Computers have become more "user friendly."
- Computers have become far more versatile.
- Computers have become far more ubiquitous.

Categories of Instructional Computer Use

As we discussed the dynamic evolution of software in education, we saw computation and programming software replaced by more complex tutorial programs; now productivity tools are taking the lead. Today we can find all three levels of software in schools. As software becomes more integral to the teaching profession, we need to think carefully about which programs are best suited to our needs, about ethical and security issues, and about the logistics of implementing software in the curriculum.

In an earlier section, we mentioned that the application of computers in education could be categorized according to the purpose for which the machines were used. One widely recognized categorizing system was proposed by Taylor in his 1980 book, *The Computer in the School: Tool, Tutor, Tutee* (Teachers College Press). Taylor suggests that computers can be organized into three major categories of use: the **tutee**—the computer is the learner or object of study; the **tutor**—the computer is the teacher; and the **tool**—the computer is an object used to perform a task.

The Computer as "Tutee"

The "tutee," or computer science orientation, was the most prevalent use of computers in the 1950s and 1960s. This pattern of use prevailed for obvious and compelling reasons—computer memory and processing speed were too limited to support complex software. As a result, very few educationally sound programs existed.

In the **tutee** category, computer hardware, software, and ethical issues of technology are the objects of study. People involved in computer programming, computer architecture, digital logic, the study of the impact of computers on society, and the ethical considerations of computer use all use the computer as tutee. Although computer programming and digital logic are primarily appropriate for students with an interest in computer science or related fields, everyone should be aware of the impact that computers are making on our lives and our society. In particular, we must recognize that many other microprocessors exist besides the microcomputers we see in our schools and homes. Microprocessors are found in most electronic equipment, including automobiles, kitchen appliances, stereo and video equipment, televisions, and video games. As such tools and other equipment become increasingly "smart," these microprocessors will increasingly affect our work, home, and play environments and our future career options.

We need people to study the ethical considerations associated with the use of computers because computer technology has advanced so quickly that our society is having difficulty establishing ethical standards regarding its appropriate use. Preeminent ethical considerations include the varied forms of **computer crime** and the issues related to **computer privacy.** These issues have important implications for all members of our society—including all students and educators. For this reason, the issues are discussed more thoroughly in the next main section.

The Computer as "Tutor"

In the **tutor** category, the computer is the teacher and the computer user is the learner. Common software products that empower the computer to tutor include drill and practice programs, tutorials, educational games, problem-solving software, and simulations. Though these programs did not become predominant in education until the middle 1980s, now many excellent programs are on the market—programs that help students develop and refine both their higher- and lower-order thinking skills. Research has demonstrated that computers can effectively increase students' skills. The ability of the computer to enhance the development of problem-solving and other higher-order thinking skills is particularly significant when we remember that these are areas where more traditional methods of instruction have not proved especially effective.

The Computer as "Tool"

The **tool** category includes applications used to enhance an individual's performance in writing or organizing information. These applications include word processing, database management, electronic spreadsheets, and drawing programs to create documents, class rosters, grading systems, charts, and graphic art. The programs in this category of educational computing have continued to increase in popularity to the point where "tool" programs are now the most widely acclaimed educational application for computers.

The hands-on exercises in this text use one of the most popular tool programs—specifically, Microsoft Works. The following chapters will help you use Microsoft Works to increase your professional productivity in writing, organization of information, numerical calculations, and production of charts. In addition, each chapter includes suggestions for integrating the use of Microsoft Works into your instruction. Finally, each chapter lists ways that you can use Microsoft Works to perform personal tasks, such as balancing your checking account and managing your address book.

Ethical Considerations of Computer Use

The rapid advance of computer technology has made it difficult for society to establish ethical standards for the appropriate use of technology. Important ethical issues can be grouped in one of two areas: **computer crime** and **computer privacy**. These issues have direct implications for students and educators.

Computer crimes include **computer theft**, **computer sabotage**, and **software piracy**. One kind of computer theft is usually perpetrated by white-collar criminals who use their authorized computer access to falsify records or misappropriate funds. Schools and businesses have problems with computer theft that involve the actual removal of the equipment from the premises. These problems can be obviated by careful security plans.

Computer sabotage is the infiltration of **computer hackers** and **computer viruses** into a computer system. Hackers are computer enthusiasts who attempt unauthorized entry to computer systems to gain illegal computer time and access confidential information. Media coverage of their crimes often results in unjustified recognition for their criminal "accomplishments." Educators can help their students realize that hackers are not heroes—on the contrary, their actions can often cause expensive and serious damage to important business and government computer systems.

Computer viruses are seemingly innocent computer programs designed to damage or destroy information stored on hard or floppy disks. Viruses gain entry into a computer system through an infected floppy disk or file received through a modem. The potentially destructive effects of computer viruses can be counteracted by using **computer vaccines**—programs that locate and eliminate computer viruses and "disinfect" any files damaged by them.

The issue of software piracy is especially important in education because piracy is so prevalent and so easily accomplished. We all know that copying a textbook is illegal, but it is also not practical in terms of the time the copying process would require and the inferior product it would produce. By contrast, computer software can be exactly duplicated in a few moments, and because it is so easy, software pirating is widespread. Nonetheless, duplicating *copyrighted* computer software is *illegal*. A legal copy of each copyrighted program must be purchased for every computer on which the program will be used. If ten students use Microsoft Works in a lab with ten computers, the school must purchase a lab set of ten programs

Computer security, a concern for every private citizen, includes **computer privacy** and **data protection** issues. Individuals have a right to protect themselves from governmental agencies, businesses, or other individuals seeking to misuse the personal information available from computer database files. Data protection measures, including passwords, disk backup techniques, and other information protection methods, insure that important data are not accidentally lost, destroyed, or intentionally exploited.

Situating Hardware for Instructional Computer Use

Computers can be found in many different places in a school, and their placement has a great influence on how the computers are used. Before choosing a location for computer equipment, certain advantages and disadvantages relating to its use should be considered. The most common places to locate computers are in a computer laboratory, in individual classrooms, in the media center, and in the administrator's office. Although administrators and the main office personnel certainly need computer access, machines situated in those locations are seldom used for instructional purposes. Therefore, in our discussion we will concentrate on the locations that facilitate laboratory or classroom instruction.

Placing Computers in a Laboratory

A **computer laboratory** generally has from ten to twenty-five machines and can be used for whole-class instruction. To be effective, there should be one machine for each student or pair of students. A computer lab is the most

In a computer lab instructional software enriches students' learning experiences.
(Courtesy of International Business Machines Corporation)

efficient way to teach word processing, keyboarding (learning to use a key-board), computer programming, and many tutorial programs. In this setting, students have an opportunity for important "hands-on" experiences and self-paced explorations. When schools hire a knowledgeable computer teacher, they have someone who can oversee the lab equipment and introduce students to a variety of computer applications. Generally, equipment can be maintained and secured far more easily in a lab than when machines are dispersed throughout the school. In addition, the computer teacher can organize and store software more efficiently in a central location, like a lab cupboard.

There are, however, disadvantages to investing in a computer lab. First, computers are not readily available for use by individual teachers, making it difficult to "seize the teachable moment." Because lab use must be scheduled, computer time is less flexible and accessible. Frequently, the lab is remote from the classroom, so students must be moved there and back, resulting in a loss of teaching time. Since schools must purchase one copy of every program used for each computer in the lab, the variety of affordable software becomes limited.

If the school hires a computer teacher, money that could be used for additional hardware or software is often sacrificed for salary. Additionally, when a special teacher is hired for the computer lab, computer instruction is often seen as a "special subject" not integrated into the regular classroom curriculum. When there is no computer teacher, labs are often used by a relatively small number of classroom teachers (the "computer enthusiasts"), meaning little or no access for some students.

Teaching a class in a computer lab requires many of the same instructional strategies that you use in any setting—careful planning, well-sequenced instructional procedures, clear instructions, flexibility, frequent use of illustrations and examples, adequate opportunity for practice, and a concise introduction to and summary of the activity. However, the level of specificity and clarity of instruction often needs to be even greater in the computer lab than elsewhere. For instance, you can improve the effectiveness of your computer lab instruction by explaining to your class, in a step-by-step fashion, the entire process they will complete *before* they have their hands on the computers. A large monitor or a **liquid crystal display screen** will help you guide your students through the procedures that they will follow independently with their computers. (A "liquid crystal display," or **LCD,** screen is a device which, when attached to a

A liquid crystal display (LCD) device can be used with an overhead projector so that a large group can view the computer display. *(Courtesy of In Focus Systems, Inc.)*

Table 2.1 Advantages and disadvantages of computers in labs

Advantages	Disadvantages
Each student (or pair of students) can have valuable "hands-on" experience with computers.	Computers are not readily accessible to the classroom teacher for professional productivity uses.
Lab settings are necessary for teaching word processing, keyboarding, and programming.	Computers are not accessible to the classroom teacher for "seizing the teachable moment."
Availability of a knowledgeable "computer teacher" can improve students' computer competence and understanding.	A "computer teacher" costs salary dollars; that may mean that computer use is not integrated into the regular curriculum.
The equipment is more easily maintained and secured in a lab than in individual classrooms.	Computer access may be inequitable for some students.
Software can be easily organized and accessed in a central location.	Purchasing a "lab set" of programs is very costly.
Whole-class instruction is possible without special management systems.	Moving students to and from the computer lab results in a loss of instructional time.

computer and placed on an overhead projector, allows the computer display to be projected on a screen or blank wall). After guiding the class through the complete process, have all the students start their computers at the same time. Next, prompt the class as a group through the beginning steps, only releasing them to work independently when you are certain they know what they are expected to do.

Whenever possible, provide students with independent guidesheets explaining the steps you want them to follow when they use computers on their own. Stop students about halfway through each work period to ask them to share discoveries, questions, problems, and insights (one good strategy to ensure that you have their attention is to ask everyone to raise both hands in the air— "show me all ten fingers"). Allow four or five minutes for troubleshooting and reorientation; then send them back to work with a clear goal in mind. About five minutes before the end of the period, it's a good idea to interrupt the students again to review and clarify the closing down procedures. One more warning a minute or so before the end of the period allows them time to save their work (if appropriate) and shut down the computers in a careful manner. Try to schedule a discussion period soon after you leave the computer lab for the class to review and discuss their computer experiences.

Although assembling computers in one room to create a laboratory is a good idea, computer labs have problems associated with them. The primary advantages and disadvantages of computer labs are summarized in Table 2.1.

Placing Computers in Individual Classrooms

When computers are placed in the classroom, they are available for individual teachers to use whenever their use is appropriate to the lesson or when a spontaneous opportunity for instruction arises. If they have a computer in their own classrooms, teachers can also use word processing, database managers, electronic spreadsheets, and other application software to enhance their professional productivity. A computer in the classroom is more likely to be integrated into the regular curriculum than taught as an isolated subject.

There are other advantages to having a computer in the classroom. One computer is less threatening for novices than a lab filled with machines. As a result, novices are more likely to try the computer out. In addition, if the machine is in the classroom, valuable instructional time is not lost moving students to and from a lab. Finally, since it is not necessary to purchase lab sets of software, teachers can purchase a greater variety of programs—those that suit their own curriculum and instructional approach.

Despite the advantages, there are problems associated with having computers in individual classrooms. Frequently, schools do not have enough computers to permit placing one machine in every classroom, and they are faced with the difficulty of determining which classrooms get computers. Often, the decision is partially based on teacher interest, but this creates equity problems. Students in the rooms of teachers who do not want computers will have no computer experience, whereas those in other rooms will have a great deal. Even if the computers are rotated from room to room, a consistent pattern of use is difficult to establish for either the teachers or the students.

When computers are dedicated to individual classrooms, the type and amount of use they get can be very irregular. In some classrooms, the computers are abandoned to the back of the room because the teacher does not know how to use them. In other classrooms, the computers are used only by the "best and brightest" students after they complete regular classwork. Both of these situations create obvious equity concerns. In classrooms where the machines are used efficiently and fairly, scheduling equal access for all students can be very time-consuming and awkward for teachers.

When a school's computers are dispersed to individual classrooms, hands-on instruction for the whole class is not possible. In addition, the computer hardware is much more difficult to maintain and secure than it is in a computer lab. Similarly, computer software is more difficult to organize and manage.

Even with the disadvantages of a classroom computer, teaching a class with a single machine is generally simpler than teaching a whole class in a lab; only one set of hands is on the computer at one time. Using a large monitor or an LCD screen can make one computer a powerful classroom teaching tool. (If your school does not have either device, encourage the administration to place one of them at the top of the next year's equipment budget.) Whenever you introduce the class to a new piece of software, use the large monitor or an LCD with an overhead projector to guide the students through the steps you want them to follow independently later. Explain to your class what you expect them to achieve by using the program before they have an opportunity to use the software.

After guiding the class through the complete process, have one or two of the students guide the others through the program. As frequently as possible, tape

Table 2.2 Advantages and disadvantages of computers in classrooms

Advantages	Disadvantages
Computers are readily available to classroom teachers for their professional productivity uses.	Individual students do not have as much opportunity for "hands-on" experience with computers.
Computers are readily accessible to classroom teachers for "seizing the teachable moment."	This setup makes it difficult to teach applications such as word processing and keyboarding.
Computer use is more likely to be integrated into the regular classroom curriculum.	The absence of a knowledgeable "computer teacher" may limit the type of computer activities that students experience.
Instructional time is maximized because students do not have to move from their classrooms.	The equipment and software are more difficult to maintain and secure in individual classrooms than in a lab.
Because "lab sets" of programs are not needed, funds are available for more varied programs, with fewer copies of each.	Whole-class, hands-on instruction is not possible.
One computer in a classroom is less threatening to a computer novice than an entire lab filled with machines.	Computer access may still be inequitable unless teachers carefully schedule computer use. Equitable scheduling can be a management problem.

independent guidesheets or have a notebook next to the computer to explain the steps students will need to follow when they use the program on their own. Periodically ask students to discuss, share, and compare their experiences on using the program so you can verify and enhance their understanding when it is appropriate

Locating computers in individual classrooms is a good idea, but this practice, like creating computer labs, has problems associated with it. The primary advantages and disadvantages of placing computers in individual classrooms are summarized in Table 2.2.

Placing Computers in Media Centers

A third common location for computers in schools is in a media center (or library). When computers are placed in the media center, they can be available for individual student use throughout the school day. Placing computers in media centers makes it possible for teachers to send a single student or a group of students to use a computer when the need arises. By locating computers in media centers, the equipment is placed under the control of personnel who are generally well versed in maintaining and organizing equipment and materials. Managing and cataloging the available software should present no difficulties for the media center staff.

Generally, media centers are already well secured, so security issues are not a matter of concern. Media center personnel can be available to assist students when they need help. The computers should be accessible whenever the center is open; the hours will probably include time before and after the school day as well as during the lunch period.

Table 2.3 Advantages and disadvantages of computers in media centers

Advantages	Disadvantages
The equipment and software are easily maintained and secured in a media center.	Individual students may not get much or any "hands-on" computer experience.
Knowledgeable media center staff are available to assist students when questions arise.	Computers are not easily available to classroom teachers for their professional productivity uses.
Computers are likely to be available throughout the school day and possibly before and after school.	Computers are not immediately available to classroom teachers for "seizing the teachable moment."
Computer programs can be well organized and managed by media center personnel.	It is difficult or impossible to teach important applications like word processing and keyboarding.
Computer use may be integrated into the regular classroom curriculum if media center staff serve as resource facilitators.	Whole class, hands-on instruction is not possible.
	Scheduling computer use may be a problem depending on the media center practices.

Among the disadvantages of having computers in media centers is that they are seldom available for whole class instruction. Frequently, some students will use the computers a great deal, whereas others will have little or no opportunity for hands-on experience. Computers in a media center are not readily accessible to classroom teachers for their own professional productivity needs or for "seizing the teachable moment." It is nearly impossible to teach word processing and keyboarding if the computers are located in the media center. Depending on the nature of the media center staff, scheduling of the computer equipment may be difficult.

The primary advantages and disadvantages of placing computers in media centers are summarized in Table 2.3.

Final Thoughts on Computer Placement

The decision about where to place computers in schools is influenced by factors including the total number of computers available, the school's philosophy, the school's faculty, and physical plant considerations. Which factor is the most critical consideration depends on the situation. If there are *no* rooms available to use for a computer lab, that option is immediately eliminated. If a school has only a few computers, creating a lab may not make sense.

We *can* make recommendations based on hardware arrangements that many schools have successfully adopted. Many schools with twenty or more computers have placed twelve to fifteen of them in a computer lab; additional computers are rotated among the entire faculty for periods of six to nine weeks. Computer carts permit the easy transport of computers from room to room. In some situations where hardware is somewhat scarce, a lab is established with all of the computers on carts. In these settings, the lab is maintained for the first quarter of the year and then dismantled so that the computers can be placed in individual classrooms. This arrangement permits whole class instruction in key areas, such as word processing and keyboarding, to take place early in the year. It also allows computers to stay in individual classrooms for the majority of the school year.

In an ideal world, schools would have enough machines to create a computer lab and to place a computer in each classroom. But regardless of the number of machines schools have, they need to provide staff development to ensure the efficient use of computers.

The primary mission of this text is to help educators develop professional productivity with word-processing, database, spreadsheet, charting, and communications software. The text's hands-on activities will introduce you to the powers of Microsoft Works, a productivity program that combines all the above applications. The word-processing exercises, for example, demonstrate how a word processor can enhance your writing capabilities; the database exercises establish how a database manager improves your ability to organize and access information. For each application, the text's exercises detail how Microsoft Works can increase productivity and effectiveness.

After you've mastered the use of word processing to satisfy your professional needs, the next logical step is to consider methods for using word processing to improve your classroom instruction. The last section of each chapter discusses strategies for using Microsoft Works instructionally. Some of these activities are more appropriate for a classroom with a set of computers in a laboratory, while others are best suited for a regular classroom with one computer and a large monitor or an LCD device. However, most of the activities can be easily modified for use in a classroom with one computer and a normal monitor.

In addition to the files supporting the text's exercises, your Works **Data** disk also contains files designed for instructional use. The use of these instructional files is discussed in the "integration" section of each chapter. Together with the strategies suggested in the integration sections, you will soon be using these files to improve your teaching as well as your productivity.

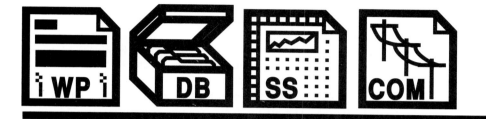

3 An Introduction to the Microsoft Works Components

Microsoft Works is an integrated software program that includes five distinct, but interrelated, productivity-enhancing computer applications. Microsoft Works can be thought of as the Swiss Army knife of application software. People purchase Swiss Army knives to give themselves a single, albeit simplified, solution to a multitude of situations requiring tools. One Swiss Army knife can serve in the stead of many powerful, highly specified tools: knife blades, screwdriver blades, scissors, corkscrews, and similar devices. Although none of the tools on a Swiss Army knife is as useful for any particular task as a dedicated tool (e.g., the long-handled screwdriver is best suited for removing deeply inset screws), the tools sufficiently satisfy the requirements of many daily tasks.

Like a Swiss Army knife, Microsoft Works admirably meets the routine needs of most computers users. Works provides users with the five major productivity applications—word processing, database management, spreadsheet manipulation, charting, and communication. In addition, Works includes the capability to develop **macros**—scripts that can automate routine tasks—in all of the applications.

Chapter 3 will give you a brief introduction to Microsoft Works. The following chapters will help you master each of its components.

Components of Microsoft Works

Word Processing

A word processor gives you the power to create, format, and manipulate text electronically; you can easily edit your letters, papers, reports, and other documents before you print them on paper. You can also control the size, shape, and style of the individual characters in the text you create and manipulate margins, spacing, justification, headers, and footers. In addition, Microsoft Works includes a spelling checker and a thesaurus that help you produce documents with well-chosen words free from spelling errors. If you don't already use a word processor for all your writing tasks, you'll soon find that its powers are indispensable. In fact, after you master one, you'll wonder how you ever managed to write anything without a word processor.

Databases

A **database** is an organized collection of information. A good example of a database is a telephone book: phone owners are organized in alphabetical order by last name. **Database managers** are programs that permit the user to access, organize, locate, arrange, and store information easily and efficiently. Whereas a phone book can only be used alphabetically, a database manager allows you to search by first or last name, street address, city, state, ZIP code, phone number, or any other category you might choose. You can arrange and rearrange the information in any of the categories into which you have the data separated, and you can store the same amount of information electronically on a disk. Before databases, this kind of organization required an extensive indexing system.

Spreadsheets

A **spreadsheet** program is a tool to use for most of your "number crunching" chores. A spreadsheet is an electronic ledger with the power to perform calculations—adding, subtracting, multiplying, and dividing—on any numbers you enter into its cells. In addition, a spreadsheet permits you to create formulas, either on your own or by using the many built-in functions that Works includes, to ask powerful "What if?" questions. For example, you can hypothetically change your mortgage interest rate, and the spreadsheet will automatically recalculate your monthly payments or the period of the loan. In addition, spreadsheets can help you greatly with all your financial matters and other tasks involving numerical calculations, including determining grades, managing your school or home budget, and balancing your checking and savings accounts.

Charting

The spreadsheet in Microsoft Works includes a program that allows you to generate charts directly from the spreadsheet data. You simply select the data you want to graph and choose the type of graph you want. The Works charting program does the rest for you. You can use the charting program to produce pie charts and bar, line, stacked bar, and mixed line and bar graphs. In addition, you can enhance the graphs that Works creates for you by adding legends, re-scaling the axes in bar or line charts, and changing the patterns or colors of the bars or pie segments.

Data Integration

Since Microsoft Works is an integrated package, you can easily pass information from one program component to another. For instance, a chart that you create can easily be added to a word-processed document. A table of figures can be copied quickly from your spreadsheet and included in a word-processed annual report. You can also share information between the database and spreadsheet to take advantage of the special powers that each application possesses.

Perhaps the most powerful form of data integration combines the database and the word processor to generate personalized form letters. With **print merging,** you can word process one document and then have it merged, or combined, with a database of five or five thousand individuals. When you print the document, you will produce letters that are automatically individualized.

Communications

Another powerful component in Works is the communications package that allows you to connect your computer with other computers around the world. To use the communications program, you must first add a modem and a telephone line to your system, but the expense is minimal. Once you have the necessary equipment, you can exchange information with other computer users worldwide. In addition, you can access vast databases of information through national network services.

Macros

One final feature of Microsoft Works is the capability to create **macros** in any of the program components. A macro is a tool that lets you assign repetitive tasks to keystroke combinations. The power to create macros is similar to having a recorder built into your computer. You first assign the macro a designated sequence of keystrokes and then a specific alpha-numeric key to use later with the **Control** (**Ctrl**) key when you want to invoke the macro. Microsoft Works stores all of your keystrokes and then "remembers" them later when you execute the designated **Control** key command sequence. In this way, macros provide a great timesaving tool.

Tutorials and Help Features

In addition to all of the wonderful components that we've already discussed in this section, Microsoft Works offers a series of hands-on tutorial lessons to help you learn the program. The tutorials can be used as stand-alone programs— that is, programs you can use by themselves without starting Microsoft Works. Alternatively, the tutorials can be accessed from within Microsoft Works if you need help while you are using the program.

Unlike the tutorials, **Help** features provided by Microsoft Works can only be used within the program; you must be using Works to access them. However, they are context-sensitive; for example, when you are using the spreadsheet program, they offer help on spreadsheet commands.

Generally, when questions arise about unfamiliar Works commands, the **Help** feature is the best place to begin looking for answers. If you cannot find the answer to your question in the help provided by Microsoft Works, the next place to look is in the reference manual that comes with Works.

Using an IBM-Compatible Computer

Many IBM-compatible programs adopt standard command structures, and all utilize similar computer techniques. You will use a number of these techniques when you work with an IBM-compatible computer, regardless of which software package you use. Table 3.1 includes many standard commands (such as **Enter** or **Return**), and Table 3.2 presents mouse techniques (such as Click or Drag). To become a competent user, you need to familiarize yourself with these commands. You do not need to have a mouse to use Works, but a mouse facilitates your use of the program.

Table 3.1 specifies and clarifies the conventions used throughout this particular text when referring to the keyboard. Keys (such as the **Enter** key or **Shift** key) appear in boldface type to emphasize their importance. Mouse techniques (such as Click or Drag) begin with a capital letter to help distinguish them from the surrounding text.

Table 3.1 Keys on the keyboard

Alt	This key (usually located to the left of the spacebar) is extremely important. Used alone, it activates the menu bar. Used with other keys, it offers keyboard shortcuts for many of the commands on the menu bar. If the IBM-compatible that you are using doesn't have a mouse, you will use the **Alt** key to access the menu bar commands.
Backspace	This is the large key located above the **Enter** key, used to remove the character to the left of the electronic position indicator known as the "cursor."
Caps Lock	This key is located below the **Tab** key and is used to select only capital letters from the keyboard. Once you press the **Cap Locks** key, it remains in effect until you press it again to "unlock" the capital letters.
Control or **Ctrl**	Located next to the **Alt** key, **Ctrl** is used in combination with other keys to issue commands and to select special characters from the keyboard. Its function is similar to the **Alt** key; it is always used in combination with other keys.
Del	The **Del** key—short for delete—is used to remove the character upon which the cursor is located. This key is usually located below the number pad keys.
down arrow	This is the key inscribed with an arrow pointing down, used to move the cursor down in documents or within dialog boxes (the messages that Works displays on the screen to help you execute commands).
End	This key, usually located on one of the number pad keys, is used to move the cursor to the righthand margin in documents.
Enter	This key is used to create a carriage return at the end of a paragraph in a word-processed document. It is also frequently used to complete commands in dialog boxes (the messages that Works displays on the screen to help you execute commands). This large "L-shaped" key, located to the right of the alphabetical keys, is sometimes called the "Return" key. In this text, the key will be referred to as the **Enter** key.
Esc	The **Escape** key, located on the upper left side of the keyboard, is used primarily to cancel commands or interrupt operations, such as printing.
Function Keys (F1–F12)	These keys are located either to the left or above the alphabetical keys. They are shortcut keys for commands. For instance, pressing the **F1** key is the quickest method for accessing Works help features.
Home	This key, usually located on one of the number pad keys, is used to move the cursor to the left hand margin in documents.
Insert or **Ins**	Usually located next to the **Del** or **Delete** key, this key is used to change the cursor from insert mode (which adds text) to typeover mode (which replaces text) in word-processed documents.
left arrow	This is the key inscribed with an arrow pointing to the left. The **left arrow** key is used to move the cursor to the left in documents or within dialog boxes (the messages that Works displays on the screen to help you execute commands).

(continued on next page)

Table 3.1 Keys on the keyboard *(continued)*

Num Lock	This key is usually located above the number pad keys. It functions similarly to the **Caps Lock** key in that it locks down when you press it and remains locked until you press it again to unlock it. It is used to activate the number keys and deactivate the **Home**, **PgUp**, **PgDn**, and **End** keys. Works displays an "NL" on the status line when the **Num Lock** key has been pressed.
Page Down or **PgDn**	This key, usually located on one of the number pad keys, is used to move the cursor down one page in the document.
Page Up or **PgUp**	This key, usually located on one of the number pad keys, is used to move the cursor up one page in the document.
Print Screen or **PrtScn**	**PrtScn** is usually located near the number pad keys and is used to reproduce the contents of the screen on paper using a printer.
right arrow	This key is inscribed with an arrow pointing to the right. The **right arrow** key is used to move the cursor to the right in documents or within dialog boxes.
Shift	Use **Shift** with other keys to produce uppercase letters and to select the characters above the number keys on the keyboard.
Spacebar	Used to insert the spaces that separate words in text in all applications, this key is also used to select options in some dialog boxes.
Tab	Use **Tab** to insert tab stops into word-processed documents, to move the cursor from location to location within dialog boxes, to move from cell to cell in spreadsheet documents (the arrow keys will also serve this function), and to move from field to field in database documents.
up arrow	This is the key inscribed with an arrow pointing up. The **up arrow** key is used to move the cursor up in documents or within dialog boxes.

Figure 3.1 shows a typical IBM keyboard. However, because keyboards differ—some have the function keys (**F1**, **F2**, etc.) to the left of the standard keys, and some have them above the standard keys—the descriptions in Table 3.1 of the placement of keys may not coincide with their placement on your keyboard.

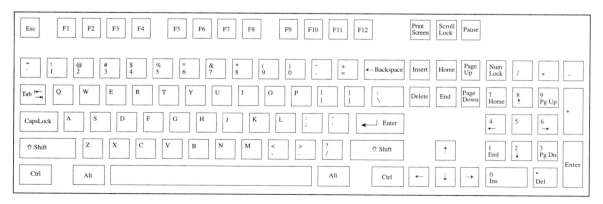

Figure 3.1 IBM keyboard

Table 3.2 Mouse techniques

mouse	The mouse is an input device that can be attached to your computer. You can use the mouse to access commands in Works more easily than you can by using the keyboard.
mouse button	This is the section in the front of the mouse that you press when you want to issue a command such as Click or Drag.
Point	This term instructs you to direct the mouse pointer toward a particular word or position on the screen.
pointer ⬆	The pointer is the small arrow displayed on the screen; its movements directly correspond to the movements of the mouse.
Click	This term instructs you to press the mouse button one time.
Double Click	When you Double Click, you press the mouse button two times in rapid succession.
Drag	To Drag, press the mouse button and move the pointer to a new location while the button is still depressed.
Shift Drag	This term instructs you to press the mouse button and hold down the **Shift** key while the mouse button is still depressed. You then release the button and continue to move the mouse—for instance, using the scroll bars—to another section of a document. This technique is useful for selecting large segments of text or data.

For additional explanation of the mouse or keyboard on your machine, consult the user's manual that came with your computer. Alternatively, you could use the tutorial software that accompanies the computer system, available from your local computer dealer.

4 Getting Started with Microsoft Works

Microsoft Works requires an IBM-compatible computer with two floppy disk drives—either 3.5 inch or 5.25 inch—or one floppy disk drive and a hard disk drive. If you have a hard disk drive, use the reference manual that comes with Microsoft Works to help you copy the various Works files from the disks to the hard disk. The **Setup** disk included with the Works package provides a very straightforward explanation of how to install Works on the hard drive. You simply follow the instructions written on the **Setup** disk, read the screen messages that Works uses to prompt the process, and insert the necessary disks when they are requested.

If you don't have a hard disk drive, you'll want to create a working copy of your Microsoft Works **Program** disk. This way, you'll always have a backup disk in case of a disk failure. You can use the **Setup** disk to help you make a working copy of the program. When you use Works without a hard disk drive, you'll need to do some "disk swapping"—that is, exchanging one disk (either 5.25 or 3.5 inch) for another of the same size. Don't worry, though; messages will appear on the screen telling you which disk you should place in which drive whenever disk swapping is required.

The exercises and instructions in this text are written specifically to work with Microsoft Works version 2.00. Many of the commands and instructions will work with an earlier version of Works, but some will not. If you do have an earlier version of Works, you may want to consider using Microsoft's software updating program, which allows registered owners to update their programs for a moderate fee.

The next three sections explain the process for getting started using Microsoft Works from a hard disk drive system or from a dual (3.5 or 5.25 inch) floppy system. Choose the set of instructions appropriate to your computer system and read them carefully; you will use them each time you begin a work session with your computer.

Disk Handling

If you use any microcomputer system, even if you have a hard disk drive, you will still have to handle floppy disks. The "floppies" that you'll use are made of mylar, covered with a magnetizable substance, and then packaged in a protective cardboard or plastic covering. Despite the fact that floppies are inexpensive and quite durable, you should treat the disks carefully. Although they hold far less data than hard disks, they can still store a large amount of information, which is worth far more than the cost of the disks themselves. The storage capacity of disks varies greatly, from less than 200 K to more than 1,000 K. Most IBM-compatible diskettes store either 360 K or 720 K, although newer disk drives can now store more than one megabyte (1.2 or 1.44 megabytes) of data.

Before a disk can be used by a computer, it must be "formatted" or "initialized" for use by that machine. When you purchase a new disk, it is like a blank record without grooves. The disk must be formatted—have concentric tracks placed on it electronically so that it can store data—for use on a particular type of computer. Therefore, disks that are initialized (or formatted) for use on a Macintosh cannot be readily used on IBM-compatible computers and vice versa.

After a disk has been formatted for use by an IBM-compatible computer, the data you produce with programs such as Microsoft Works can be stored on it. To format a disk for use with an IBM-compatible, you must use the **Format** command available from your operating system. Different operating systems have slightly different formatting commands, so you should consult your DOS manual to guide you through the formatting process. Except in the case of disk failure, once a disk has been formatted, it does not have to be reformatted.

Several cautions for handling disks are worth noting:

- Keep your disks away from extreme temperatures—heat or cold.
- Avoid bending or folding your disks.
- Keep your disks away from magnets (including any magnetic fields such as those in monitors and televisions).

- Keep your disks stored in their jackets (or sleeves) to minimize their exposure to dust. Keep them stored in boxes or disk containers.
- Whenever possible, mark on the labels before putting them on the disks. If you must mark on a label while it's on the disk, use a felt-tip pen. (These cautions are particularly true for 5.25 inch disks).

For the most part, these cautions are simple common sense. The most important caution of all is to *make sure that you have a backup*—a second copy—*of all the important information you have stored on computer disks.* In addition, store your backup disks somewhere separate from the original copy of the disk. If you adopt this practice, you will only be annoyed by disk failure, not dismayed. With a backup, your data can always be retrieved.

Using a Hard Disk Drive System

You will find that using Microsoft Works from a hard disk drive is speedy and simple. First, however, you will need to make a working copy of Microsoft Works on your hard disk drive. Once you have installed Microsoft Works on your hard disk, the only disk that you will need is your Works **Data** disk for storing your files.

Making a Working Copy of the Program Disk

Your first task is to use the **Setup** disk to help you install Works on your hard disk drive by creating a subdirectory and calling it "Works." Subdirectories are similar to folders in a file drawer; they help you organize the data on your hard disk drive so that information is more easily located. They will also help you keep your Microsoft Works files separate from the files of any other programs that you store on the hard disk drive. If you need additional help using the **Setup** disk, consult the reference manual that comes with Works.

To install a working copy of Microsoft Works on your hard disk drive, follow these steps:

1. Turn the computer on, using the switch on the back of the machine. Next, locate the monitor switch (usually on the side or back of the equipment) and turn it on as well.
2. Wait while the computer loads the system software from the hard disk into the computer's memory. The first message you may see is a request for the current date and time. If you don't want to enter that data, you can simply press the **Enter** key twice to ignore the requests. However, when you enter the current information, your computer dates your files when it saves them. These procedures help you keep track of your work sessions, so it is usually worth the trouble to enter the current date. After entering the date in the requested form (for example, 09/15/92), press the **Enter** key. Then enter the time and press the **Enter** key.

3. In a few moments, you'll usually see a **C>** prompt on the screen. The **C>** indicates that the hard disk drive is the default drive (that is, the drive that is active when the system starts up); the floppy disk drive will be identified as the **A>** drive.

4. Place the Works **Setup** disk in the **A>** drive and lock the disk in. (The technique for locking a disk in a disk drive varies. Some drives lock disks in place automatically, whereas other drives require users to manually secure the disks. Read the manual that comes with your computer if you are not certain how to secure disks in your drive.) Now type **A:** and press the **Enter** key to instruct the computer that the floppy disk drive will now be the active drive. When the **A>** prompt appears on the screen, the floppy disk drive is active.

5. Type **Setup** and press the **Enter** key. In a few moments, questions and instructions will appear on the screen. Responding to the screen messages will allow you to configure the Works **Program** disk so that it will operate most efficiently with your computer system.

6. Accept the suggested **C>** drive (the designation for your hard disk drive) by pressing the **Enter** key, and follow the screen instructions.

7. When you finish installing Microsoft Works on your hard disk drive, store the original **Program** disk in a safe place and only use the new copy as your working disk.

You now have Microsoft Works on your computer system and are ready to start using the program.

Starting Works Using a Hard Disk Drive System

After the Works program is installed on your hard disk drive, you are ready to store documents on your Works **Data** disk. Remember the following procedure; you'll practice it each time that you use Works. To use the program with a *hard disk drive system*:

1. Turn the computer on with the switch on the back or side of the machine. Next, locate the monitor switch (usually on the side or back of the equipment) and turn it on as well.

2. Wait while the computer loads the system software from the hard disk into the computer's memory. The first message you see is a request for the current date and time. Remember, if you don't want to enter that data, you can simply press the **Enter** key twice to ignore the requests. For now, use the keyboard to enter the date in the requested form and press the **Enter** key. Then use the keyboard to enter the time in the requested form and press the **Enter** key.

3. When you see the **C>** prompt on the screen (indicating that the hard disk drive is the active drive), you can access the Microsoft Works subdirectory you created when you used the **Setup** disk. Use the keyboard to type **CD Works** and press the **Enter** key. This command, **CD Works**, instructs the computer to **C**hange the **D**irectory to the subdirectory named **Works**.

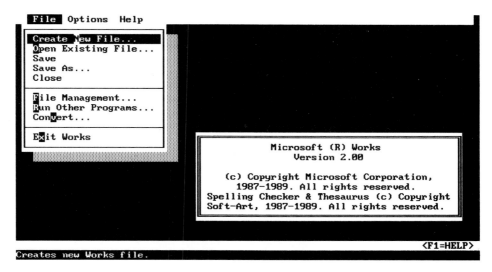

Figure 4.1 Microsoft Works opening screen display

4. Place your Works **Data** disk in the **A>** drive and lock in the disk.
5. To start the program, type **Works** and press the **Enter** key.
6. Now the program is loaded into the computer's RAM. You will see the open-ing screen display identifying the version of Works that you are using and the limited menu bar with **File**, **Options**, and **Help** commands available. The choices available under the **File** menu (**Create New File**, **Open Existing File**, etc.) are displayed for your convenience (Figure 4.1).

   You are now ready to use Microsoft Works.

Quitting Works Using a Hard Disk Drive System

The process for quitting Microsoft Works and turning off your computer is simple with a hard disk drive. Although Works will tell you if you haven't saved your files, always remember to do this yourself before you exit Works. Follow these steps when you are ready to quit using Microsoft Works:

1. Press the **Alt** key (the one to the left of the space bar) to activate the menu bar commands. Note that the first letters on the command words, **F**ile, **O**ptions, **H**elp, are highlighted. You can now access the list of commands beneath these words on the menu bar by pressing the appropriate letter—**F**, **O**, or **H**.
2. Press the **F** (for **F**ile) key to access the file commands.
3. When you see the **File** command menu, press the **X** (for E**x**it) key to quit Works.

4. In several moments, you'll see **C>** displayed on the screen, indicating that you have exited the program and are now using the operating system from the hard disk drive.
5. You can safely remove your disks. Unlock the disk drive, remove your **Data** disk, and replace it in its carrying case.
6. Reach behind the computer and turn off the power switch. Locate the power switch for the monitor and turn it off as well.

Using a Dual 5.25 Inch Disk Drive System

If you are using two 5.25 inch disk drives, you'll need the following disks each time you use Microsoft Works with an IBM-compatible computer:

- a disk containing a copy of the disk operating system (**DOS**)
- a copy of the Microsoft Works **Program** disk
- a copy of the Microsoft Works **Accessories** disk
- the formatted Works **Data** disk that came with the text

You will also need several other disks when you are performing certain tasks. When you want to check the spelling in your document or use the help features that Works provides, you'll need the Microsoft Works **Spell and Help** disk. When you want to use the thesaurus to help you choose the best word for a particular passage, you'll need the Microsoft Works **Thesaurus** disk. When you wish to have a lesson to help you improve your understanding of Works, you'll need to use one of the three tutorial disks—**Learning Works 1**, **Learning Works 2**, **Learning Works 3**—that come with Microsoft Works. Finally, when you first make a working copy of your Works **Program** disk, you will need to use the **Setup** disk to configure your copy of Works to fit your system's graphic and printing options. Although that sounds like a lot of disks, most of the time you'll only need to use your **Program** disk and your **Data** disk.

Making a Working Copy of the Program Disk

Before you can begin this section, you will need a blank 5.25 inch floppy disk to use as your new working **Program** disk. To make a working copy of the **Program** disk with dual 5.25 inch floppy disk drives, follow these steps:

1. Place the copy of the **DOS** (disk operating system) disk in the boot drive (generally the lefthand or uppermost disk drive); this is the disk drive that first operates when the computer system is turned on. Lock in the disk.
2. Turn the computer on, using the switch in the back of the machine. Next, locate the monitor switch (usually on the side or back of the equipment) and turn it on as well.
3. Wait while the system software is loaded from the **DOS** disk into the computer's memory. The first message you see is the system request for the

current date and time. If you don't wish to enter that data, you can simply press the **Enter** key twice to ignore the requests. However, if you comply with the request, your computer will date your files when it saves your documents. These procedures help you keep track of your work sessions, so it is usually worth the trouble to enter the current date. Use the keyboard to enter the date in the requested form (for example, 09/15/92), and press the **Enter** key. Then enter the time in the requested form and press the **Enter** key again.

4. In a few moments, you will see an **A>** prompt on the screen. The **A>** indicates that the boot drive (with the copy of the **DOS** disk) is the active drive; the other floppy drive will be identified as the **B>** drive. Use the handle to unlock the **A>** drive and remove the **DOS** disk.

5. Now place the Works **Setup** disk in the **A>** drive. Again, lock the disk in the drive.

6. Type **Setup** and press the **Enter** key. In a few moments, questions and instructions will appear on the screen. Responding to the screen messages will allow you to configure the **Program** disk so that it will operate most efficiently with your particular computer system.

7. Place the blank 5.25 inch disk in the **B>** drive, and respond to the screen prompts to create a new working copy of the **Program** disk.

8. After you finish making a working copy of the **Program** disk, store the original **Program** disk in a safe place and only use the new copy.

You are now ready to create documents using your working copy of the Works program.

Starting Works Using a Dual 5.25 Inch Disk Drive System

To use Microsoft Works with dual 5.25 inch floppy disk drives, follow these steps each time you use the program:

1. Place the copy of the **DOS** disk that came with your computer in the boot drive (the lefthand or uppermost disk drive); this is the disk drive that first operates when the computer system is turned on. Lock the disk in the drive.

2. Turn the computer on, using the switch in the back of the machine. Next, locate the monitor switch (usually on the side or back of the equipment) and turn it on as well.

3. Wait while the system software is loaded from the **DOS** disk into the computer's memory. When you see the request for the present date and time, either press the **Enter** key twice to ignore the requests or enter the date, press the **Enter** key, enter the time and press the **Enter** key again.

4. In a few moments, you'll see the **A>** prompt on the screen (indicating that the boot drive where you placed the copy of the **DOS** disk is the active drive). Unlock the disk drive and remove the **DOS** disk.

5. Place the **Program** disk in the **A>** drive and lock it in.

6. Place your Works **Data** disk in the other disk drive—the **B>** drive—and lock it in.

7. Since you want to start the program, type in **Works**, and press the **Enter** key.

8. Now the program is loaded into the computer's memory. You will see the opening screen display identifying the version of Works that you are using and showing the limited menu bar with **File**, **Options**, and **Help** commands available. The choices available under the **File** menu—**Create New File**, **Open Existing File**, etc.—are displayed for your convenience (see Figure 4.1 on page 37).

You are now ready to use Microsoft Works.

Quitting Works Using a Dual 5.25 Inch Disk Drive System

With dual 5.25 inch disk drives, quitting Microsoft Works and turning off your computer requires some disk exchanging. Although Works will let you know if you haven't saved your files, always remember to save your document before exiting the program. Follow these steps when you are ready to quit using the program:

1. Press the **Alt** key (the one to the left of the space bar) to activate the menu bar commands. Note that the first letters on the command words, **F**ile, **O**ptions, **H**elp, are highlighted. The menus of commands beneath those words on the menu bar can now be accessed by pressing the appropriate letter—**F**, **O**, or **H**.
2. Press the **F** (for **F**ile) key to access the file commands.
3. When you see the **File** command menu, press the **X** (for E**x**it) key to quit Works.
4. In several moments, you'll see a message asking you to insert the disk containing the **Command.Com** file. This file is part of the operating system contained on the **DOS** disk. When you see that message appear on the screen, unlock the **A>** drive and remove the **Program** disk.
5. Now place the **DOS** disk in the **A>** drive. Lock in the disk and press the **Enter** key.
6. In a few moments, you will see an **A>** prompt displayed on the screen, indicating that you have exited the program and are now using the operating system. You can safely turn off the computer system and remove your **DOS** disk.
7. Reach behind the computer and turn off the power switch. Locate the power switch for the monitor and turn it off as well.

Using a Dual 3.5 Inch Disk Drive System

If you are using two 3.5 inch disk drives, you'll need the following disks each time you use Microsoft Works with an IBM-compatible computer:

- a disk containing a copy of the disk operating system (**DOS**)
- a copy of the Microsoft Works **Program** disk
- the formatted Works **Data** disk that came with the text

You will also need several other disks when you are performing certain tasks. When you want to check the spelling in your document, to use the help features that Works provides, or to use Works' thesaurus to help you choose the best word in a particular passage, you'll need the Microsoft Works **Spell, Help, and Thesaurus** disk. When you wish to have a lesson to help you improve your understanding of Works, you'll need to use one of the two tutorial disks— **Learning Works 1 and 2,** or **Learning Works 3**—that come with Microsoft Works. Finally, when you first make a working copy of your Works **Program** disk, you will need to use the **Setup** disk to configure your copy of Works to fit your system's graphic and printing options. Although that may sound like a lot of disks, most of the time you'll only need your Microsoft Works **Program** disk and your Works **Data** disk.

Making a Working Copy of the Program Disk

Before you can begin this section, you will need a blank 3.5 inch floppy disk to use as your new working **Program** disk. To make a working copy of the **Program** disk with dual 3.5 inch floppy disk drives, follow these steps:

1. Place the copy of the **DOS** (disk operating system) disk in the boot drive (generally the lefthand or uppermost disk drive); this is the disk drive that first operates when the computer system is turned on.
2. Turn the computer on, using the switch in the back of the machine. Next, locate the monitor switch (usually on the side or back of the equipment) and turn it on as well.
3. Wait while the system software is loaded from the **DOS** disk into the computer's memory. The first message you see is the system request for the current date and time. If you don't wish to enter that data, you can simply press the **Enter** key twice to ignore the requests. However, if you comply with the request, your computer will date your files when it saves your documents. These procedures help you keep track of your work sessions, so it is usually worth the trouble to enter the current date. Use the keyboard to enter the date in the requested form (for example, 09/15/92), and press the **Enter** key. Then enter the time in the requested form and press the **Enter** key again.
4. In a few moments, you'll see an **A>** prompt on the screen. The **A>** indicates that the boot drive (with the copy of the **DOS** disk) is the active drive; the other floppy drive will be identified as the **B>** drive. Press the button to eject the **DOS** disk from the drive.
5. Now place the Works **Setup** disk in the **A>** drive.
6. Type **Setup** and press the **Enter** key. In a few moments, questions and instructions will appear on the screen. Responding to the screen messages will allow you to configure the **Program** disk so that it will operate most efficiently with your particular computer system.
7. Place the blank 3.5 inch disk in the **B>** drive, and respond to the screen prompts to create a new working copy of the **Program** disk.

8. After you finish making a working copy of the **Program** disk, store the original **Program** disk in a safe place and only use the new copy.

You are now ready to create documents using your working copy of the Works program.

Starting Works Using a Dual 3.5 Inch Disk Drive System

To use Microsoft Works with dual 3.5 inch floppy disk drives, follow these steps each time you use the program:

1. Place the copy of the **DOS** disk in the boot drive (the lefthand or upper disk drive); this is the disk drive that first operates when the computer system is turned on.
2. Turn on the computer, using the switch in the back of the machine. Next, locate the monitor switch (usually on the side or back of the equipment) and turn it on as well.
3. Wait while the system software is loaded from the **DOS** disk into the computer's memory. When you see the request for the present date and time, either press the **Enter** key twice to ignore the requests or enter the date, press the **Enter** key, enter the time, and press the **Enter** key again.
4. In a few moments, you'll see an **A>** prompt on the screen (indicating that the boot drive where you placed the copy of the **DOS** disk is the active drive). Press the button to remove the **DOS** disk from the disk drive.
5. Place the **Program** disk in the **A>** drive.
6. Place your Works **Data** disk in the other disk drive—the **B>** drive.
7. Since you want to start the program, type Works, and press the **Enter** key.
8. Now the program is loaded into the computer's memory. You will see the opening screen display identifying the version of Works that you are using and showing the limited menu bar with **File**, **Options**, and **Help** commands available. The choices available under the **File** menu—**Create New File**, **Open Existing File**, etc.—are displayed for your convenience (see Figure 4.1 on page 37).

You are now ready to use Microsoft Works.

Quitting Works Using a Dual 3.5 Inch Disk Drive System

With dual 3.5 inch disk drives, quitting Microsoft Works and turning off your computer requires some disk exchanging. Although Works will let you know if you haven't saved your files, always remember to save your document before exiting the program. Follow these steps when you are ready to quit using the program:

1. Press the **Alt** key (the one to the left of the space bar) to activate the menu bar commands. Note that the first letters on the command words, **F**ile, **O**ptions,

Help, are highlighted. The menus of commands beneath those words on the menu bar can now be accessed by pressing the appropriate letter—**F**, **O**, or **H**.

2. Press the **F** (for **F**ile) key to access the file commands.
3. When you see the **File** command menu, press the **X** (for E**x**it) key to quit Works.
4. In several moments, you'll see a message asking you to insert the disk containing the **Command.Com** file. This file is part of the operating system contained on the **DOS** disk. When you see that message appear on the screen, press the button to eject the **Program** disk and remove it from the drive.
5. Now place the **DOS** disk in the **A>** drive, and press the **Enter** key.
6. In a few moments, you will see an **A>** prompt displayed on the screen, indicating that you have exited the program and are now using the operating system.
7. Press the buttons to eject your Works **Data** disk and the **DOS** disk, remove them from the disk drives, and place them in their carrying cases.
8. Reach behind the computer and turn off the power switch. Locate the power switch for the monitor and turn it off as well.

Using the Microsoft Works Tutorials

The tutorial lessons provided with Microsoft Works offer in-depth explanations and practice situations designed to help you master this software independently. The tutorials can be used as stand-alone lessons or they can be accessed from within the Works program itself. For example, if you need help with an application, **while you are using the program,** you needn't exit Works to have the lesson. Microsoft Works provides you with the option of using tutorials appropriate to the application you are using while working in the program.

First we will discuss the procedures for using the tutorials while you are already working in Microsoft Works and then address the stand-alone option.

Using the Tutorials within Works

You can access the tutorials while you are using Works by using either the mouse or the keyboard. Using a mouse, follow these steps:

1. Point to the **Help** command on the menu bar.
2. Press the mouse button on **Help** and Drag the pointer down to **Works Tutorial**.
3. When **Works Tutorial** is highlighted, release the mouse button. You have now selected the tutorial.

Using the keyboard, simply hold down the **Shift** key and press the **F1** key. This combined keystroke automatically places you in the tutorial lessons.

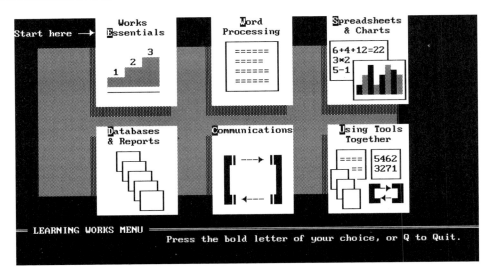

Figure 4.2 Microsoft Works Tutorials main menu

When you see the opening screen (Figure 4.2), you can easily proceed by following the prompts. The tutorials are designed for independent use by computer novices. The command options offered throughout the series of lessons are easily understood. Each lesson provides instruction and some practice situations. When using the tutorials within Works, you have the power to interrupt the lessons by quitting and resuming the use of Microsoft Works whenever you wish.

In addition, Works allows you to navigate through the lessons by holding the **Control** (**Ctrl**) key down. A menu entitled **Course Control** will pop up. The **Course Control** menu allows you to move quickly (forward or backward) through a lesson, print the lesson on paper, receive a lesson summary, return to the previous menu, or quit the Works Tutorials.

To use the **Course Control** menu, hold the **Ctrl** down and press one of the highlighted keys (while continuing to hold down the **Ctrl** key). Holding the **Ctrl** key down and pressing the **M** (**M**enu) key, for example, will return you to the menu of the current section. Figure 4.3 shows the menu of the **Works Essentials** section.

The **Course Control** menu facilitates your use of the lessons themselves. It keeps you from having to complete a lesson you don't need or from missing an explanation you would like to have repeated. The **Course Control** menu is available any time you are working on a lesson, but not when the main menus are displayed. The menus already provide you with the navigational control you need to move easily through the tutorials.

There are several subtle advantages to using the tutorials within Works as opposed to using them as stand-alone lessons. When you access the tutorials from Works, the program automatically places you in a tutorial corresponding to

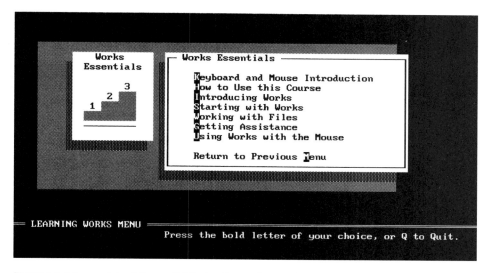

Figure 4.3 Menu of the Microsoft Works Tutorials **Works Essentials** section

the application you are using. For instance, if you are using the word processor and don't know how to use tabs, hold the **Shift** key down and press the **F1** key while using the **Tab** dialog box; the tutorial that appears on the screen explains how to use tabs. Similarly, if you access the tutorials from within the spreadsheet, the tutorial will explain the appropriate spreadsheet topic. For instance, if you wanted to know how to use the financial functions provided in the spreadsheet, the tutorial could explain the necessary procedures in a few moments. This context-sensitive nature of the tutorials provides the specific instruction you need quickly and efficiently.

The procedure for quitting the tutorials from within the Works program is easier than the stand-alone tutorials. When you quit, the tutorials return you to your place in the application, not to the operating system. For instance, if you press the **Shift** and **F1** keys to get a lesson on the use of borders while you are word processing a report, you are returned to the exact position in your report when you finish the tutorial. You don't have to restart Works or reopen the word-processed report to continue writing.

The next section explains how to use the Microsoft Works tutorials as stand-alone lessons using either a hard drive or a dual floppy disk drive system. Read the section that corresponds to your system.

Using the Tutorials Independently

To receive instruction on using Works without starting the program, you can use the tutorials by themselves. The procedure that allows you to use the tutorials as stand-alone lessons is similar to the steps that start up Works.

If you are using a *dual floppy disk drive system,* follow these steps:

1. Place your working copy of the **DOS** disk in the boot drive. Lock in the disk.
2. Turn on the computer and the monitor.
3. Wait while the system software is loaded from the **DOS** disk into the computer's RAM. Respond to the request for the current date and time as explained in the last section.
4. In a few moments, you'll see an **A>** prompt on the screen; unlock the disk drive and remove the **DOS** disk.
5. Place the **Learning Works 1** disk in drive **A>**. Again, lock in the disk.
6. Since you want to use the Microsoft **Works Tutorials,** type Learn, and press the **Enter** key.

In a few moments, you will be presented with requests and instructions. Carefully read the screen messages and use the keyboard to respond appropriately. With a 5.25 inch dual disk drive system, the **Learning Works 1** disk is the only disk you'll need if you request lessons on **Works Essentials** or most word-processing topics. With a 3.5 inch dual disk drive system, the **Learning Works 1 and 2** disk contains the lessons on word-processing, spreadsheet, and database topics. When you request lessons on topics not stored on the disk you are using, Works will prompt you to exchange that **Learning Works** disk for the appropriate one. In that case, simply remove the disk, insert the requested disk, and press the **Enter** key.

If you are using a *hard disk drive system,* follow these steps:

1. Turn on the computer using the switch in the back or on the side of the machine. Next, locate the monitor switch and turn it on as well.
2. Wait while the system software is loaded from the hard disk into the computer's memory. Respond appropriately to the system's request for the present date and time.
3. In a few moments, you will see a **C>** prompt on the screen. Access the Microsoft Works subdirectory by using the keyboard to type CD Works, and press the **Enter** key.
4. Since you want to use the Microsoft **Works Tutorials**, type Learn, and press the **Enter** key.

In a few moments, you will be presented with requests and instructions. Carefully read the screen messages and use the keyboard to respond appropriately. Since the lessons from all three of the **Works Tutorials** are stored on your hard disk drive, you won't need to handle any floppy disks.

Once you are in the lessons, the instructions are basically the same as those provided in the previous section, **Using the Tutorials Within Works.** The **Course Control** menu is still available to help you easily navigate through the tutorials. To use the **Course Control** menu, hold the **Ctrl** key down and simultaneously press one of the highlighted keys**.** Remember, this option can be accessed from within any of the lessons but is not available when the main menus are displayed.

Recall the two differences between using the tutorials independently or within Works mentioned in the previous section. The tutorials are not context-sensitive when used independently from the Works program, so you must navigate through the main menu each time you use them. Also, when you quit the tutorials, you are returned to the operating system (and the **A>** or **C>** prompts), *not* back to the program.

When you have had sufficient tutoring for one session, follow these steps to exit the tutorials and turn off your computer:

1. If a menu is displayed on your screen, simply press the **Q** (**Q**uit) key to exit the tutorials. If you are in the middle of a lesson, hold down the **Ctrl** key and press the **Q** (**Q**uit) key once**.**

If you are using a *dual floppy disk drive system,* follow these steps:

2. When you see a message appear on the screen asking you to insert the disk containing the **Command.Com** file, unlock the disk drive and remove the **Learning Works 1** disk.
3. Insert the **DOS** disk, lock it in, and press the **Enter** key.
4. In a few moments, you'll see an **A>** prompt displayed on the screen, indicating that you have exited the tutorial and are now using the operating system. You can safely remove your disks and turn the computer system off.

If you are using a *hard disk drive system,* follow these steps:

2. When you see **C>** displayed on the screen (indicating you are now using the operating system from the hard disk drive), unlock the disk drive, and remove your Works **Learning Works 1** disk.
3. Turn off the computer and the monitor.

Using the Microsoft Works Help Features

The **Help** features in Microsoft Works can be accessed only while you are using the program. The procedures for using the **Help** features are similar to those for using the tutorials within Works. Like the tutorials, the **Help** features are context-sensitive—that is, they can simplify your searching process by offering help or lessons relative to the component of Works in which you are presently working. Therefore, when you are working with the word processor and need help, for example, you don't have to search through lists of suggestions referring to databases or spreadsheets.

In addition, the procedures for exiting the **Help** and tutorial components are similar. Both programs return you to the application and the document you were working on when you accessed them. When you are finished using the **Help** features, Works returns you to the place from which you sought help.

You can activate the **Help** features by using either the mouse or the keyboard. *To use the mouse,* follow these steps:

1. Point to the **Help** command on the menu bar.
2. Press the mouse button and Drag the pointer down, selecting **Using Help** by highlighting it.
3. Release the mouse button.

To use the keyboard, simply press the **F1** key. This keystroke automatically places you in the **Help** layer.

Whichever technique you use, you will soon notice the **Microsoft Works Help** index window displayed in the middle of the screen (Figure 4.4).

When you see the **Help** screen, you can proceed easily by following the offered prompts and suggestions. The **Help** layer is designed to be used independently, and the command options offered are easily understood and applied.

The **Help** layer is organized in indices, with a context-specific index available for each of the **Help** categories. These indices serve to expedite the process of searching for help and include: **B**ASIC SKILLS, **I**NTRODUCING THE TOOLS, **K**EYBOARD, **M**OUSE, **C**OMMANDS, and **P**ROCEDURES. Each category has an alphabetical index of sub-topics with detailed explanations clarifying the use of a particular aspect or command structure of Microsoft Works. If you find you need an even more detailed explanation than the **Help** layer provides, you can access the tutorials directly from the **Help** layer by choosing the **L**esson option shown at the bottom of the screen.

Once you have entered the **Help** layer, you can navigate through the features with the mouse or the keyboard. To change **Help** categories with a mouse, Point to the category you wish and Click the mouse button. To change categories with

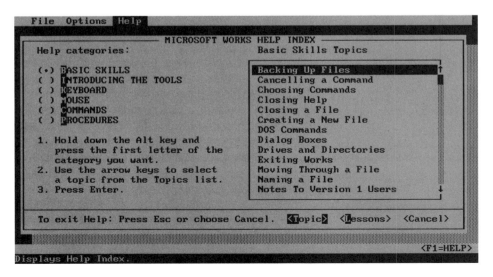

Figure 4.4 Microsoft Works **Help** index

the keyboard, hold down the **Alt** key and press the key corresponding to the first letter of the category you wish to access (for instance, press the **C** key for the **C**ommands index or the **P** key for the **P**rocedures index).

Once you are in the category you seek, you can use either the mouse or keyboard to select the specific commands that you want clarified. Using a mouse, Point to the command you want to have explained and Click the mouse.

Using the keyboard:

1. Use the arrow keys to highlight the command you want explained and then press the **Enter** key.
2. If the command you want to have clarified is not visible, activate the **scroll bars** to the right of the **Help** screen with the arrow keys or the mouse pointer. This will reveal any commands that are hidden from view.
3. Highlight the sought-after command and press the **Enter** key.

Once you locate the command or feature that you want clarified, you can use the **scroll bars** to the right of the **Help** screen to help you find the instructions you seek. Remember: if the explanation provided in the **Help** overlay is not sufficient, you can always request a lesson from the **Works Tutorial** by selecting the **L**esson option.

As an example of this process, imagine that the thirty-page document you have created is single-spaced and you decide it should be double-spaced. You could use the mouse or the keyboard to highlight the text manually, but you'd prefer a shortcut, if one exists. You hope Works has a command available to highlight all of the text in the document. You notice the **All** option under the **Select** command on the menu bar. It sounds good, but, being prudent, you want to make sure it does what you think it will. What should you do?

Using the keyboard:

1. Hold down the **Alt** key, then the **S** (for **S**elect) key, and press the **down arrow** to highlight the **All** option under the **Select** menu.
2. Press the **F1** key to get help with the command. An explanation of the **Select All** command will appear on the screen. By choosing the **Select All** command, you can indeed highlight all the text in the document and double-space the entire paper in one step.
3. Exit the **Help** layer by pressing the **Esc** key, or choose the **Cancel** button with the mouse or arrow keys.

The **Help** features provide useful and efficient answers to your questions without your having to consult manuals or your friends. When you want a comprehensive lesson, choose the tutorials that Microsoft Works provides. If you want a quick answer to clarify a momentary confusion, the **Help** layer in Works is the place to start.

5 Focusing on Word Processing

Word-processing programs permit the user to process, not just type, text. Instead of writing with ink or pencil as you normally do, when you word process, you write with light electronically. Word processors offer wonderful powers to everyone who considers writing an important task. Certainly, most professionals find that the word processor is an indispensable tool. With a word processor, you can easily change, move, or remove any characters, words, sentences, or paragraphs you have entered. The style of the characters, the spacing and justification of the text, and the margins of a document can all be altered instantaneously with a word processor.

The power of word processing is often compared to that offered by an enhanced electric typewriter. In fact, there is very little difference between the latest electric typewriters and the original word-processing programs. However, the difference between a standard electric typewriter and a modern word-processing program is dramatic. Text you create with a typewriter cannot be altered without using white-out or retyping. Changing the sequence, emphasis, or format of text you create with a typewriter is laborious and time-consuming.

To illustrate the difference between a standard electric typewriter and a word processor, imagine two secretaries producing a dictated letter. Tom uses a standard electric typewriter without a memory; Wendy uses a computer with a word-processing program. Each must first enter the letter's text using their machines. This portion of the task requires roughly the same amount of time with either typewriter or word processor. Once the letter is completed, Tom takes his letter from the typewriter while Wendy, having stored her letter on a data disk, is still printing a copy of it with her printer. So far, the efficiency advantage seems slightly in Tom's favor.

After the text is entered, however, the powers of the word processor become more evident. The secretaries detect several errors when they proofread the letter. Tom will have to retype the entire letter, but Wendy can simply correct the errors on screen and reprint the letter. Now suppose the supervisor decides the letter must be double-spaced, not single-spaced, and that the left and right margins should be changed from 1 inch to 1.25 inches. Again, Tom has to retype the letter from scratch. Wendy has only to add margin setting commands and a simple double-space command before she prints a new copy of the letter.

Finally, imagine that the same letter must be sent to five different individuals. The only differences will be the individual's name and address and a sentence or two to personalize the letter. Tom will have to retype an entirely new letter for each receiver; Wendy will only have to make the name, address, and unique sentence changes for each letter on screen and then print out a new letter for each person.

Several minutes after she receives the requests, Wendy will have delivered the six letters, including the suggested changes, and be ready for her next task. Tom, on the other hand, will probably still be retyping the original letter to eliminate the errors he detected while proofreading. Next week, if more copies of the letter must be sent to more individuals, Tom will have to start all over again. Wendy will simply copy the letter from her data disk, change the date and other details, and print the new letters in a very short time. Expand this scenario to a week or month of professional tasks, and the advantages of word processing become obvious.

An Introduction to Word Processing

Word processing derives its name from the idea that the user engages in a total writing process. Word processing goes beyond merely entering words on a sheet of paper; it produces both the text itself and its ultimate appearance.

In some ways, a word processor gives the writer the same creative freedom as a pen or a pencil. However, writing with a word processor is much less labor intensive than writing by hand. Because you create your text electronically, you can easily change, move, or remove any character, word, sentence, or paragraph without sacrificing hours of labor.

Although the power of word processing is often compared to that of an enhanced electric typewriter, a modern word-processing program such as Microsoft Works provides dramatic and powerful advantages to the writer. For instance, text you create with a typewriter cannot be altered without using white-out or retyping. With a word processor, however, you can change the sequence, emphasis, or format of your text quite easily. The style of the characters, the spacing and justification of the text, and the margins of the document can all be altered after you have word processed the text. Many word-processing programs (including Microsoft Works) even allow the writer to add illustrations and charts to the documents and merge data stored in computerized form.

The keyboard for a word processor is similar to a typewriter keyboard, but with some important differences. With a typewriter, the typist must press the carriage return at the end of each line, listening for the sound of the little bell that all typists learn to use as a gauge. With a word processor, you can type continuously without having to remain conscious of the ends of lines and without having to press the carriage return except to create new paragraphs. This **word-wrap** capability (so named because text automatically moves down or "wraps" to the next line) allows you to continue typing while the words automatically move to the next line.

As the characters are being entered and as the text wraps, a **cursor** indicates the writer's position on the monitor. The cursor, a blinking point of light, moves up, down, right, and left and can highlight individual words, single lines, or whole paragraphs. You can move the cursor to any position on the screen by using the mouse or the arrow keys on the keyboard. When not in use, the cursor remains a blinking light indicating your current position in the text. As you enter text by typing at the keyboard, the cursor moves along with the text.

To move to another part of the document, you scroll up or down by using the arrow key or pointing the mouse to the **scroll bars** on the right and bottom of the screen. Scrolling quickly moves the cursor to the new location in the text. Since the entire document you create is in the computer's memory, you do not need to remove or replace separate sheets of paper if you wish to move to another page. By moving the cursor, you can easily move to other parts of the text.

When you first begin a new document, the margins and spacing will already be set at default (or standard) settings by the computer. With Microsoft Works, the top and bottom margins are set to 1 inch, the left margin is set to 1.3 inches and the right margin is set to 1.2 inches. If you wish to change the margins, simply command the computer to make the changes you want. You can also change the spacing from the default single-space setting to other spacings. The standard alignment for text is from the left, but you can center or right justify text, or even have it aligned on both the right and left margins (called fully justified).

Word processors also let you change the style of letters with the use of simple keystroke commands. You can produce text that is normal, **boldfaced,** underlined, *italicized*, ~~strikethrough~~, or a combination of all. Most word processors allow you to create superscribed text (for example, with exponents: X^2) or

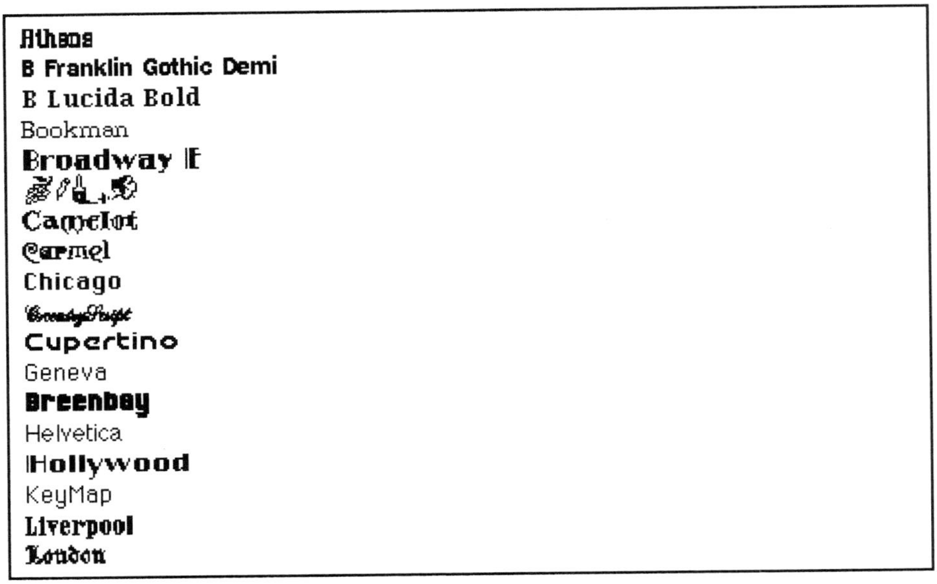

Athens
B Franklin Gothic Demi
B Lucida Bold
Bookman
Broadway E
〰〰〰〰
Camelot
Carmel
Chicago
Crossing Script
Cupertino
Geneva
Greenbay
Helvetica
Hollywood
KeyMap
Liverpool
London

Figure 5.1 Examples of different font styles

subscribed text (for example, with formulas: H_2O). Beyond that, word processors typically offer you the power to choose the size of individual letters or words and the font you wish to use.

A font is a particular style of lettering—thick or thin, formal or casual. A variety of different fonts are available, some especially well suited for a business environment, others most appropriate for informal documents (Figure 5.1).

Among the most important and convenient advantages of word processors are the powers they give writers to save, edit, delete, and change text. By pressing the **Backspace** key, for instance, you can delete a previously mistyped letter or eliminate as much text as you want. You can also use the mouse to highlight whole sections of text for rewriting or for moving sections to different parts of the document. You can move text to different areas or insert completed text in a new position without retyping, cutting and pasting paper, drawing arrows, or any of the other traditional techniques writers have used when working with their texts. Obviously, such capabilities make revision and editing very easy.

When you are finished with a writing session, you can save what you have produced by executing a simple **Save** command. The computer stores what you have written on a hard or floppy disk. Although you will probably always print out a hard (paper) copy, that copy will not be the only one accessible; the computer will have stored other copies for you to work with later.

During the past five years, word-processing programs (including Microsoft Works) have added features that address the content of documents as well as the text itself. Many programs now include a spell checker and a thesaurus, and some even provide grammar and writing style checkers. With these features, the computer can flag apparently misspelled words, recommend alternative words, indicate erroneous sentence structures, and provide the definitions of unrecognized words directly on the computer screen.

Now it's your turn to use these features for yourself. In the next section, you will master many of the powers of the Microsoft Works word processor. You will learn to create a new document, edit an existing document, change text characteristics (including justification, style, font, size, and spacing), check your spelling, and print out a word-processed document.

Creating and Saving a New Word-Processed Document

Getting Started

To start the Microsoft Works application, use the same procedure that you used when completing the section, **Using the Microsoft Works Tutorials.** Follow these steps to start Works with a *hard disk drive system:*

1. Turn on both the computer and monitor.
2. Wait while the system software is loaded from the **DOS** disk into the computer's memory. Respond appropriately to the system request for the current date and time.
3. When you see a **C>** prompt on the screen, access the Works subdirectory by typing **CD Works** and pressing the **Enter** key.
4. Place your Works **Data** disk in the **A:** drive and lock in the disk.
5. Type **Works** and press the **Enter** key.
6. When the program is loaded into the computer's memory, you will see the Works opening screen display.

To use Microsoft Works with *dual 5.25 inch floppy disk drives,* follow these steps:

1. Place the copy of the **DOS** disk in the boot drive and lock in the disk.
2. Turn on both the computer and monitor.
3. Wait while the system software is loaded from the **DOS** disk into the computer's memory. Respond appropriately to the system request for the current date and time.
4. When you see the **A>** prompt on the screen, unlock the disk drive and remove the **DOS** disk.
5. Place the Works **Program** disk in the **A:** drive and lock in the disk.
6. Place your Works **Data** disk in the **B:** drive and lock in the disk.
7. Type **Works** and press the **Enter** key.
8. When the program is loaded into the computer's memory, you will see the Works opening screen display.

To use Microsoft Works with *dual 3.5 inch floppy disk drives,* follow these steps:

1. Place the copy of the **DOS** disk in the boot drive.
2. Turn on both the computer and monitor.
3. Wait while the system software is loaded from the **DOS** disk into the computer's memory. Respond appropriately to the system request for the current date and time.
4. When you see the **A>** prompt on the screen, remove the **DOS** disk.
5. Place the Works **Program** disk in the **A:** drive.
6. Place your Works **Data** disk in the **B:** drive.
7. Type **Works** and press the **Enter** key.
8. When the program is loaded into the computer's memory, you will see the Works opening screen display.

If you need additional help getting to this point, see the **Getting Started with Microsoft Works** sections in this text.

Opening a New Word-Processed Document

Issue the command to open a new document by pressing the **N** (for Create **N**ew File) key. Next instruct Works that you want to open a new word-processed document by pressing the **W** (for **W**ord Processor) key. In a few moments, Works copies the word-processor program into memory and displays a blinking cursor to indicate you can now enter text (Figure 5.2).

Now that you are in the Works word processor, you can see the **menu bar** across the top of the screen; you will use this later to select special commands.

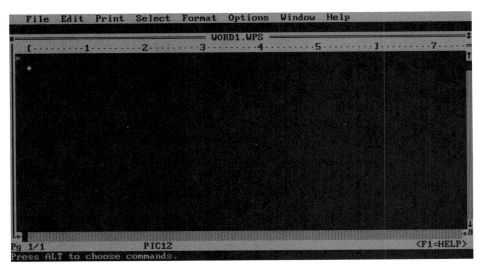

Figure 5.2 Word processor blank document screen before any text has been entered

The **title box** is below the menu bar. Works has placed **WORD1.WPS** in the title box, indicating that you have just started a new word-processing document without assigning it a name. The **.WPS** is an extension that Works uses to indicate that the document is created with the word processor. Since the new document is still unnamed, Works suggests the file name, **WORD1.WPS.** The **ruler** appears below the file name, showing the width of the document in inches. You will use the ruler later when you format your document.

The blinking cursor appears in the upper left corner of the blank screen, indicating the point at which you can enter text. After you have entered some text, you will be able to move the cursor with the mouse or the arrow keys, thus controlling where in the document you enter characters. If you are using a mouse, the **scroll bars** appearing to the right and below the blank word-processing screen will help you navigate through long or wide documents (Figure 5.3).

Figure 5.3 Word processor scroll bar

Creating an Opening Day Letter

Figure 5.4 shows a typical "opening of school" letter that educators often send to parents in the fall to provide them with valuable information about the new school year. You will gain some practice using the word processor by entering this letter into the computer.

As you type the letter into the word processor, replace the words that are all capitals (YOUR NAME, YOUR OFFICE ADDRESS, or YOUR STREET ADDRESS) with your personal information. As you enter text, press the **Enter** key *only* when you want to start a new line—after you have finished typing your name or your office address. If you make a mistake, press the **Backspace** key to remove the character to the left of the cursor's position. If the error is not immediately to the left of the cursor's position, use the **right arrow, left arrow, up arrow,** or **down arrow** keys to position the cursor to the right of the mistake and then use the **Backspace** key.

Once you start typing the body of the letter, the text-wrap capability of the word processor will let you keep typing without having to enter carriage returns.

YOUR NAME
YOUR OFFICE ADDRESS
YOUR STREET ADDRESS
YOUR CITY, YOUR STATE YOUR ZIP CODE

August 23, 1991

Dear Grant Public School families:

Welcome back! It is nearly September and time to start planning another exciting school year. School will begin on September 4th and the hours will remain the same as last year. The school day will begin at 8:30 and will dismiss at 2:40.

Registration for students will take place in the auditorium on August 31, from 10:00 in the morning to 4:00 in the afternoon. If your child is entering our district for the first time, you will need to bring a registration packet. Students must be 5 years old before October 1st to enter Kindergarten, and 6 years old before October 1st to enter first grade. Students entering our school district for the first time must bring their immunization records from a physician or medical clinic.

We have had enrollment changes, and as a result, some staff changes. Teachers report to work on September 2nd and have a full schedule of inservice meetings before the first day of school. I know you want to know classroom assignments, especially in the primary grades, where there may be some changes. I wish I could tell you now, but I have to wait until after registration to know precisely how we will be organized this year.

Thank you for your cooperation in making this the start of a great school year.

Sincerely Yours,

YOUR NAME

Figure 5.4 An opening day letter

Press the **Enter** key only at the end of each paragraph or any line that ends before the right margin. When you finish typing, you will store the information on the data disk provided with this text so that you can use it later.

Using the keyboard:

1. Type your name, using the **Shift** key to capitalize the first letter in your first and last names. (If you accidentally press the **Caps Lock** key, all the charac-

ters you type will be uppercase letters. If you press the **Caps Lock** key a second time, the text will return to lowercase letters.)

2. After the last letter in your last name, press the **Enter** key once.

Note that the cursor moves to the lefthand margin of the next line, in position for you to type your office address.

3. Use the **Shift** key again to capitalize the first letter in your office (or school) address.
4. After the last letter in your address, press the **Enter** key again.
5. Repeat the process for the remainder of the letterhead information, the date, and the greeting. Remember, if you make a mistake, just use the **Backspace** key to remove the character to the left of the cursor.

Saving Your Letter

Remember, once the computer is turned off, the information temporarily stored in it is lost unless it has been saved onto a disk. When you finish entering the letter into the computer, therefore, store the information on your data disk so that it will be available for future use. To store (or save) your letter on the disk, follow these steps:

1. Press the **Alt** key and then the **F** (for **F**ile) key (or use the mouse to point to the **File** command on the menu bar).
2. Press the **A** (for Save **A**s) key to select the **Save As** command (or press the mouse button, Drag the pointer down the options on the pull-down menu until you highlight the **Save As** choice, and release the mouse button). Note the **Save file as** dialog box displayed on the screen (Figure 5.5).

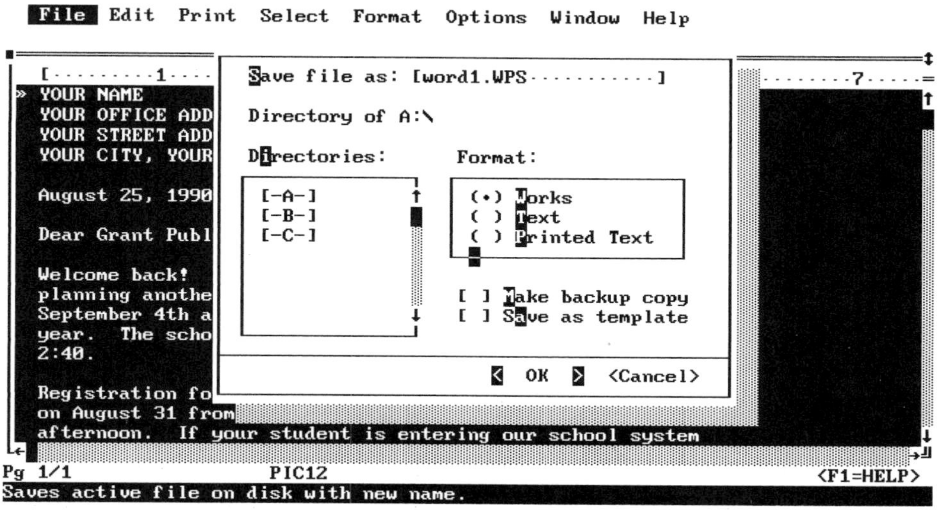

```
 File  Edit  Print  Select  Format  Options  Window  Help

  [········1····    Save file as: [word1.WPS············]       ········7····
» YOUR NAME
  YOUR OFFICE ADD    Directory of A:\
  YOUR STREET ADD
  YOUR CITY, YOUR    Directories:        Format:

  August 25, 1990    [-A-]              (•) Works
                     [-B-]              ( ) Text
  Dear Grant Publ    [-C-]              ( ) Printed Text

  Welcome back!
  planning anothe                      [ ] Make backup copy
  September 4th a                      [ ] Save as template
  year.  The scho
  2:40.
                                        ◀  OK  ▶  <Cancel>
  Registration fo
  on August 31 from
  afternoon.  If your student is entering our school system

Pg 1/1            PIC12                                    <F1=HELP>
Saves active file on disk with new name.
```

Figure 5.5 Save file as dialog box, used to name and save files to specific disks or directories

3. Works suggests that you save the document using the name **WORD1.WPS** on the active disk (the Works **Program** disk if you are using a dual floppy system, or the Works subdirectory if you are using a hard disk drive system). You need to change the disk on which the document will be stored and then change the name of the document.

4. Instruct Works to save the file on your Works **Data** disk. While holding down the **Alt** key, press the **I** (for Directories) key. When the blinking cursor appears in the **Directories** dialog box, press the **down arrow** until you highlight the letter of the disk drive containing your Works **Data** disk (the **[-A-]** drive if you are using a hard disk drive system, or the **[-B-]** drive if you're using a dual floppy system) and press the **Enter** key. This procedure makes your Works **Data** disk the active disk. Notice the **Directory of** line in the dialog box now shows that the active directory is the drive holding your Works **Data** disk (an **A:** with a hard disk drive system, a **B:** with a dual floppy system).

5. Press the **Tab** key to move to the **Save file as** dialog box. Use the keyboard to type a new file name for your letter. You can use up to 8 characters to name your files, but you *cannot use spaces*. Let's choose a simple name for this file: **LETTER**. Type LETTER and press the **Enter** key. Works will quickly store the letter you just typed on your Works **Data** disk under the name, **LETTER.WPS**. Works adds the **.WPS** extension to your file to show that it is a word-processed file. (In later exercises, Works will use the **.WDB** extension to indicate a database file and the **.WKS** extension to represent a spreadsheet file.)

6. To make sure you have succeeded in saving the file on the disk, press the **Alt** key, then the **F** (for **F**ile) key, and then the **O** (for **O**pen Existing File) key to select the **Open Existing File** command. (Or use the mouse to point to the **File** command on the menu bar, press the mouse button, Drag the pointer down to highlight the **Open Existing File** choice, and release the mouse button.)

7. Examine the **File to open** dialog box displayed on the screen. Your file, **LETTER.WPS**, will be listed among the files shown in the **Files** box.

8. Once you have verified that your file exists on your Works **Data** disk, press the **Esc** key to cancel the **Open Existing File** command and return to your word-processed file.

Exiting Works

Since you know that your text is stored on your Works **Data** disk under the name **LETTER.WPS**, you can safely exit Works without worrying about losing the information in your file. At this point, we'll practice exiting the program and shutting down the computer. To do so, follow these steps:

1. Press the **Alt** key, then press the **F** (for **F**ile) key to access the file commands.

2. When you see the **File** command menu, press the **X** (for E**x**it) key to quit Works.

3. With a *hard disk drive system*, you'll soon see the **C>** prompt on the screen, indicating that you have exited Works. You can safely remove your disk and turn off the computer system. With a *dual floppy drive system,* you'll see a message asking you to insert the disk containing the **Command.Com** file. When that message appears on the screen, remove the Works **Program** disk, insert the **DOS** disk, and press the **Enter** key. The **A>** prompt you see on the screen indicates you have exited Works.

4. Unlock the disk drive, remove your Works **Data** disk, and replace it in its carrying case. (With a dual floppy system, remove the **DOS** disk as well.)

5. Reach behind the computer and turn off the power switch. Locate the power switch for the monitor and turn it off as well.

Formatting and Printing a Word-Processed Document

Getting Started

In your next exercise you will enhance the appearance of your letter (by adding boldfacing, underlining, centering, and other formatting) and print the final version on paper. To begin, you must bring the letter you typed and saved on your Works **Data** disk back into the memory of the computer.

Follow these steps to start Works with a *hard disk drive system:*

1. Turn on both the computer and monitor.

2. When you see the system request for the current date and time, use the keyboard to enter the information in the requested form.

3. When you see a **C>** prompt on the screen, type CD Works and press the **Enter** key.

4. Place your Works **Data** disk in the **A:** drive and lock the disk in the drive.

5. Type Works and press the **Enter** key. When the program is loaded into the computer's memory, you will see the Works opening screen display.

To use Microsoft Works with either *3.5 inch* or *5.25 inch floppy drive systems,* follow these steps:

1. Place the copy of the **DOS** disk in the boot drive, lock the disk in the drive, and turn on both the computer and monitor.

2. When you see the system request for the current date and time, use the keyboard to enter the information in the requested form.

3. When you see the **A>** prompt on the screen, remove the **DOS** disk, place the Works **Program** disk in the **A:** drive, and then place your Works **Data** disk in the **B:** drive.

4. Type Works and press the **Enter** key. When the program is loaded into the computer's memory, you will see the Works opening screen display.

If you need additional help getting to this point, see the **Starting Works** sections that explain in greater detail the start-up procedures using floppy or hard disk drive systems.

Opening the LETTER.WPS File

When you see the opening screen, instead of creating a new word-processed document as you did for the last exercise, you will open an existing file, **LETTER.WPS.** To open the **LETTER.WPS** file stored on your Works **Data** disk, follow the same steps you used to verify that your file was saved on your Works **Data** disk:

1. Press the **O** (for **O**pen Existing File) key. Note the **File to open** dialog box displayed on the screen (Figure 5.6).
2. Works lists the files on the active disk (the **Program** disk if you are using a dual floppy system, or on the Works subdirectory if you are using a hard disk drive system). Next, you need to make the disk drive containing your Works **Data** disk—either the **[-A-]** or **[-B-]** drive—the active directory so you can access the **LETTER.WPS** file stored there.
3. While holding down the **Alt** key, press the **I** (for D**i**rectories) key. When the blinking cursor appears in the **Directories** dialog box, press the **down arrow** until you highlight the letter of the disk drive containing your Works **Data** disk (the **[-A-]** drive if you are using a hard disk drive system; the **[-B-]** drive if you are using a dual floppy system) and press the **Enter** key. This makes your Works **Data** disk the active disk. Notice the **Directory of** line in the dialog box now shows that the active directory is the location of your Works **Data** disk (an **A:** with a hard disk drive system, a **B:** with a dual floppy system) and the **Files** box displays the files on your Works **Data** disk.
4. Hold down the **Alt** key and press the **F** (for **F**iles) key. When you see the blinking cursor in the **Files** dialog box, use the **down arrow** to highlight your **LETTER.WPS** file and press the **Enter** key.

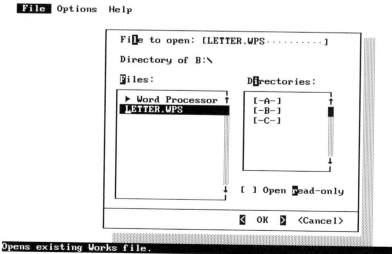

Figure 5.6 **File to open** dialog box

5. Works will copy the **LETTER.WPS** file from the disk and place the copy in the computer's memory. In a few moments, you should see your letter displayed on the screen.

Using the Works Setting to Modify the Screen Display

When you first start Works, the default screen setting is for text display instead of graphics display. When Works is set for text display, it operates more quickly, but you cannot see special characters such as underlined and italicized letters on the screen. However, you can easily change the default settings and change the colors displayed on the screen to suit your own tastes and needs. This is a good time to change the screen display to ensure that the formatting changes you will make in the upcoming exercises will be easily visible on the screen—as well as on paper after you print the document.

To change the screen display, follow these steps:

1. Press the **Alt** key, then the **O** (for **O**ption) key to access the **Option** menu, and the **W** (for **W**orks Settings) key to choose the **Works Settings** dialog box. (Or use the mouse to Point to the **Option** menu, press the mouse button and Drag the pointer down to highlight the **Works Settings** option, and release the mouse button.)

Examine the many options that are available in the **Works Settings** dialog box (Figure 5.7). The **Country** box lets you choose foreign symbols, such as the currency sign (dollar sign or pound sign, etc.). The **Units** box allows you to set the printer settings in units of measure other than inches. With the **Screen Color** box, you can choose which colors the screen will display on the borders and background.

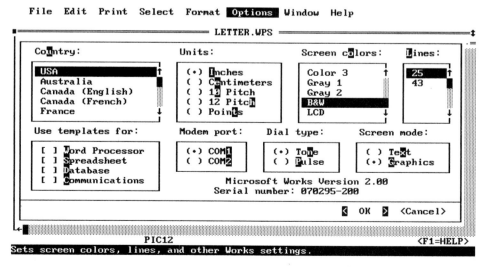

Figure 5.7 Works Settings dialog box

2. You can experiment with the screen colors on your own after you change the **Screen mode** to graphics display. To change the screen display so that formatting changes are visible on the screen, hold down the **Alt** key and press the **G** (for **G**raphics) key to choose the **Graphics Screen** mode. (Or use the mouse to Point to the parentheses to the right of the **Graphics** option and Click the mouse button.) Note that a dot appears between the parentheses to confirm that the **Screen mode** is now set to **Graphics**.

(If you do not wish to experiment with changing the screen color now, you can press the **Enter** key to exit the **Works Settings** dialog box and return to your **LETTER.WPS** document. If you would like to change the screen colors, follow the procedures listed below. Keep in mind, however, that the color choices you will be presented with and the quality of the screen display on your monitor will depend on the graphics capability of your system.)

3. To change the screen color, hold the **Alt** key down and press the **O** (for **Co**lor) key, then use the **down arrow** to highlight your color choice. When you have selected the color you wish, press the **Enter** key to exit the **Works Settings** dialog box and return to your **LETTER.WPS** document. If you don't like the resulting color, return to the **Works Settings** dialog box by pressing the **Alt** key, then the **O** (for **O**ption) key and choose a different color setting.

When you decide on the color setting you prefer, return to your **LETTER.WPS** document and begin the next exercise.

Setting Up Works for Your Printer

In the next procedure, you will make sure that Works is set up to print with your printer. Although you won't print your letter until you finish reformatting it, one of the formatting changes that you will make—altering the size of the characters you use—will not function unless you have already selected a printer capable of printing graphics. Therefore, to set Works up to print with your dot matrix or laser printer, follow these steps:

1. Press the **Alt** key, then the **P** key to access the **Print** menu (Figure 5.8).
2. Press the **S** (for **S**etup) key. (Or use the mouse to Point to the **Print** menu, press the mouse button, Drag the pointer down to highlight the **Printer Setup** option, and release the mouse button.)

Examine the options presented in the **Printer Setup** dialog box (Figure 5.9). The choices that you see may well differ from those shown here. You established which printer choices are displayed here when you installed Works using the **Setup** disk. If you wish to change the printer choices on your working copy of the Works **Program** disk, you can use the **Setup** disk to do so.

The **TTY** option represents a Teletype model that will not print graphics. If the **TTY** option is the only choice you see, you will have to use the **Setup** disk to add a printer capable of printing graphics or skip the section on changing the

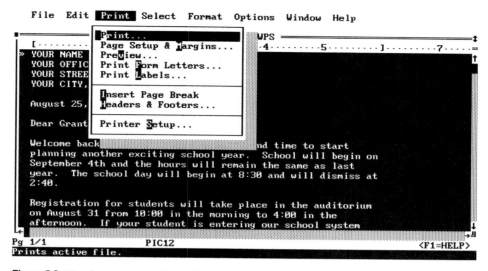

Figure 5.8 Word processor **Print** pull-down menu

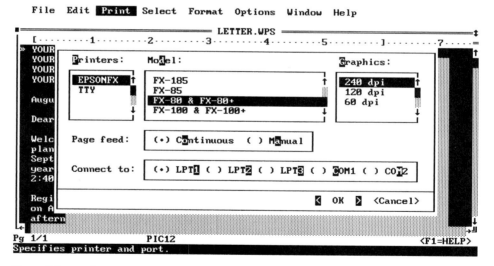

Figure 5.9 Word processor **Printer Setup** dialog box

size of characters. If you have printers listed other than the **TTY** model, follow these steps to instruct Works to use one of them:

1. The blinking cursor should already be in the **Printers** box. If not, hold down the **Alt** key and press the **P** key (or use the mouse) to place the cursor in the **Printers** box.

2. Use the **up** or **down arrow** keys (or the mouse) to highlight the printer you want.

Notice the changed options presented in the **Model** and **Graphics** boxes when you select a new printer. The **Graphics** box lets you determine the number of dots per inch (**DPI**) that your printer will use when it prints your documents. The higher the number, the greater the resolution (that is, the better the quality of the printout), but the longer the printing process. For the moment, you don't need to change these settings, so proceed with the next step:

3. Press the **Enter** key to select the printer with graphic capabilities and return to your word-processed document. Now you are ready to enhance the appearance of your letter.

Formatting the Letter—Justification and Boldface

The first change you'll make to your letter is to center the letterhead that you created. To change text in any way, you must first select or highlight it.

1. Make sure that the cursor is on the first letter of your first name in the letterhead. To select the letterhead text, hold down the **Shift** key and press the **down arrow** key four times to highlight all the text in the first four lines. (Or use the mouse to position the cursor to the left of the first letter in your name, press the mouse button, Drag the cursor down to highlight the letterhead text, and release the mouse button.)

If you have highlighted all four lines of the letterhead, you are ready for the next step. If not, release the **Shift** key and press any arrow key once (or click the mouse button once) to turn off the highlighting, return the cursor to the top of the document, and try the steps again.

2. Press the **Alt** key, then the **T** key to access the **Format** menu (Figure 5.10).

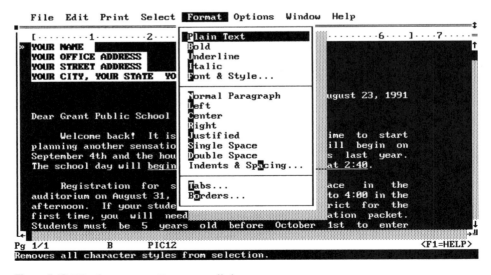

Figure 5.10 Word processor **Format** pull-down menu

3. Press the **C** key to **Center** the text. (Or use the mouse to Point to the **Format** menu, press the mouse button, Drag the pointer down to highlight the **Center** option, and release the mouse button.) Notice that the text you selected, still highlighted, is now centered.

You could perform this same task more easily by using a keyboard shortcut. To center highlighted text with the shortcut method, hold down the **Ctrl** key and press the **C** (for **C**enter) key. This method is quicker than using the menu bar, but it requires you to remember the shortcut commands.

In general, you'll find that many shortcut commands are available in Works (see **Appendix A**), and you'll probably remember the ones you use most often. However, to maintain a simple format within this text, the exercise instructions typically will include only one method for executing a command. When you want to see if a shortcut exists, refer to **Appendix A**.

For now, you'll make the text in the letterhead boldfaced so that it stands out more clearly. This time, you'll use the keyboard shortcut method to complete the task.

1. Since the text is still highlighted from the last exercise, simply hold down the **Ctrl** key and press the **B** (for **B**oldface) key.
2. Next, press any of the arrow keys (or click the mouse button) once to "deselect" the text—that is, turn off the highlighting to indicate that the text is no longer selected for formatting. The letterhead is both centered and in boldface type.

Now you'll move the date to line it up on the right instead of the left margin.

1. First, use the arrow keys or the mouse to move the cursor to the left of the date.
2. Next, hold down the **Shift** key and press the **right arrow** key to highlight the entire date, August 23, 1991. (Or press the mouse button, Drag the cursor to the right to highlight the date, and release the mouse button.) If you highlight too little or too much text, release the **Shift** key and press any arrow key (or click the mouse button) once to turn off the highlighting and repeat the process.
3. Press the **Alt** key, then the **T** key to access the **Format** menu, and the **R** key to **Right** align the text. (Or use the mouse to Point to the **Format** menu, press the mouse button, Drag the pointer down to highlight the **Right** option, and release the mouse button.) Notice that the text you selected, still highlighted, now lines up on the right margin of the page.
4. Release the **Shift** key and press any arrow key once to deselect the highlighted text.

Formatting the Letter—Spacing and Underlining

When you created the letter you did so in single-spaced format. Your next task is to make the body of the letter double-spaced.

1. Use the arrow keys or the mouse to move the cursor to the left of the first word of the letter.
2. Hold the **Shift** key and press the **down arrow** key until you highlight the entire letter. (Or press the mouse button, Drag the cursor down to highlight the whole letter, and release the mouse button.)
3. Press the **Alt** key, then the **T** key to access the **Format** menu.
4. Press the **D** key to **d**ouble-space the body of the letter. (Or use the mouse to Point to the **Format** menu, press the mouse button, Drag the pointer down to highlight the **Double Space** option, and release the mouse button.) Notice that the text you selected, still highlighted, is now double-spaced.

The next task is to improve the appearance of some of the text by using underlining. You want to be certain that parents pay particular notice to the school's opening and closing hours. You will underline school hours so that parents will be sure to see them.

1. Use the arrow keys or the mouse to move the cursor to the left of the phrase "begin at 8:30" (in the fourth line of the letter's body).
2. Hold the **Shift** key and press the **right arrow** key to highlight the phrase "begin at 8:30." (Or press the mouse button, Drag the cursor to the right to highlight the phrase, and release the mouse button.) If you highlight too little or too much text, release the **Shift** key and press any arrow key (or click the mouse button) once to turn off the highlighting and repeat the process.
3. Press the **Alt** key, then the **T** key to access the **Format** menu.
4. Press the **U** key to **u**nderline the selected phrase. (Or use the mouse to Point to the **Format** menu, press the mouse button, Drag the pointer down to highlight the **Underline** option, and release the mouse button.) Notice that the phrase, still highlighted, is now underlined.
5. Use the arrow keys or the mouse to move the cursor to the left of the phrase "dismiss at 2:30." Hold the **Shift** key and press the **right arrow** key to highlight the phrase "dismiss at 2:30." (Or press the mouse button, Drag the cursor to the right to highlight the phrase, and release the mouse button.) If you highlight too little or too much text, release the **Shift** key and press an arrow key (or click the mouse button) once to deselect the text and repeat the steps.
6. Hold down the **Ctrl** key and press the **U** (for **U**nderline) key (this method is the keyboard shortcut for underlining).
7. Press any arrow key (or click the mouse button) once to deselect the highlighted text.

Now two of the more important phrases are underlined so parents can identify them more easily.

Formatting the Letter—Character Size

The last formatting change you'll make to your letter is to increase the size of some of the characters in the text to make them particularly noticeable to the parents. In fact, this time you'll use both characters of larger font size and bold-face style to make the text concerning the registration procedures especially recognizable. Many of the formatting steps will be very familiar by now, but we'll still repeat them systematically.

1. Use the arrow keys or the mouse to move the cursor to the left of the word *Registration* (the first sentence in the second paragraph).
2. Hold the **Shift** key and press the **right arrow** key to highlight the entire sentence. (Or press the mouse button, Drag the cursor to highlight the sentence, and release the mouse button.) If you highlight too little or too much text, press an arrow key (or click the mouse button) once to deselect the text and repeat the steps.
3. Press the **Alt** key, then the **T** key to access the **Format** menu.
4. Press the **F** key to access the **Font & Style** dialog box. (Or use the mouse to Point to the **Format** menu, press the mouse button, Drag the pointer down to highlight the **Font & Style** option, and release the mouse button.)

Examine the options presented in the **Font & Style** dialog box (Figure 5.11). Notice that you can change the style of characters—bold face, italic, underline, or strikethrough—by using this dialog box instead of the other methods you have used.

5. Hold down the **Alt** key and press the **F** key to access the **Fonts** box.
6. Press the **down arrow** once to highlight the first font choice provided. (Or use the mouse to Point to the first font listed in **Fonts** box and Click the mouse button.) The first font is probably **Pica**, but may be different depending on which printer you selected with the **Printer Setup** dialog box.

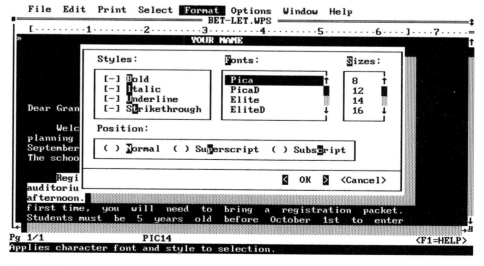

Figure 5.11 Word processor **Font & Style** dialog box

7. Note that there are now different sizes offered in the **Sizes** box to the right of the **Fonts** box. The sizes are listed in points; the larger the number, the larger the character size (64 points equals one inch). You'll select size **14** to make the highlighted characters more distinctive. (If you don't have the size **14** option available, choose any font size larger than **10**.)
8. Hold down the **Alt** key and press the **S** key to access the **Sizes** box.
9. Press the **down arrow** key to highlight the **14** (or use the mouse to Point to the **14** in **Sizes** box and Click the mouse). Now press the **Enter** key to exit the **Font & Style** dialog box and return to your word-processed document.
10. Hold down the **Ctrl** key and press the **B** (for **B**oldface) key. The sentence is now in a larger font size and in boldface type.

Notice that, although you cannot distinguish changes in character size, fewer words appear on each line because the characters are larger. Look at the display line across the bottom of the screen. Notice that it lists **PIC14** to indicate that the highlighted text is now in size 14 Pica characters. Even though you cannot see the larger characters on the screen, you will be able to see them when you print the letter on paper.

Saving and Printing the Letter

The final activity you will perform with this word-processed document will be to print the letter on paper. Before you print a document, however, it's always a good idea to save it on a data disk to make sure you don't lose it. To replace the old version of the letter with the newly enhanced one, follow these steps:

1. Press the **Alt** key and then the **F** (**F**ile) key (or use the mouse to point to the **File** command on the menu bar).
2. Press the **S** key to **Save** the document using the same name, **LETTER.WPS.** (Or press the mouse button, Drag the pointer down the options on the pull-down menu until you highlight the **Save** choice, and release the mouse button.) You have now replaced the earlier version of the file with the enhanced one.

Now we'll use the print preview capability to inspect the document. This display is referred to as "Greeking." Its purpose is to allow you to see the format of your document as it will appear on paper, not to permit any editing. Proof-reading should take place in the word processor, not in the print preview overlay. If you approve of the spacing, margins, and other features of the document, then you can safely print it. To preview a document prior to printing it, follow these procedures:

1. Press the **Alt** key and then the **P** key to access the **Print** menu (or use the mouse to point to the **File** command on the menu bar).
2. Press the **V** key to access the **Print Preview** dialog box (or use the mouse to Point to the **Preview** option and Click the mouse button).

3. If you do not want to change any of the options here, press the **Enter** key to select the **Preview** choice (or use the mouse to Point to the **Preview** option and Click the mouse button).

If you are using a *dual floppy drive system,* you will see a message asking you to insert the **Accessories** disk, the one containing the print preview overlay. Follow the screen messages to prompt you through the disk swapping process. With a *hard disk drive system,* you will not need to exchange disks and should soon see your document displayed on the screen in small, nearly indistinguishable characters.

If you want to change the document in some way before you preview it, press the **Esc** key to cancel the **Preview** option and return to the document. Next, use the editing features to make the document changes you wish. When the document is finished and you are ready to print it, repeat the previous steps to accomplish that task.

In this case, your letter does not fit on one page, and you can only see the first page of it. To see the second page, press the **Pg Dn** key located on the right of the keyboard. To see the first page again, press the **Pg Up** key.

If you are satisfied with the appearance of the letter, press the **P** (for **P**rint) key. The default settings, the ones already installed on Works by Microsoft, are sufficient for the task of printing this letter. (Before you begin printing, make certain that the printer you are using is turned on and properly connected to your computer.) In a few moments, your first word-processed document should be printed on paper.

At this point you may want to exit Works and shut down your computer. If so, follow the shut-down procedures listed in previous exercises; for additional help, consult the complete instructions listed on pages 60–61.

If you want to continue working with the program now, follow these steps to close the current document **LETTER.WPS** without exiting Works:

1. Press the **Alt** key and the **F** (for **F**ile) key.
2. Press the **C** key to select the **Close** command. The current document **LETTER.WPS** is no longer in the computer's memory, but Microsoft Works still is. You are now ready to begin the next section without having to restart Works.

Spell Checking a Word-Processed Document

Getting Started

In the next activity, we will check the spelling of an error-filled version of the letter you typed in the first exercise. To begin, you must bring a copy of the file from your Works **Data** disk into the computer's memory. Once the file has been copied into the computer's memory, you will check the spelling of the letter. The file, **BAD-LET.WPS**, is identical to the one you typed except for the many typing and spelling mistakes it contains.

If you have exited Works, then use the same procedures to start Works that you have used in the preceding exercises. If you need additional help, consult the more detailed instructions presented in the **Getting Started** section on pages 55–56.

Opening the BAD-LET.WPS File

When you see the opening Works screen, you will open an existing file, **BAD-LET.WPS.** To open the file (which is stored on your Works **Data** disk), follow the same steps you used to open your **LETTER.WPS** file for the previous exercise:

1. Press the **O** key to select the **Open Existing File** command (or use the mouse to highlight the **Open Existing File** choice and release the mouse button).
2. To make the disk drive containing your Works **Data** disk the active directory, hold down the **Alt** key and press the **I** (for Directories) key.
3. When the blinking cursor appears in the **Directories** dialog box, press the **down arrow** until you highlight the letter of the disk drive containing your Works **Data** disk (the **[-A-]** drive if you are using a hard disk drive system, the **[-B-]** drive if you are using a dual floppy system) and press the **Enter** key.
4. Hold down the **Alt** key and press the **F** key. When the blinking cursor appears in the **Files** dialog box, use the **down arrow** to highlight the file **BAD-LET.WPS**, then press the **Enter** key.
5. Works will copy the **BAD-LET.WPS** file from the disk and place the copy in the computer's memory. In a few moments, you will see the document displayed on the screen.

Automated Spell Checking of BAD-LET.WPS

To check the spelling of the new document, follow these steps:

1. Press the **Alt** key and then the **O** key to access the **Options** menu (or use the mouse to highlight the **Options** command and Click the mouse button).
2. Press the **S** key to access the **Check Spelling** option (or use the mouse to highlight the **Check Spelling** option and Click the mouse button).

If you are using a *floppy disk drive system,* you will have to exchange disks during the spell-checking process. Works must collect the words in your document and compare them to the words in the dictionary on the **Spell and Help** disk. You will have no difficulties if you follow the messages on the screen telling you which disk to insert. If you are using a *hard disk drive system,* you won't have to swap disks at all.

3. When the comparing process is complete, Works will display the **Correct Spelling** dialog box. Notice that the word *familees* is identified as a **Mis-**

spelled Word and placed in the **Replace with** box. This indicates that the word *familees* is not in the Works dictionary and Works suspects it is misspelled.

4. Hold the **Alt** key down and press the **S** (for **S**uggest) key to have Works suggest alternative spellings for *familees*. Notice that the word *families* is highlighted in the **Suggestions** box, indicating that Works is providing it as the alternative for the word *familees* (Figure 5.12).

5. To select *families* to replace *familees*, press the **Enter** key to choose the **Change** option.

6. Notice that the word *families* quickly replaces the word *familees* in the document.

7. Now the word *neerly* is in the **Unknown** box. To have Works suggest alternative spellings for *neerly*, hold the **Alt** key down and press the **S** key. (Or use the mouse to Point to the **Suggest** option and Click the mouse button.) Note that the word *nearly* is highlighted in the **Suggestions** box, indicating that Works is providing it as the alternative for the word *neerly*. To replace *neerly*, press the **Enter** key to choose the **Change** option.

8. The word *schol* is now in the **Replace with** box. To have Works suggest alternative spellings for *schol*, again hold down the **Alt** key and press the **S** key. (Or use the mouse to Point to the **Suggest** option and Click the mouse button.) Notice now that the word *school* is highlighted in the **Suggestions** box. To replace *schol*, press the **Enter** key to select the **Change** option.

9. The word *School* is now highlighted in the document, but the word *School* appears in the **Replace with** box. Based on the last correction you made (*school* replacing *schol*), Works suggests *School* as the correct spelling. Since that recommendation is correct, press the **Enter** key to select the **Change** option.

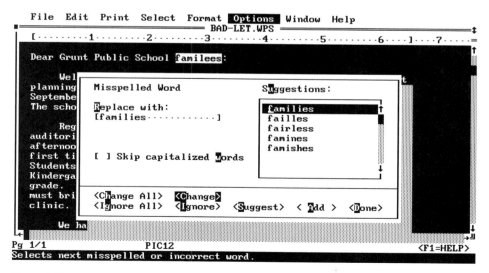

Figure 5.12 Spelling dialog box with suggested option selected

The **BAD-LET.WPS** file contains four additional misspelled words: *befor,* *enterring, imunization,* and *fysician.* Using the same procedures just described, try to correct these errors on your own.

10. Finally, note that the word *inservice* is now in the **Unknown** box. Although Works does not recognize the word, *inservice* is spelled correctly. Therefore, we want to tell Works to add *inservice* to the dictionary so that it will be recognized the next time we use the spell checker. Press the **A** key to **Add** *inservice* to the dictionary (or use the mouse to Point to **Add** and Click the mouse button). The next time you correct the spelling of a document containing the word *inservice,* Works will not flag it as a possibly misspelled word.

Manual Spell Checking

Works now displays a message box informing us that the spell-checking process is complete. The words we've corrected are the only incorrect words in this document that the Works spelling checker will identify. However, it is also important to note the words that the Works spelling checker does not catch. For instance, the name of the school, *Grant* Public School, was accidentally misspelled *Grunt* Public School in this document. Because *Grunt* is a word that is already in the Microsoft Works dictionary, it was not identified by the spell checker as an error. We will change other words—*Grunt, two,* and *wear*—on our own without using the Works spelling checker. To do so, press the **Enter** key to continue. Now we'll have to check the other words ourselves.

1. Press the **Pg Up** key several times until the letterhead at the beginning of the document appears on the top of the screen. Use the arrow keys to place the cursor between the letters *u* and *n* in the word *Grunt.* Press the **Backspace** key once to remove the letter *u* and use the keyboard to replace it with the letter *a.*

2. To make the next change, you will use the **Replace** command. This command lets you quickly locate and replace a word that you wish to change without having to scroll through a document to locate it. In this case, the word *two* in the second sentence of the second paragraph is misused. Hold down the **Alt** key, then the **S** key to choose the **Select** command on the menu bar, and then press the **R** key to select the **Replace** command. (Or use the mouse to Point to the **Select** command on the menu bar, Drag the pointer down the menu bar to select the **Replace** command, and release the mouse button.) When the **Replace** dialog box appears, type two into the **Search for** line, press the **Tab** key once to move the cursor to the **Replace with** line, and type to. (This procedure instructs Works to replace the *two* with the word *to.*) Press the **Alt** key, then press the **R** to choose the **Replace** command (or use the mouse to Point to the **Replace** button and Click the mouse button). This instructs Works to prompt you on the screen before it replaces the word. Generally that is a

good practice so that Works does not change words that you did not want to have replaced. Notice the word *two* is highlighted on the screen in context so that you can see where in the document it occurs. Press the **Enter** key (or use the mouse to Point to the **Yes** button and Click the mouse button) to replace the word *two* with the word *to*. Works displays a message on the screen to inform you that you found the only occurrence of *two* in this document, so press the **Enter** key.

3. Finally, let's replace the word *wear* in the third sentence of the third paragraph. You can use the same procedure that you used before to make this change. Press the **Alt** key, the **S** key to choose the **Select** command on the menu bar, and the **R** key to select the **Replace** command. (Or use the mouse to Point to the **Select** command on the menu bar, Drag the pointer down the menu bar to select the **Replace** command, and release the mouse button.) When the **Replace** dialog box appears, type wear into the **Search for** line, press the **Tab** key once to move the cursor to the **Replace with** line, and type where. (This procedure instructs Works to replace *wear* with the word *where*.) Press the **Alt** key, then press the **R** key to choose the **Replace** command. (Or use the mouse to Point to the **Replace** button and Click the mouse button.) *Wear* is highlighted on the screen, so press the **Enter** key (or use the mouse to Point to the **Yes** button and Click the mouse button). When Works displays the **No more occurrences** message, press the **Enter** key (or use the mouse to Point to the **OK** button and Click the mouse button) to return to the document.

Saving the Better Letter File

You have now finished correcting the **BAD-LET.WPS** document and can store the corrected version of the document on your Works **Data** disk under the name, **BET-LET.WPS** (for Better Letter). To do so, follow these steps:

1. Press the **Alt** key and then the **F** key (or use the mouse to point to the **File** command on the menu bar).
2. Press the **A** key to select the **Save As** command (or press the mouse button, Drag the pointer to highlight the **Save As** option, and release the mouse button).
3. Works suggests that you save the document on the active disk using the name, **BAD-LET.WPS**, on your Works **Data** disk.
4. Since the directory is correct, use the keyboard to type BET-LET.WPS. Press the **Enter** key.

At this point you may want to exit Works and shut down your computer. If so, follow the shut-down procedures listed in previous exercises; for additional help, consult the complete instructions listed on pages 60–61.

If you want to continue working with the program now, follow these steps to close the current document **BET-LET.WPS** without exiting Works:

1. Press the **Alt** key and the **F** (for **F**ile) key.
2. Press the **C** key to select the **Close** command. The current document **BET-LET.WPS** is no longer in the computer's memory, but Microsoft Works still is. You are now ready to begin the next section without having to restart Works.

Using the Works Thesaurus

Getting Started

The next activity will add one final enhancement to the opening day letter you've created. Microsoft Works includes a thesaurus as part of the program package. Although the concept of using a thesaurus is not new, having one included as part of Works means that you do not have to leave your work on the computer, locate a thesaurus, look up the word that you would like to replace, find a suitable synonym, and enter it into the computer text. Instead of following that onerous process, the electronic thesaurus allows you to press the thesaurus keystroke combination; Works will do the rest.

To use the thesaurus, you must have a document in the computer's memory and have the cursor positioned on the word for which you want Works to suggest alternatives. To begin, then, bring a copy of the file, **BET-LET.WPS,** from your Works **Data** disk. Once the file has been copied into the computer's memory, you will use the thesaurus to improve the letter.

Use the same procedures to start Works that you have used in the preceding exercises. If you need additional help, consult the more detailed instructions presented in the **Getting Started** section on pages 55–56.

Opening the BET-LET.WPS File

When you see the opening Works screen, you'll open an existing file, **BET-LET.WPS.** To open the file (stored on your Works **Data** disk), follow the same steps you always use to open existing files:

1. Press the **O** (for **O**pen Existing File) key to select the **Open Existing File** command (or use the mouse to highlight the **Open Existing File** choice and release the mouse button).
2. Hold down the **Alt** key and press the **I** (for D**i**rectories) key. When the blinking cursor appears in the **Directories** dialog box, press the **down arrow** to highlight the letter of the disk drive containing your Works **Data** disk; then press the **Enter** key.
3. Hold down the **Alt** key and press the **F** (for **F**iles) key. When the blinking cursor appears in the **Files** dialog box, use the **down arrow** to highlight the file **BET-LET.WPS**; then press the **Enter** key.

4. Works will copy the **BET-LET.WPS** file from the disk and place the copy in the computer's memory. In a few moments, you should see the document displayed on the screen.

Using the Thesaurus to Improve Word Selection

To use the Works thesaurus to improve the word selection in the **BET-LET.WPS** document, follow these steps:

1. Use the arrow keys (or the mouse) to position the cursor on the word *exciting* in the second line of the letter. Let's see if the Works thesaurus can suggest a more interesting word than *exciting*.
2. Press the **Alt** key and then the **O** key to access the **Options** menu (or use the mouse to highlight the **Options** command and Click the mouse button).
3. Press the **T** key to activate the **Thesaurus** (or use the mouse to highlight the **Thesaurus** option and Click the mouse button).

If you are using a *floppy disk drive system* you will have to exchange disks during the synonym-searching process since Works compares the word in your document with the words on the 5.25 inch **Thesaurus** disk or the 3.5 inch **Spell/ Help and Thesaurus** disk. You will not have difficulties if you follow the screen messages. If you are using a *hard disk drive system,* you won't have to swap disks at all.

4. When the comparing process is complete, Works will display the **Thesaurus** dialog box (Figure 5.13).

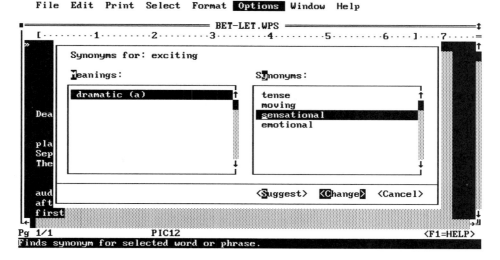

Figure 5.13 Word processor **Thesaurus** dialog box

Notice that the meaning of the word *exciting* is listed as "dramatic," and the synonyms listed in the **Synonyms** box include *sensational*. Let's imagine that you prefer the word *sensational* to *exciting*. Press the **Tab** key once to enter the **Synonyms** box, then use the **down arrow** key to highlight *sensational*. (Or use the mouse to highlight *sensational* and Click the mouse button.)

5. When you have highlighted *sensational,* hold down the **Alt** key and press the **C** (for **C**hange) key to replace *exciting* with *sensational*.

In a few moments, the words are exchanged and you have returned to the document. Use the same procedures to examine other words in the document. Remember to position the cursor on the word for which you want alternatives. If you want Works to find a substitute for several words (for instance, the two words *take place*), use the **Shift** key and the arrow keys (or use the mouse) to highlight the words and then activate the thesaurus. Words for which you may want to explore the powers of the Works thesaurus include: *start, planning, remain, take place,* and *especially.*

Saving the BET-LET.WPS File

When you have finished enhancing **BET-LET.WPS**, you can store the improved version of the document on your Works **Data** disk using the same name. To do so, follow these steps:

1. Press the **Alt** key and then the **F** key (or use the mouse to point to the **File** command on the menu bar).
2. Press the **S** key to select the **Save** command (or press the mouse button, Drag the pointer down the options to highlight the **Save** choice, and release the mouse button).

In a few moments, Works will replace the original version of the document on your Works **Data** disk with the improved version that you just completed.

At this point you may want to exit Works and shut down your computer. If so, follow the shut-down procedures listed in previous exercises; for additional help, consult the complete instructions listed on pages 60–61.

If you want to continue working with the program now, follow these steps to close the current document **BET-LET.WPS** without exiting Works:

1. Press the **Alt** key and the **F** (for **F**ile) key.
2. Press the **C** key to select the **Close** command. The current document **BET-LET.WPS** is no longer in the computer's memory, but Microsoft Works still is. You are now ready to begin the next section without having to restart Works.

Creating Text Macros in a Word-Processed Document

Getting Started

You were introduced to macros in an earlier section. Now it's time for you to create a simple text macro. You'll be able to create macros in any of the program components by following the same procedures described here. After you see how to create a macro for a word-processed document, you may want to use macros for all repetitious tasks in each of Works' components.

You'll create a macro that will automatically enter your letterhead, center the letterhead text, and then make it boldface type. The same process can be used to create simple keystroke equivalents for any groups of words that you type frequently. For example, if you work in the Colorado Public School District, a single key combination (such as holding down the **Ctrl** key while pressing the **S** key) could be recorded as a macro for typing the school district name.

First, let's open a new word-processed document and then create the macro. Use the same procedures to start Works that you have used in the preceding exercises. If you need additional help, consult the more detailed instructions presented in the **Getting Started** section on pages 55–56.

Open a new document by pressing the **N** (for Create **N**ew File) key. Tell Works that you want to open a new word-processed document by pressing the **W** (for **W**ord Processor) key. When the blinking cursor appears on the screen, Works is ready for you to begin typing.

Recording a Macro

Now you can create your own macro.

1. Hold down the **Alt** key and press the slash key (/) to access the **Macro options** dialog box (Figure 5.14).
2. Press the **Enter** key to select the **Record Macro** command. As the name suggests, this command will let you record a macro. Soon you will see the **Record Macro** dialog box displayed on the screen. The cursor is now in the

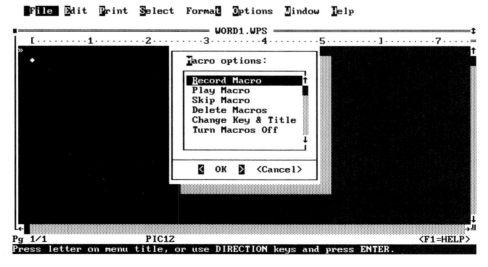

Figure 5.14 Word processor **Macro options** dialog box

Playback key box—the place to indicate the combination of keystrokes you want to use to invoke this macro.

3. Hold down the **Ctrl** key and press the letter **L** (for **L**etterhead); this assigns the **Ctrl-L** keystroke combination to this macro.

4. Press the **Tab** key to move the cursor to the **Title** box. Within this box, you will enter a brief title for the macro to remind yourself later of what function the macro serves.

5. Type Letterhead, then press the **Enter** key to indicate you are ready to start recording your macro. From this point on, every keystroke you use will be recorded, including any mistakes. A word of caution: record your macros slowly and carefully.

6. Type your own letterhead information carefully. Press the **Enter** key after each line of text and continue until you have completed your full letterhead name and address. To clarify the instructions, let's illustrate how to complete the exercise for an imaginary situation:

Ms. Ann G. Jones
647 Grant Street
Buffalo, NY 14219

To enter this letterhead, you would first type Ms. Ann G. Jones and press the **Enter** key. Next you would type 647 Grant Street and press the **Enter** key. Then you would type Buffalo, NY 14219 and press the **Enter** key twice. After practicing with the simulation, use the same steps to complete a letterhead appropriate for you.

7. Use the **Shift** key and the arrow keys (or the mouse) to highlight the letterhead you've just typed. First, use the **up arrow** key to move the cursor under the first letter in your first name; then hold down the **Shift** key and press the **down arrow** key until the entire letterhead is highlighted.

8. Now hold down the **Ctrl** key and press the **C** key to **Center** the selected text.

9. You'll now use the keyboard shortcut to boldface the letterhead by holding down the **Ctrl** key while pressing the **B** (for **B**old) key.

10. Finally, deselect the text by pressing the **down arrow** key until the cursor is below your letterhead.

11. To indicate the end of a macro, you must tell Works to stop recording your keystrokes. To accomplish this, hold down the **Alt** key and press the / key to access the **Macro options** dialog box. Notice the suggested option in the dialog box is the **End Recording** choice. Since you want to stop recording the macro, press the **Enter** key to accept the **End Recording** choice. You are done creating your first macro.

Using a Macro

Let's test your new macro in a new word-processed document.

1. Open a new document by pressing the **Alt** key, then the **F** (for **F**ile) key, and finally, the **N** key.

2. Now tell Works that you want to open a new word-processed document by pressing the **W** key. You are now in a new word-processed document, ready to test your new macro.

3. To invoke the macro you created, hold down the **Ctrl** key while pressing the **L** (for **L**etterhead) key. You can watch while the computer does the typing for you, creating a letterhead that you can use to start each letter you write. This same process can be used to automate any repetitive text, such as your school name, the names of your students, or frequently used expressions such as "educational computing" or "elementary school computing programs."

The macros you create are automatically saved in an "init" file, provided you quit Microsoft Works by using the **Exit Works** option under the **File** menu. (Init files are utility files that are automatically opened when you open the applications to which they correspond.) If you don't quit Works in this manner (for instance, if you simply turn off the computer before exiting the program), the macros that you create will be lost. If you use the **Exit Works** option when you quit the program, the macro init file is automatically saved and will re-open each time you start Works.

When using macros, take care not to assign macros to keystroke combinations that already have Works commands assigned to them. For instance, if you assign a macro to the **Ctrl-C** keystroke combination, you will disable the **Ctrl-C** keystroke shortcut that centers text. Use **Appendix A** to determine which keystroke combinations have already been allocated to other commands.

At this point you may want to exit Works and shut down your computer. If so, follow the shut-down procedures listed in previous exercises; for additional help, consult the complete instructions listed on pages 60–61.

If you want to continue working with the program now, follow these steps to close the current document without exiting Works:

1. Press the **Alt** key and the **F** (for **F**ile) key.

2. Press the **C** key to select the **Close** command. The current document is no longer in the computer's memory, but Microsoft Works still is. You are now ready to begin the next section without having to restart Works.

Accessing a Previously Defined Macro

Getting Started

To access a particular macro whenever you use Microsoft Works, you will only need to remember the keystroke combination that you assigned to it (**Ctrl-L** in the case of the letterhead text). To practice accessing a macro, repeat the usual steps for starting Works with a new word-processed file. If you need additional help, consult the more detailed instructions presented in the **Getting Started** section on pages 55–56.

Using a Previously Defined Macro

Once you have a new word-processed document open, you can access the macro file. Although you cannot see it displayed anywhere on the screen, your macro (and other macros you may have defined) will now be available to you. Try the letterhead macro one more time to make certain it is still available. Hold down the **Ctrl** key and press the **L** (for **L**etterhead) key to invoke the macro. Now wait a few moments and watch the macro do the typing for you.

If a macro that you've defined fails to function, the best solution is to delete it and create another one from scratch. To delete a macro (or to inspect the list of macros that you've already created), hold down the **Alt** key and press the **/** key to access the **Macro options** dialog box. Use the **down arrow** (or the mouse) to highlight the **Delete Macros** command, then press the **Enter** key to select that option. Soon you will see the **Macros** dialog box displayed on the screen, listing your Letterhead macro.

The **Macros** dialog box displays all the currently available macros. It also lets you delete any macros you no longer use, or any that do not function as expected. To delete a macro, use the arrow keys or the mouse to highlight it, then hold down the **Alt** key and press the **L** (for De**l**ete) key. If you happen to delete a macro that you like, you can recreate it by following the same simple steps that you first used. If you choose not to delete your macro, simply press the **Esc** key once to cancel the **Delete Macros** command and return to your document.

Exiting Works

Now you can create, save, and delete macros. Since the word-processed document you have opened was only used to practice your macro, you don't need to save it. You can now exit Works and ignore the reminder that you have not saved your file. To exit the program and shut down the computer, use the same steps that you have used in the preceding exercises. If you need additional help, consult the more detailed instructions presented in the **Exiting Works** section on pages 60–61.

Integrating Word Processing into the Instructional Process

Now that you are familiar with the powers of the Microsoft Works word processor, let's examine several strategies for integrating word processing into your classroom instruction. Some of the activities suggested in this section can be used effectively with a single computer in a classroom, whereas others are more appropriate for a computer lab. You can enhance the presentation of most of the strategies by using a large monitor or an LCD with an overhead projector. This way the computer display can be easily read by the whole class. All the activities can be modified to suit the instructional style of the teacher, the available equipment, the grade level of the students, and the objectives of the lesson.

Process Writing in a Word-Processing Environment

If computers were used only to help students improve their writing abilities, their presence in schools would be fully justified. With practice on your word processor, you can feel free from concerns about the appearance and formatting of your writing and concentrate on the content. Word processing can do the same thing for your students.

Process writing—a procedure that includes draft writing, editing, revising, and publishing—has been advocated in the teaching of composition for many years. Getting students to adopt this approach is often difficult because in the revision cycle, they literally have to write the paper again. That sounds like work to students (and it is). If you replace paper and pencil with word-processing software, writing becomes manageable, even enjoyable, for students.

To begin, teach your students the basic word-processing commands they will need to use the program effectively; avoid teaching them all of the "bells and whistles" that Works provides. Stick to the fundamentals they will need to load, edit, save, and print their papers. They can learn additional commands as they need them. Teaching process writing with a word processor, however, means more than simply teaching your students the various commands and powers available. The ultimate goal is to teach them how to use a word processor to edit and revise their text.

To demonstrate the revision process, you might project a word-processed writing sample for the class to view by using a large monitor or an LCD with an overhead projector. (If you do not have the necessary equipment, distribute paper copies of the sample to each student.) For the first guided revision session, read the sample with the class and solicit suggestions for clarifying and improving the text. Demonstrate the standard editing procedures, such as deleting or inserting words and rearranging text to improve readability. Illustrate the relationship between the author's voice and the students' understanding.

Once the sample revisions are complete, print out the document and photocopy it so that students can compare the original to the revised version. In subsequent lessons, ask for student volunteers to be the author whose paper the class will help revise. (It helps to prepare the volunteer before the class session.) This practice serves many instructional purposes. Seeing the work of fellow students is generally quite interesting to the class, so they are likely to be attentive. In addition, a classmate's authorial voice is similar to their own and easier to understand than commercial or teacher-prepared material. Also, by having a student guide the discussion and revision session, you are shifting the instructional focus from the teacher to the students—often an interesting and empowering experience for them.

Related Activities

- Have each student keep a portfolio of original and revised papers to document their improvement in writing over the course of the year.
- In each session, rotate students playing the teacher's role so that all students have the opportunity to guide the revision process. With poor writers, prepare them beforehand by helping them with the revisions.
- Prepare your class before the first revision session by discussing appropriate and inappropriate suggestions from the class. Use a brainstorming session to establish a set of agreed-upon rules to guide student responses during the sessions.
- Display the original and revised copies of student work on a bulletin board so that students can view the improvement process.
- Have your students practice their word-processing and revision skills by pairing them with younger students. The older students might enter their younger partner's text, print out the finished papers, and then read the work to them.

Guiding Brainstorming Sessions

Word processing can be used very effectively to guide your students in brainstorming sessions on a variety of topics. Typically, the teacher's role in brainstorming sessions is to record students' suggestions on the blackboard as they make them. When the brainstorming session is over, the class often reviews the listed suggestions and determines which of them are most important, perhaps even prioritizing or sequencing them.

How can a word processor assist in this procedure? A brainstorming session must be quick-paced or the students' enthusiasm for suggesting ideas quickly fades. By running a word processor connected to a large monitor or LCD, the teacher (or a student with keyboarding skills) can enter student responses and all the students can see the responses displayed as quickly as they are made.

When the time comes to review and prioritize the suggestions, you can use the Works word-processing features to facilitate and enhance the process. With the cut and paste features you can rearrange the ideas in order of importance, you can use style features, such as boldface and larger character size, to accentuate especially important ideas, you can rely on the spelling checker to eliminate any misspellings. When the final list is ready, you can print out a polished version and make copies for all the students several minutes after the brainstorming session ends.

If you don't have a large display device available, you can quickly print out some draft copies of your list and distribute them to small groups of students. The groups can discuss the relative importance of the different suggestions and reach a consensus. A final list can be created and copied so that everyone has a copy.

Related Activities

- Use an initial brainstorming session for students to suggest procedures that should be followed during subsequent brainstorming sessions.
- Use a brainstorming session to come up with a set of class rules that should be followed throughout the school year.
- Have students suggest ideas for class projects that they might undertake to improve the community.
- Solicit suggestions for class projects that students might undertake to improve the school.
- Have students take over the role of keyboard entry and discussion guide after you have adequately modeled the procedures you expect. You can then take a seat with the class and brainstorm with the students.

Resequencing a Set of Instructions

Resequencing instructions is a good activity to introduce your students to cut and paste commands. Under the **Edit** command, use the **Move** command to "cut" text, reposition the cursor, and then press the **Enter** key to "paste" the text in its new location. First, create a series of sequenced instructions, such as how to check a book out of the library, prepare a research paper, or conduct a science experiment. This exercise is designed to reinforce a familiar procedure, not to introduce a topic.

Next, create a set of instructions listed out of sequence on the word processor. Show the students how to use the cut and paste commands to move the instructions from one location to another.

When the students understand the necessary procedures, have them use the computer(s) independently, printing out the completed set of instructions. Students can then share their results in pairs.

Related Activities

Once they are familiar with the activity, have the students generate additional examples for their classmates to rearrange. Additional instructional set ideas include:

- the steps to use when adding two numbers
- the steps needed to go from school to the library
- the steps to follow when studying chapters in science texts
- the steps to follow when studying chapters in social studies texts
- the steps to use to divide three digit numbers by one digit numbers
- the procedures to follow at the beginning of the school day
- the procedures to follow in a fire drill
- the procedures to follow at the end of the school day
- the steps to follow when solving a math word problem

Developing Practice Skill Sheet Exercises

You can use the Works word processor to produce worksheets that teach your students word-processing skills and skills in other disciplines at the same time. Instead of giving your students worksheets on paper, prepare exercises for your students to complete on screen. When the assignment is complete, the students can either print their exercises on paper or resave the document with a new file name.

You can produce the worksheets in many different formats. In the sample below, students can use the word processor's **Delete** command to remove the unwanted option, leaving their selection in place. For example, in language arts class, students could practice grammar skills by completing exercises such as the following:

The girl's mother *was/were* happy with the *girls'/girl's* progress.

By deleting, typing, and printing the corrected sentences on paper, students can practice their word-processing skills and reinforce content area concepts at the same time.

Related Activities

When they are familiar with the activity, have your students generate additional practice sheets for their classmates to rearrange. Additional worksheet ideas include:

- review sheets for history (dates, characters, events)
- review sheets for science (elements, properties, clouds)
- review sheets for literature (characters, authors, genres)
- review sheets for mathematics (operations, terminology)
- review sheets for foreign language (vocabulary, grammar)
- review sheets for geography (countries, landmarks, cities)
- review sheets for sociology (terminology, trends)

Resequencing the Events in a Story

Resequencing events is another good activity for introducing your students to the word processor's cut and paste commands. First, enter a list of events from a story that the students have already read, but place the events in the wrong chronological order. The story that you choose should be one with which the students are already familiar.

Next, demonstrate the procedures for using the cut and paste commands to reorder the events so that they are in the correct chronological sequence. Then the students can work on the activities independently, either printing or resaving the complete exercises.

Related Activities

When your students are familiar with this activity, ask them to generate additional exercises for their classmates to rearrange. Additional exercise ideas include:

- resequencing historical events (explorers, American history)
- resequencing scientific events (discoveries, inventions)
- resequencing plot actions (classics, independent reading)

Creating Collaborative Stories

Creating stories together provides students the opportunity to practice their word-processing skills, their creative writing skills, and their group process skills. This activity is conducted most effectively in a computer lab. During the exercise, your students will create collaborative stories in groups. Give your students a topic to focus their writing, allow time to brainstorm appropriate story ideas, and then ask each student to begin drafting a story on his or her computer.

After about fifteen minutes, tell the students to complete the sentence they are writing and then exchange computers with another student in their group. Have the students read the story now displayed on their computers and continue it in the way they believe the original author had intended.

After another fifteen minutes, interrupt the students, ask them to complete the sentence they are writing, and then exchange computers once again. After one final fifteen minute period, interrupt the students again, ask them to complete the sentence they are writing, and then have them return to their original computer.

Ask them to read their stories, use the Works spell checker to correct any misspellings, and then print them on paper. The group stories can be posted on the bulletin board or used in class as an exercise to discuss the author's voice.

Commenting on Student Word-Processed Writing

Instead of having students print out their writing assignments on paper, you can insert your comments and corrections directly into the computer. Load your students' files in the standard manner, reading and responding to their work on the computer screen. Once you have inserted your comments, use the mouse or the keyboard to highlight them and change the character style to ~~strikethrough~~ (or a font of your preference) to distinguish them from the students' writing.

When you finish commenting on the students' work, resave it on their data disks. When the students load their writing again, they can read your comments and incorporate your suggestions into their papers. When the corrections are complete, the students can delete your comments from their work before resaving and printing it out on paper.

Additional Activities

Educational Activities

Creating Open House invitations

Writing letters marking the beginning and ending of a school year

Producing requests for parent volunteers

Creating announcements for Parent Conferences

Producing invitations for parents to attend their children's performances

Producing permission slips for field trips

Creating progress monitors

Creating lesson plans

Formatting overhead transparency masters

Creating routine communication to parents reporting their children's accomplishments and difficulties

Generating tests

Creating student assignments and guide sheets

Writing reports

Responding to requests for grant proposals

Producing instructional notes

Generating feedback and comments on student work

Producing conference proposals

Teaching students composition and process writing skills

Generating bulletin board labels

General Activities

Maintaining your correspondence

Generating reminders

Producing lists

Writing a diary

Creating messages

6 Focusing on Database Managers

With a database management program, you can electronically store and access large amounts of data with great speed and efficiency. You can easily maintain and organize equipment inventories, student and parent information, or the location of your most important resource materials.

The index card file is the standard metaphor for an electronic database manager. You probably have an index card file where you store information according to major topics. Within each category, file cards further delineate the information contained there. This manual system works well when you are not storing a large amount of data. As the amount of information grows, however, the system becomes imprecise, slow, and bulky. The more information you accumulate, the more difficult it is to store and access data in an efficient and timely fashion.

With an electronic database manager, you can easily store the same amount of information on a single disk that would fill many index card files. The savings in physical storage area is dramatic. Even more impressive, however, is how easy it is to access and manipulate information once the data have been entered into an electronic database. Let's examine a more concrete situation.

Consider your information management needs as a classroom teacher. You must decide how to organize important student records—with an index card file or with an electronic database file. If you use an index card system, each student will have an index card with his or her name on it. Each index card will contain information such as date of birth, place of birth, parents' names, home address, home telephone number, parents' work telephone numbers, doctor's name, math group, reading group, bus number, allergies, names and ages of siblings, favorite foods, and pets. If you create an electronic database file, each student will be represented by a unique record (conceptually similar to a separate index card). The same types of information (date of birth, place of birth, etc.) will be stored in the fields (another term for categories).

Either information management system—index card system or the electronic database—will contain the same student information. Each will require about the same amount of time to create. How do you decide which system will be the most useful?

Consider several important points when determining which system will best satisfy your needs—for example, the ease of accessing information, the flexibility of organizing information, and the space required to store the information. The electronic database is clearly the more efficient system for all these considerations. With a database, you can easily arrange information alphabetically or numerically, organize information according to certain criteria (e.g., "all girls"), and store it magnetically on a disk. With an index card system, however, the information is clumsy to store and difficult to access. If you want information about Sally Jones, for instance, you can search for her index card and find what you seek. But if you want data about all the girls in the class, you must look through every girl's index card to locate the information you want. The data remain organized by one criteria—alphabetically by the last name of each student.

Imagine that your principal asks you for lists of your students arranged according to math group, reading group, and last name. Next, the Room Mother asks you for a list of your students born during December or January for a birthday display on the bulletin board. In addition, the librarian wants a list of the students in your class who have pets, including the types of pets they have. You are frequently asked to generate many lists like these. It sounds like a lot of work for you.

Being pragmatic, you decide to deal with the principal's request first. Let's examine how the requests could be satisfied using the index card and electronic database systems. If you have only an index card system, you have to go through each index card to compile the list of students by math groups. Then, you have to go through the index cards again to compile the list by reading groups. Next, you go through the cards again and compile the alphabetical list. You type those three lists and send them to the principal's office.

To satisfy the requests of the Room Mother and the librarian, you again search through each of the index cards to find the students who were born in December or January and type those names. Finally, you search again for the students who have pets and carefully list the number and type of pet next to each name. These lists are also sent on their way. Even if the index card system is compressed into a series of information tables, the process promises to be labor intensive.

Let's call an electronic database management program to your rescue. Once you create an electronic database file, instead of an index card system, to maintain student data, you can save yourself a great deal of time and effort. After the file is created, the principal's requests can be easily satisfied. You quickly arrange the file according to math groups and print the list on your printer. Next, you arrange the file according to reading groups and print that list. Then you arrange the file according to last name and print a third list.

You now search your database file for the students who were born in December or January and print the resulting list for your Room Mother. Finally, you satisfy your librarian's request by using the database program to identify which of your students have pets. When the search is complete, you print a list of those students matched with their pets. The entire operation takes you less than ten minutes.

If you expand this simple scenario to include the routine record management requirements you have each school year, the savings in time and effort, accuracy, and efficiency are undeniable. Electronic database management programs leave you with more time to do what you enjoy most—teach—by simplifying your routine record-keeping chores.

An Introduction to Database Managers

Computerized database managers offer users many advantages in the organization and manipulation of information. Just as word processors greatly extend the capabilities of electronic typewriters, database managers extend the powers of filing cabinets filled with folders and file boxes of names and addresses. In the next section you will learn to use the powers of the Microsoft Works database. But first, let's go over some standard database terminology.

Four terms are used to describe how data are entered and organized—**file, record, field,** and **data entry** (listed here from general to specific). A **file** is a collection of all the information you have available on a particular subject. In the case of your class, a file would contain all the information you have on all the students in the class. The file of your class will be divided into **records,** one record for each student. The record for an individual student—Ann Eldredge, for example—would include all the information you have about her. **Fields** are categories into which your records are organized. The fields in Ann's record include her first and last name, her gender, her parents' names, their home address(es) and telephone number(s), their work numbers, Ann's doctor's name and telephone number, and any other important information about Ann. In your database, the field, First Name, would have the specific **data entry,** Ann, and Eldredge would be the data entry in the Last Name field.

On the database screen, data are generally shown in either **list** or **form** display. In list display, data are arranged in columns and rows; the rows represent records, and the columns correspond to fields. The list display is used to view many records at the same time. Sometimes, however, it is necessary to see *all* the information in one record at the same time. In that case, the form display is the option to choose. In the form display, field names are listed down the left side of the screen with the corresponding data entries to the right.

With an electronic database, you have the capability of switching displays from one arrangement to another with just a simple keystroke. Furthermore, each display can be custom-formatted and changed as often as you like. For example, you can modify the sequence of the fields (or columns) in a list display; you can increase or decrease the width of individual columns or groups of columns; you can change the justification (left, right, or center) of the data in any field. In each case, the modifications are quick and easy to effect.

Perhaps the most important powers of an electronic database are the **Sort** and **Search** capabilities. When you **sort** information, you arrange and rearrange a database file according to numeric or alphabetical characteristics. For example, you could easily arrange your students in alphabetical order according to last name and then rearrange the file according to ZIP code, math group, age, or gender. Even when you rearrange data this way, each record maintains its original data entries.

When you instruct your database manager to **search**, it selects particular records from a large file according to certain criteria. You could produce an alphabetical list of girls only, or a list of the boys in the highest reading group, or a roster of girls on the gymnastics team who rode a particular bus home. With an electronic database, any of those searches could be quickly completed.

With database managers you can also update the information in your files; it's easy to add a new student to the existing file or delete the record of a departing student from the file. If you decide to add a new field to your database halfway through the term, you simply name the new field and then add the appropriate data entries for each student.

Finally, database managers have powerful reporting tools for generating print-outs of the information that they contain. You can print out some or all of the data in either list or form display, and you can print it vertically or horizontally. In addition, you can add calculated fields to the report so that totals and averages can be completed automatically.

In the next few sections, you will learn to create a new database file, edit an existing file, use both form and list views, sort a file, search a file, and generate and print out a database report.

Creating and Saving a New Database Document

Getting Started

Use the same procedures to start Works that you have used in the preceding exercises. If you need additional help, consult the more detailed instructions presented in the **Getting Started** section on pages 55–56.

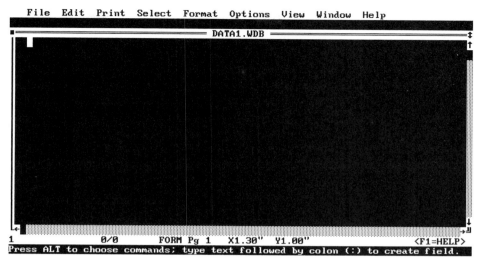

Figure 6.1 Database manager opening blank screen in form display

Opening a New Database Document

When you see the opening Works screen, issue the command to open a new document by following these steps:

1. Press the **N** (for Create **N**ew File) key.
2. Press the **D** (for **D**atabase) key to instruct Works that you want to open a new database document.

In a few moments, Works will copy the database program into memory and display the blank database screen of the new document, **DATA1.WDB** (Figure 6.1). The **.WDB** extension identifies the document as a database just as the **.WPS** extension indicated a word-processed document.

For your first database project, you'll develop a file to maintain your student records. You will begin creating the student record database by naming the fields (or categories) for the information you are going to include in the database file.

Naming New Fields

When you create a database file, you first designate the names of the fields or categories of information the database will include. In this exercise, you'll create a simple database for twenty-five students. Each student record will contain six fields: First Name, Last Name, Street Address, City, State, Zip Code. At the bottom of the screen a display line reads, "type text followed by a colon (:) to create field." Any text that is followed by a colon in this form screen of the database functions as a field name. To create the necessary fields for your database, follow these steps:

1. Type **First Name:** and press the **Enter** key. (Be certain to remember the colon.) Note that a dialog box appears on the screen, suggesting that the field width should be 20 characters. Ten characters is sufficient for your students' first names, so type **10** and press the **Enter** key to set the field width. Next, press the **down arrow** key once to skip a line between fields.

2. Type **Last Name:** and press the **Enter** key. (Be certain to remember the colon.) Again, note that the dialog box appears on the screen, suggesting that the field width should be 20 characters. Fifteen characters is sufficient for your students' last names, so type **15** and press the **Enter** key to set the field width. Press the **down arrow** key once to skip a line between fields.

3. Type **Street Address:** and press the **Enter** key. When the field width dialog box appears on the screen, press the **Enter** key to set the width at 20 characters, and then press the **down arrow** key once.

4. Type **City:** and press the **Enter** key. Ten characters is sufficient for the city names, so type **10** in the field width dialog box and press the **Enter** key. Press the **down arrow** key once.

5. Type **State:** and press the **Enter** key. Since you'll use the state abbreviations, type **2** in the field width dialog box and press the **Enter** key. Then press the **down arrow** key once again.

6. Type **Zip Code:** and press the **Enter** key. Since you'll use standard five-digit ZIP codes, type **5** when the field width dialog box appears. Press the **Enter** key to set the field width.

Those are all the fields you need for this database. Now you are ready to enter the information into the fields.

Entering Information into the Fields

You have been working in the Works form (or single record) screen. Notice the menu bar across the top of the screen; you will use it later to select commands. The **title box** appears below the menu bar, as it did on the word processing screen. Below the title are the fields that you just created: First Name, Last Name, etc. Although you can't see it, there is an empty box to the right of each field name where you can place information pertaining to each student. Use the **up arrow** key (or the mouse) to move the cursor to highlight the First Name field, then press the **right arrow** key once to reveal the empty box. This box is the ten-character field you created in the last exercise. Press the **Tab** key to move down to the other fields. You'll notice that some of the boxes are smaller than the others; you determined the width of those fields with the field width dialog box.

When you want to move back up to the previous fields, hold down the **Shift** key and press the **Tab** key. Now let's create a file of five student records. We begin by entering information about one student.

1. While holding down the **Shift** key, press the **Tab** key to move the cursor to the empty box at the right of the First Name field. Notice that the box is now

highlighted. Type **Paul** and press the **Tab** key. Note that Paul appears in the box, and the Last Name field is now highlighted.

2. Type **Allen** and press the **Tab** key. Note that Allen appears in the Last Name field and the Street Address field is now highlighted.

3. Type **422 Rockwell Rd.** and press the **Tab** key. The address appears in the Street Address field and the City field is now highlighted.

4. Type **Buffalo** and press the **Tab** key. The city name appears in the box, and the State field is now highlighted.

5. Type **NY** and press the **Tab** key. The state name appears in the box, and the Zip Code field is now highlighted.

6. Type **14220** and press the **Tab** key. After entering information into the last field, all the information disappears from the boxes and the First Name field of the second student record is now highlighted.

Look to the left of the First Name field in the bottom lefthand corner of the screen. The number 2 indicates that this is indeed the second student record. To reassure yourself that the information for Paul Allen has not been lost, hold down the **Shift** key and press the **Tab** key one time to display the first record. The number 1 has replaced the number 2 in the lower left corner of the screen, showing that Paul Allen's information belongs to the first record. Now press the **Tab** once to return to the second (blank) record and enter information on Jane Anderson.

1. Type **Jane** and press the **Tab** key. Note that Jane appears in the box and the Last Name field is highlighted.

2. Type **Anderson** and press the **Tab** key. Note that Anderson appears in the box and the Street Address field is highlighted.

3. Type **342 Elmwood Ave.** and press the **Tab** key. Again, the address appears in the box and the City field is highlighted.

4. Type **Buffalo** and press the **Tab** key. Buffalo appears in the box and the State field is highlighted.

5. Type **NY** and press the **Tab** key. NY appears in the box and the Zip Code field is highlighted.

6. Now type **14222** and press the **Tab** key.

Again, note that all the information disappears from the boxes and the First Name field of the third student record is highlighted. The number 3 to the left of the First Name field at the bottom of the screen tells you that this is the third student record. Hold down the **Shift** key and press the **Tab** key one time, displaying the second record. Once you are assured that the information for Jane Anderson has not been lost, press the **Tab** key once to return to the third (blank) record.

1. Now type **Jim** and press the **Tab** key.
2. Type **Blanchard** and press the **Tab** key.
3. Type **174 Linwood Ave.** and press the **Tab** key.
4. Type **Buffalo** and press the **Tab** key.
5. Type **NY** and press the **Tab** key.

6. Now type **14218** and press the **Tab** key. Again, all the information disappears from the boxes and the First Name field (of the fourth student record) is highlighted. The number 4 appears to the left of the First Name field to inform you that this is the fourth student record.
7. Now type **Fred** and press the **Tab** key.
8. Type **Bland** and press the **Tab** key.
9. Type **642 Elmwood Ave.** and press the **Tab** key.
10. Type **Buffalo** and press the **Tab** key.
11. Type **NY** and press the **Tab** key.
12. Now type **14219** and press the **Tab** key. The information disappears from the boxes and the First Name field is highlighted. The number 5 appears to the left of the First Name field to tell you that this is the fifth student record.
13. Type **Oliver** and press the **Tab** key.
14. Type **Casey** and press the **Tab** key.
15. Type **671 Main St.** and press the **Tab** key.
16. Type **Buffalo** and press the **Tab** key.
17. Type **NY** and press the **Tab** key.
18. Now type **14220** and press the **Tab** key. The information disappears from the boxes and the First Name field for the sixth student record is highlighted.

Saving the Database

You now have a database document consisting of five records (or students—e.g., Paul Allen), with each record containing six fields (or categories—e.g., First Name) of information. Before you complete the database, first copy the file to your data disk to make certain that you don't lose the information. You can store this partially completed version of the file on your Works **Data** disk under the name **STUDENT**. To do so, follow these steps:

1. Press the **Alt** key and then the **F** (for **F**ile) key. (Or use the mouse to point to the **File** command on the menu bar.)
2. Press the **A** key to select the **Save As** command. (Or press the mouse button, Drag the pointer down the options on the menu until you highlight the **Save As** choice, and release the mouse button.) Note the **Save file as** dialog box displayed on the screen. Works suggests that you save the document using the name, **DATA1.WDB**, on the active disk (on the Works **Program** disk, if you are using a dual floppy system, or on your Works subdirectory if you are using a hard disk drive system). You need to change both the name of the document and the disk on which it will be stored.
3. To instruct Works to save the file on your Works **Data** disk, hold the **Alt** key and press the **I** (for D**i**rectories:) key. When you see the blinking cursor in the **Directories** dialog box, press the **down arrow** key until you highlight the letter of the disk drive containing your Works **Data** disk (the **[-A-]** drive if you are using a hard disk drive system, or the **[-B-]** drive if you are using a dual

floppy system) and press the **Enter** key. Notice the **Directory of** line in the dialog box now shows that your Works **Data** disk is the active directory.

4. Type STUDENT and press the **Enter** key. Works will quickly store the file you just created on your Works **Data** disk under the name, **STUDENT.WDB**. Remember, Works adds the **.WDB** extension to your file name to show that it is a database file.

Completing the Database

When the computer has finished copying your **STUDENT.WDB** file to your Works **Data** disk, you can safely continue working on the file without worrying about losing any information. Follow the same procedures to complete your database by entering the student information listed in Table 6.1. (The first five lines are information you have already entered.)

Table 6.1 STUDENT.WDB database

First Name	Last Name	Address	City	State	ZIP Code
Paul	Allen	422 Rockwell Rd.	Buffalo	NY	14220
Jane	Anderson	342 Elmwood Ave.	Buffalo	NY	14222
Jim	Blanchard	174 Linwood Ave.	Buffalo	NY	14218
Fred	Bland	642 Elmwood Ave.	Buffalo	NY	14219
Oliver	Casey	671 Main St.	Buffalo	NY	14220
George	Cooper	400 Grant Rd.	Buffalo	NY	14222
Jessie	Cooper	418 W. Ferry St.	Buffalo	NY	14220
Doug	Craft	230 Grant Rd.	Buffalo	NY	14217
Sally	Dale	234 Bird Ave.	Buffalo	NY	14219
James	Dunlop	674 Linwood Ave.	Buffalo	NY	14222
Bill	Grant	114 Delaware Ave.	Buffalo	NY	14209
Sarah	Johnson	160 Linwood Ave.	Buffalo	NY	14216
John	Johnstone	762 Elmwood Ave.	Buffalo	NY	14213
Margaret	Jones	41 Harbor St.	Buffalo	NY	14216
Catherine	Kelly	142 Rockwell Rd.	Buffalo	NY	14219
Nancy	Kennedy	41 W. Ferry St.	Buffalo	NY	14222
Robert	Martin	741 Main St.	Buffalo	NY	14217
Tricia	Palmer	361 Delaware Ave.	Buffalo	NY	14222
Annie	Phelps	414 Delaware Ave.	Buffalo	NY	14222
Elizabeth	Phillips	135 Green St.	Buffalo	NY	14219
Greg	Plander	13 Shore Drive	Buffalo	NY	14222
Mike	Reich	701 Claussen Dr.	Buffalo	NY	14216
Julie	Reichman	451 Elmwood Ave.	Buffalo	NY	14213
David	Shore	851 Fox Rd.	Buffalo	NY	14217
Samantha	Tramper	431 Bird Ave.	Buffalo	NY	14213

Because you have already entered all the information for the first five students, begin with George Cooper for record six and add the next twenty records to create a database of twenty-five students.

If you accidentally mistype information or skip an entry in your database, don't panic—you can easily correct any mistakes. To correct an entry, simply hold down the **Shift** key and press the **Tab** key to move to the field containing the information you want to change. Once that field is active, the data contained there appears on the **display line** beneath the menu bar. To change the entry, type the correct data and press the **Enter** key. Your new entry will replace the unwanted information.

Re-saving the Database File

When you have completed the task of entering the student records, you will have a database document consisting of twenty-five records (that is, twenty-five students—e.g., Samantha Tramper), with each record containing six fields (that is, categories—e.g., City) of information. Before you manipulate the database, make certain that you don't lose the information. Therefore, copy the database document to your Works **Data** disk. You can replace the partially completed file (already stored on your Works **Data** disk under the name **STUDENT.WDB**) by pressing the **Alt** key, then pressing the **F** (for **F**ile) key, and then pressing the **S** (for **S**ave) key. The saving process replaces the database file of only five students with the new version containing twenty-five students.

Exiting Works

When the computer has finished copying your new **STUDENT.WDB** file to your Works **Data** disk, you can exit Works and shut down the system without worrying about losing any data. To exit the program and shut down the computer, use the same steps that you have used in previous exercises. If you need additional help, consult the more detailed instructions presented in the **Exiting Works** section on pages 60–61.

If you want to continue working with the program now, follow these steps to close the current document, **STUDENT.WDB**, without exiting Works:

1. Press the **Alt** key and the **F** (for **F**ile) key.
2. Press the **C** key to select the **Close** command.

The current document, **STUDENT.WDB**, is no longer in the computer's memory, but Microsoft Works still is. You are now ready to begin the next section without having to restart Works.

Manipulating and Printing a Database Document

Getting Started

During this exercise, you will learn to manipulate and print the information stored in your database file, **STUDENT.WDB.** The maneuvers you'll practice will include sorting (or arranging) the database alphabetically and numerically, as well as searching and querying the database for specific information. Finally, you'll print your database document on paper.

Use the same procedures to start Works that you have used in the preceding exercises. If you need additional help, consult the more detailed instructions presented in the **Getting Started** section on pages 55–56. If you only closed your database document and did not exit Works at the end of the previous section, you are ready to reopen the **STUDENT.WDB** file.

Opening the STUDENT.WDB File

When you see the opening Works screen, you will be able to open the file, **STUDENT.WDB**. To open the file from your Works **Data** disk, follow these steps:

1. Press the **O** key to select the **O**pen Existing File command (or use the mouse to highlight the **Open Existing File** choice and release the mouse button).
2. Hold down the **Alt** key and press the **I** (for D**i**rectories) key. When the blinking cursor appears in the **Directories** dialog box, press the **down arrow** key to highlight the letter of the disk drive containing your Works **Data** disk, and press the **Enter** key.
3. Hold down the **Alt** key and press the **F** (for **F**ile) key. When the blinking cursor appears in the **Files** dialog box, use the **down arrow** key to highlight the file **STUDENT.WDB** and press the **Enter** key.
4. Works will copy the **STUDENT.WDB** file from the disk and place a copy in the computer's temporary memory. In a few moments, you will see the database document displayed on the screen.

Exploring the Database Form Display

Notice that your screen still only displays one record at a time. As you know, this is the Form (or single record) display (Figure 6.2).

When you open the **STUDENT.WDB** file, the screen should display an empty record, number 26—the record after the last one you completed (Samantha Tramper). You already know how to move from one field to another using the **Tab** key. Let's go through some additional operations and features of the form display.

1. To move from one record to another, hold down the **Crtl** key and press the **Page Up** or **PgUp** key to move to the previous record, then the **Page Down** or **PgDn** key to move to the next record. (Or use the mouse to Point to the **up arrow** above and the **down arrow** below the scroll bar to the right of the screen.)

   Let's try moving through the records using the **Crtl** key with the **Page Up** and **Page Down** keys. Hold down the **Crtl** key and press the **Page Up** key. Your screen should now display the information about Samantha Tramper,

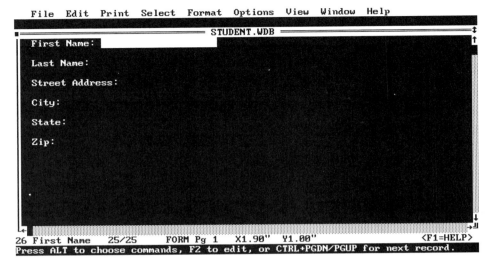

Figure 6.2 Database manager: the form, or single record, display

record number twenty-five (notice the 25 at the bottom left of the screen). Each time you hold down the **Ctrl** key and press the **Page Up** key, you will move to the previous record. Each time you hold down the **Crtl** key and press the **Page Down** key, you should move to the next record. Try moving between records for a few minutes until you are proficient at the task.

2. Hold down the **Crtl** key and press the **Home** key to return to the first record in your document, Paul Allen (or use the mouse and the **up arrow** above the scroll bar). Notice that although the information in all the fields is visible, you can only see one record at a time.

3. Now use the **Tab** key or the **Shift** and the **Tab** keys to move the cursor to the data box to the right of the Street Address field. Notice that the address (422 Rockwell Rd.) is displayed both there and in the area below the **File** command in the menu bar across the top of the screen. That part of the screen is known as the **display line**.

The display line shows all the data that are in the field, regardless of the field size in the form display (a Works field can contain a maximum of 256 characters). If you've typed too many characters to display in a particular field, some of the characters will no longer be visible in the field box. However, you can still view the entire entry on the display line. Let's change the size of the Street Address field temporarily to illustrate the usefulness of the display line. When the Street Address field is highlighted, follow these steps:

1. Press the **Alt** key and then press the **T** (for Forma**t**) key to access the **Format** menu.

2. Press the **Z** (for Field Si**z**e) key to change the field width.

3. Replace the current field width of 20 characters (displayed in the dialog box) by typing **10** and pressing the **Enter** key.

Notice that in the form display only 422 Rockwe appears in the field. However, the display line shows the entire address, 422 Rockwell Rd. This illustrates that data are not lost, even if the size of the field is too small to display all the information.

Let's change the size of the Street Address field back to the original size so that the entire addresses are visible. With the Street Address field still highlighted, follow these steps:

1. Press the **Alt** key and then the **T** (for Forma**t**) key to access the **Format** menu.
2. Press the **Z** (for Field Si**z**e) key to alter the field width.
3. Change the current field width of 10 characters to **20** and press the **Enter** key.

Use this process with some of the other fields (First Name, Last Name, or City) so that data boxes to the right of the fields fit the size of the data they contain. Don't worry if you make one of the boxes too small to show all the data it contains; you can change the size of any one by the same process you are now using. Practice expanding and contracting the data boxes until you are comfortable with the process.

Exploring the Database List Display

For the moment, you'll leave the form display and examine the list display. A screen display in table format, like the one you used to enter the student information for the other twenty student records in this database, is known as the list (or multi-record) display (Figure 6.3).

```
 File   Edit   Print   Select   Format   Options   View   Window   Help
"Paul
================================ STUDENT.WDB ================================
      First Name   Last Name     Street Address      City    State   Zip
1     Paul         Allen        422 Rockwell Rd.     Buffalo   NY    14220
2     Jane         Anderson     342 Elmwood Ave.     Buffalo   NY    14222
3     Jim          Blanchard    174 Linwood Ave.     Buffalo   NY    14218
4     Fred         Bland        642 Elmwood Ave.     Buffalo   NY    14219
5     Oliver       Casey        671 Main St.         Buffalo   NY    14220
6     George       Cooper       400 Grant St.        Buffalo   NY    14222
7     Jessie       Cooper       418 W. Ferry St.     Buffalo   NY    14220
8     Doug         Craft        230 Grant Rd.        Buffalo   NY    14217
9     Sally        Dale         234 Bird Ave.        Buffalo   NY    14219
10    James        Dunlop       674 Linwood Ave.     Buffalo   NY    14222
11    Bill         Grant        114 Delaware Ave.    Buffalo   NY    14209
12    Sarah        Johnson      160 Inwood Ave.      Buffalo   NY    14216
13    John         Johnstone    762 Elmwood Ave.     Buffalo   NY    14213
14    Margaret     Jones        41 Harbor St.        Buffalo   NY    14216
15    Catherine    Kelly        142 Rockwell Rd.     Buffalo   NY    14219
16    Nancy        Kennedy      41 W. Ferry St.      Buffalo   NY    14222
17    Robert       Martin       741 Main St.         Buffalo   NY    14217
18    Tricia       Palmer       361 Delaware Ave.    Buffalo   NY    14222
1 First Name      25/25      LIST                              <F1=HELP>
Press ALT to choose commands, or F2 to edit.
```

Figure 6.3 Database manager: the list, or multi-record, display of the **STUDENT.WDB** document

To change the screen to list display, follow these steps:

1. Press the **Alt** key and then press the **V** key to access the **View** menu.
2. Press the **L** (for **L**ist) key.

Notice that the information is now displayed in rows and columns. Each row in the list display represents a single record; each column represents a field. The list display can show information from no more than eighteen records on one screen. However, if there are many fields in a database document, you frequently cannot see all the fields on the same screen in the list display.

You can return to the form display again by following these steps:

1. Press the **Alt** key and then press the **V** key to access the **View** menu.
2. Press the **F** (for **F**orm) key.

If you have gone to the form display, now return to the list display so you can examine it more closely. Press the **Alt** key, then the **V** key, and then the **L** (for **L**ist) key.

Let's exchange the position of the first two columns, so that the table displays the Last Name field before the First Name field rather than the other way around. To rearrange fields, follow these steps:

1. Position the cursor on any data entry in the First Name field.
2. Hold down the **Shift** key and press the **F8** key. This selection will highlight the entire First Name field.
3. Press the **Alt** key and then the **E** key to access the **Edit** menu.
4. Press the **M** (for **M**ove) key to prepare to move the field. Notice the message, **Select new location and press ENTER. Press ESC to cancel.** displayed on the bottom of the screen. The new field location can be selected by using either the cursor movement keys or the mouse.
5. The field to be moved will be inserted to the left of the current (highlighted) field, so press the **right arrow** key twice to position the cursor in the Street Address field. Press the **Enter** key.

The field sequence is now Last Name, First Name, then Street Address. You can exchange the position of any two fields using this same method. Practice changing field positions several times until you are confident that you can position fields wherever you want in the list screen. Once you're confident with this skill, return the list screen display to its original order (First Name, Last Name, Street Address, City, State, Zip Code). Then we'll look at some of the other powers databases provide.

Using the Database Sorting Powers

Now let's explore the database powers for arranging or sorting information either numerically or alphabetically. The **STUDENT.WDB** file is presently arranged in alphabetical order by student last name. Imagine that you needed your docu-

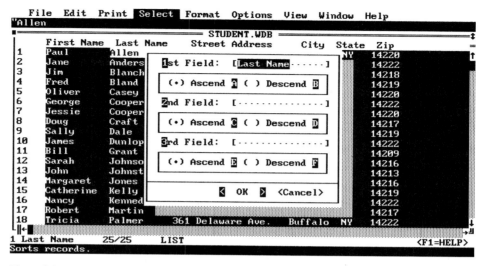

Figure 6.4 Database **Sort** dialog box with Last Name as the first sort field

ment arranged in reverse alphabetical order by student last name, perhaps to create a new seating arrangement for your class. To create this sort of alphabetical arrangement, follow these steps:

1. Use the arrow keys (or the mouse) to position the cursor on any data entry in the Last Name field.
2. Press the **Alt** key and then press the **S** key to access the **Select** menu.
3. Press the **O** (for Sort Records) key to sort (or arrange) the records. Notice the **Sort** dialog box appears on the screen, showing that you can sort the database document according to three different fields (Figure 6.4).

If the student population of your entire school was in a database file, this multi-field sorting feature would let you first arrange the file numerically according to grade level. You could next arrange the data alphabetically by teacher's last name so that classes of the same grade level were kept together. Finally, each individual teacher's class list could be arranged alphabetically by student last name. This entire sorting process could be accomplished with one procedure.

For now, you only need to sort your database according to one field, Last Name, so follow these steps:

1. Hold down the **Alt** key and press the **B** (to choose the **Descend** option) to sort the database by last name in descending alphabetical order. Note that the black dot in the circle to the left of the **Descend** option shows that you have selected reverse alphabetical order.
2. Press the **Enter** key to accept that choice, and observe that all the records are arranged according to student last name instantaneously. Samantha Tramper is now the first record because hers was the last name on the class list.

Setting Field Attributes

We will execute a numerical sort in a moment, but first let's explore how we can establish the characteristics, or attributes, of information stored in any field. With the exception of the Zip Code field, all of the fields we have in our database are text fields, meaning that they will be treated as alphabetical characters. We do not need to perform any mathematical operations on the city, state, or even street address fields. For a field to be considered a numeric field, its data must consist of numbers only, with no alphabetical characters.

The Zip Code field, however, is a purely numeric field; therefore, we need to specify it as a numeric rather than a text field. To have Works treat Zip Code as a numeric field, we need to set the attributes of that field. To do so, follow these steps:

1. Use the arrow keys (or the mouse) to position the cursor anywhere in the Zip Code field.
2. Press the **Alt** key and then the **T** key to access the **Format** menu.
3. Press the **X** (for Fi**x**ed) key to select a fixed number of decimal places.

In the **Number of Decimals** dialog box that appears, the highlighted **2** suggests that the default setting for decimals is two places. If we accepted this answer, each five-digit ZIP code would be followed by a decimal point and two zeros. Clearly, that's not appropriate in our case. In fact, we do not want any decimal places, so we will eliminate them by instructing Works to display the ZIP code entries as integers without decimal places. To accomplish this task, follow these steps:

1. Press the **0** (zero) key.
2. Press the **Enter** key to return to the database. You can now arrange your file numerically according to ZIP Code.

With the cursor still positioned on one of the data entries in the Zip Code field, follow these steps to arrange the records by ZIP code:

1. Press the **Alt** key and then press the **S** key to access the **Select** menu.
2. Press the **O** (for S**o**rt Records) key to sort (or arrange) the records.
3. When the **Sort** dialog box appears, use the keyboard to replace the Last Name entry in the **1st Field** box by typing Zip Code.
4. Hold down the **Alt** key and press the **B** (to choose the **Descend** option) to sort the database by ZIP code in descending order.
5. Verify that a black dot appears to the left of the **Descend** option. If so, press the **Enter** key to accept the choice. The document is now arranged from the highest ZIP code to the lowest, with the 14222 ZIP codes listed first.

You can control other attributes of the data you include in your database fields by using the **Format** menu. This menu allows you to specify the numeric format (fixed, currency, comma, percent, exponential, true/false, or time/date), font, style (bold, italics, or underline), and justification (left, right, or center) of the information in a field. The choices serve the purposes that their names suggest, so go ahead and try a few on your own.

Using the Database Searching Powers

Now let's examine the searching capabilities a database can provide. Imagine that you needed to locate all the students who lived on Delaware Avenue, perhaps because a family emergency required a neighbor to help transport a student home. With a database of only twenty-five students, this is not a major task. But if the database were considerably larger, locating the information quickly and easily would be difficult without the database search capability.

To identify all the students who live on Delaware Avenue, follow these steps:

1. Press the **Alt** key and then the **S** key to access the **Select** menu.
2. Press the **S** (for **S**earch) key to search the database for particular records. Notice that the **Search** dialog box provides a place for you to enter the data you seek.
3. Use the keyboard to enter **Delaware**.
4. Hold down the **Alt** key and press the **A** (for **A**ll) key to select all the records that match the "Delaware" criterion.
5. Verify that a black dot appears to the left of the **All records** option and then press the **Enter** key to apply the search.

The screen displays only three records, those of Annie Phelps, Tricia Palmer, and Bill Grant. These are the only three records—students—with a Delaware Avenue address. If you wish to see all the records again, not just those of the three students living on Delaware Avenue, follow these steps:

1. Press the **Alt** key and then the **S** key to access the **Select** menu.
2. Press the **L** (for Show All Records) key to display all records again. Notice that all the student records are visible on the screen.

Using the Database Querying Powers

One limitation of the database searching feature is that you can only search for one criterion (for instance, "Delaware") at a time. If you wanted to locate a record according to more than one criteria—a student named Cooper who has a ZIP code of 14222, for instance—you would need to use the database querying powers. Let's examine the querying capabilities of the Works database that can perform such an operation. Again, for a database of only twenty-five students, this is not a major task. However, if the database were large, the ability to quickly locate information satisfying multiple criteria makes the database querying capacity very useful.

To locate the student named Cooper who has a 14222 ZIP code, follow these steps:

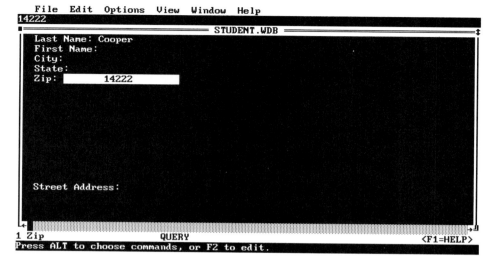

Figure 6.5 Database query screen with the criteria Last Name = Cooper and Zip Code = 14222 displayed

1. Press the **Alt** key and then press the **V** key to access the **View** menu.
2. Press the **Q** (for **Query**) key to query the database for particular records. Notice that the **Query** screen lists all of the fields in the database. This is where you enter the data you seek (Figure 6.5).
3. Use the **Tab** key (or the **Shift** and **Tab** keys together to move back up the fields) to position the cursor in the data box to the right of the Last Name field. Type **Cooper** and press the **Enter** key.
4. Use the **Tab** key (or the **Shift** and **Tab** keys) to position the cursor in the data box to the right of the Zip Code field and enter **14222**. Press the **Enter** key.
5. Press the **F10** key to apply the query and display the record with Cooper in the Last Name field and 14222 in the Zip Code field.

Notice that the screen displays the record of George Cooper, the only student named Cooper whose ZIP code is 14222. To see all the records again, follow these steps:

1. Press the **Alt** key and then the **S** key to access the **Select** menu.
2. Press the **L** (Show All Records) key to display all records again. Notice that all the student records are visible on the screen.

Use the database query features whenever you wish to match more than one criterion. For advanced uses of the querying powers, consult your reference manual or use the Microsoft **Works Tutorials**.

Printing the Database

Your next task will be to print the information from your database in a simple table. To print the information, follow these steps:

1. Press the **Alt** key and then press the **P** key to access the **Print** menu.
2. Press the **M** (Page Setup & **M**argins) key to change the left and right margins so that the document will fit on one page. Notice that the **Page Setup & Margins** dialog box appears on the screen.
3. Hold down the **Alt** key and press the **E** (L**e**ft margin) key to position the cursor in the **Left margin** box.
4. Use the keyboard to enter **.5** (for one-half inch) in the box, then press the **Tab** key to move the cursor to the **Right margin** box.
5. Type **.5** in the **Right margin** box, then press the **Enter** key to accept both settings. Your document will now fit on a single page.

The next step will be to preview the table on the screen before you print it on paper. To preview the database table, follow these steps:

1. Press the **Alt** key and then press the **P** key to access the **Print** menu.
2. Press the **V** key to pre**v**iew the document on the screen. Notice that the **Print Preview** dialog box appears on the screen.
3. Hold down the **Alt** key and press the **L** (for Print record and field **l**abels) key to instruct Works to include the field names at the top of the columns when it prints the database. Verify that an **X** appears to the left of the **Print record and field labels** option, indicating that it has been selected.
4. Hold down the **Alt** key and press the **P** key to **p**review the document on the screen.
5. If the document—shown in the "Greeking" display (Figure 6.6)—appears as you wish, press the **P** key to **p**rint the document on paper.

If you want to make changes before you print, press the **Esc** key to cancel the printing process and return to the database document. Make the changes that

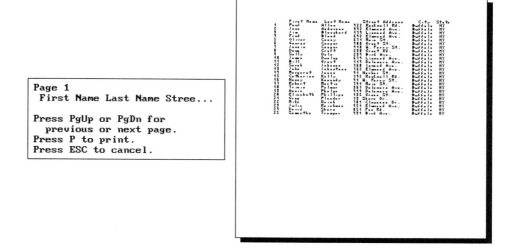

Figure 6.6 Database document shown in **Print Preview** display

you wish within the database, or use the **Print** menu commands to change the document's margins. When you have made your changes, repeat the previous steps to complete printing the document. Remember, if you are using a 5.25 inch floppy disk drive system, you will have to exchange disks to access the print preview layer, but Works will prompt you when it needs you to insert the **Accessories** disk.

Re-saving the Database File

That's the last database exercise you'll undertake with the **STUDENT.WDB** document. Although none of the changes that you made to your **STUDENT.WDB** file during these exercises is especially valuable, it's a good habit to save your documents before you close them. To save the document on your Works **Data** disk, follow these steps:

1. Press the **Alt** key and then the **F** (for **F**ile) key.
2. Press the **S** key to select the **Save** command. In a few moments, Works will store the changed version of the document on your Works **Data** disk.

Exiting Works

Once you have printed your report and are confident that it has been stored on your Works **Data** disk, you can safely exit Works without worrying about losing the information in your document. To exit the program and shut down the computer, use the same steps that you have used in the previous exercises. If you need additional help, consult the more detailed instructions presented in the **Exiting Works** section on pages 60–61.

If you want to continue working with the program now, follow these steps to close the current document, **STUDENT.WDB**, without exiting Works:

1. Press the **Alt** key and the **F** (for **F**ile) key.
2. Press the **C** key to select the **Close** command.

The current document, **STUDENT.WDB**, is no longer in the computer's memory, but Microsoft Works still is. You are now ready to begin the next section without having to restart Works.

Developing and Printing a Database Report

Getting Started

During this exercise you'll develop and print a database **report form.** The report-generating powers of Works let you design far more complex printouts than the simple table you created in the last section. A database file can contain many different report formats, each format satisfying the requirements of a particular situation. The report formats are saved as part of the database file, so once you design a format, you can use it over and over. In this exercise you will use the **CLASSES.WDB** database file that is stored on your Works **Data** disk.

Use the same procedures to start Works that you have used in the preceding exercises. If you need additional help, consult the more detailed instructions presented in the **Getting Started** section on pages 55–56.

Opening the CLASSES.WDB File

When you see the opening Works screen, you want to copy the **CLASSES.WDB** file into the computer's memory. To open the file from your Works **Data** disk, follow these steps:

1. Press the **O** key to select the **O**pen Existing File command.
2. Hold down the **Alt** key and press the **I** (for **D**irectories) key. When the blinking cursor appears in the **Directories** dialog box, press the **down arrow** key to highlight the letter of the disk drive containing your Works **Data** disk, then press the **Enter** key.
3. Hold down the **Alt** key and press the **F** (for **F**iles) key. When the blinking cursor appears in the **Files** dialog box, use the **down arrow** key to highlight the file, **CLASSES.WDB**, then press the **Enter** key.
4. Works will copy the **CLASSES.WDB** file from the disk and place the copy in the computer's temporary memory. In a few moments, you will see the database document displayed on the screen.

Viewing and Printing a Database Report

The **Report** layer within the Works database is the tool you will use to print more complicated reports of the information stored in databases. To access the **Report** layer, you will use the commands available under the **View** menu on the menu bar. One report is already stored within the **CLASSES.WDB** document to demonstrate the report features. To access that report, follow these steps:

1. Once the **CLASSES.WDB** document is open in the computer's memory, press the **Alt** key, then press the **V** (for **V**iew) key.
2. Press the number **1** key to select the report titled **Master List**. In a few moments, the first part of the report will be displayed on the screen. Examine the report screen (Figure 6.7).
3. Press the **Enter** key to display the next part of the report. Continue to press the **Enter** key until you reach the end of the report. Then you will automatically be returned to the beginning of the report with the formatting commands needed to produce the report displayed on the screen.

The commands you see on the screen define the **Master List** report that you just viewed. The entries preceded by the equal signs (for instance, =Last Name) represent field entries. The other information on the screen (for instance,

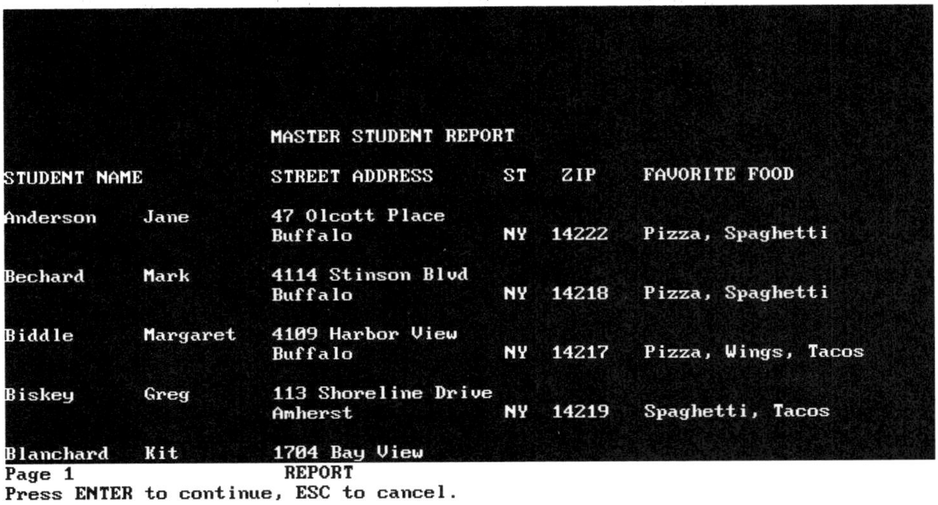

MASTER STUDENT REPORT

STUDENT NAME		STREET ADDRESS	ST	ZIP	FAVORITE FOOD
Anderson	Jane	47 Olcott Place Buffalo	NY	14222	Pizza, Spaghetti
Bechard	Mark	4114 Stinson Blvd Buffalo	NY	14218	Pizza, Spaghetti
Biddle	Margaret	4109 Harbor View Buffalo	NY	14217	Pizza, Wings, Tacos
Biskey	Greg	113 Shoreline Drive Amherst	NY	14219	Spaghetti, Tacos
Blanchard	Kit	1704 Bay View			

Page 1   REPORT
Press ENTER to continue, ESC to cancel.

Figure 6.7 Database **Master List** report display

MASTER STUDENT REPORT) is simply text inserted to enhance the report. To print this report, follow these steps:

1. Press the **Alt** key and then the **P** key to access the **Print** menu.
2. Press the **V** (for Pre**v**iew) key to access the **Print Preview** dialog box and examine the document on the screen.
3. Hold down the **Alt** key and press the **P** (for **P**review) key to see the document on the screen in the familiar Greeking display (Figure 6.8).

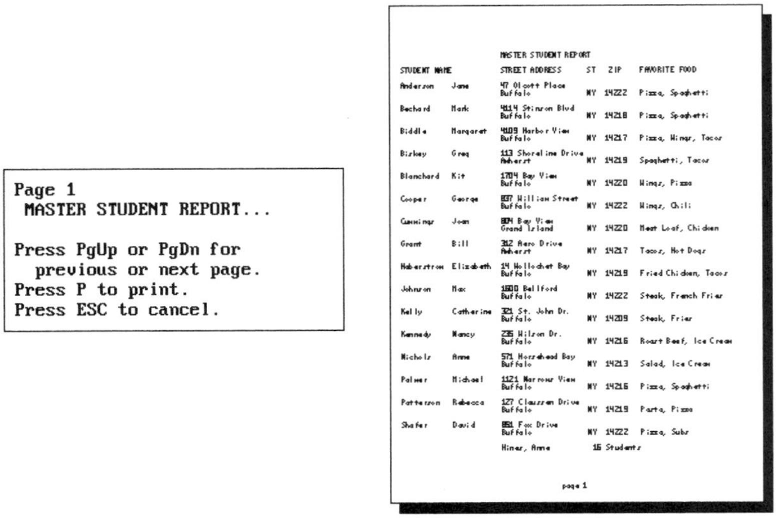

Page 1
  MASTER STUDENT REPORT...

Press PgUp or PgDn for
  previous or next page.
Press P to print.
Press ESC to cancel.

Figure 6.8 Database **Print Preview** display of **Master List** report

4. Press the **Page Down** key to view the subsequent pages of the report. When you have approved the report's appearance on the screen, press the **P** key to **p**rint it on paper.

5. When the printing process is complete, press the **F10** key to exit the report overlay and return to the list display.

Remember, if you're using a 5.25 inch floppy disk drive system, you'll have to exchange disks to access the print preview layer, but Works will tell you when to insert the **Accessories** disk.

Developing a Database Report

Now it's your turn to generate your own database report. The report generator is very powerful, but it is also complex. The four basic steps to creating a report are:

1. Establish the sequence of the report and define any **break fields** you will use in the report.

A break field causes the printing of a subtotal line each time the data entry in the field differs from that in the previous record. In the sample report, the Teacher field was a break field. Each time the teacher name changed in the data record, the **Total Number of Students** subtotal was printed.

2. The second step is to define the format (or layout) of the report in terms of **labels, data, functions,** and **document features.**

Labels are text that do not change throughout a report (for instance, the title and the column headings). Functions are the built-in mathematical operators that Works provides, such as COUNT, AVG, SUM, and MAX. Document features include headers and footers—text lines printed at the top or bottom of each page of the report—that enhance the appearance of the report. In the **Master List** report, the **page #** command is an example of a footer.

3. Name the completed report.

4. Store the completed report on disk in a database file. Reports are saved within the same file as the database document on which they are based. Once a report has been saved, it can be printed using the procedures described earlier.

Creating a Database Report

In this part of the exercise, you will create from scratch the **Master List** report that you just previewed. To establish the break fields in the report, follow these steps:

1. Once the **CLASSES.WDB** document is open in the computer's memory, press the **Alt** key, then press the **V** (for **V**iew) key.

2. Press the **N** (for **N**ew Report) key to develop a new report titled **New List**. In a few moments, a default report will be displayed on the screen.
3. Press the **Esc** key to cancel the default screen display and display the report definition screen.
4. Press the **Alt** key, then the **S** key to access the **Select** Menu.
5. Hold down the **Alt** key and press the **O** (for S**o**rt) key to access the **Sort Field** Menu.
6. Use the keyboard to type Teacher into the **1st Field** prompt box.
7. Hold down the **Alt** key and press the **G** key to select the **Break G** option.
8. Hold down the **Alt** key and press the **2** key to select the **2nd Field** prompt box.
9. Use the keyboard to type Last Name into the **2nd Field** prompt box and press the **Enter** key to end the sorting process.

Notice that the report definition screen is again displayed. The break fields have now been established. Next, you will add labels to your report. To do so, follow these steps:

1. Use the arrow keys (or mouse) to move the cursor to **Column C**.
2. Use the keyboard to type the report title, MASTER STUDENT REPORT, and then press the **Enter** key.
3. Use the **left arrow** key (or mouse) to move the cursor to **Column A**. Then use the **down arrow** key (or mouse) to move the cursor to the first line labelled **Intr Page**.
4. Replace the Last Name text that appears there by typing Student Name and pressing the **Enter** key.
5. Use the **right arrow** key (or mouse) to move the cursor to the First Name entry, press the **Delete** (or **Del**) key, and then press the **Enter** key to remove the entry.
6. Use the **right arrow** key (or mouse) to move the cursor to the cell in **Column G** currently containing the text entry, Teacher. Next, press the **Alt** key and then the **E** (for **E**dit) key to access the **Edit** menu.
7. Press the **D** key to access the **Delete** option, then press the **C** key to delete a column, and press the **Enter** key to confirm the choice.
8. Use the **right arrow** key (or mouse) to move the cursor to the cell in **Column D** currently containing the text entry, City. Next, press the **Alt** key and then the **E** (for **E**dit) key to access the **Edit** menu.
9. Press the **D** key to access the **Delete** option, then press the **C** key to delete a column, and press the **Enter** key to confirm the choice.
10. Use the **down arrow** key (or mouse) to move the cursor to any cell in the row labeled **Summ Teacher**. Next, press the **Alt** key and then the **E** key to access the **Edit** menu.
11. Press the **I** key to access the **Insert** option, then press the **Enter** key to insert a row.
12. When you see the **Type** dialog box, use the arrow keys (or mouse) to highlight the **Record** option and press the **Enter** key. Then press the **down arrow** key once to deselect the row.

13. Use the arrow keys to move the cursor along the newly inserted record row to the cell beneath the label, **Street Address**. Use the keyboard to type =City and press the **Enter** key.

14. Use the arrow keys to move the cursor to the row labelled **Summ Teacher**. Next, press the **Alt** key and then the **E** key to access the **Edit** menu.

15. Press the **I** key to access the **Insert** option, then press the **Enter** key to insert a row.

16. When you see the **Type** dialog box, use the arrow keys (or mouse) to highlight the **Summ Teacher** option and press the **Enter** key. (You will now repeat steps 14, 15, and 16 two more times to create three **Summ Teacher** rows.)

17. Press the **Alt** key, then the **E** key to access the **Edit** menu. Press the **I** key to access the **Insert** option, then press the **Enter** key to insert a row. In the **Type** dialog box, use the arrow keys to highlight the **Summ Teacher** option and press the **Enter** key.

18. Press the **Alt** key, then the **E** key to access the **Edit** menu. Press the **I** key to access the **Insert** option, then press the **Enter** key to insert a row. In the **Type** dialog box, use the arrow keys to highlight the **Summ Teacher** option and press the **Enter** key.

19. Now press the **down arrow** key once to deselect the row.

20. Use the arrow keys to move the cursor to the **Column A** cell of the first **Summ Teacher** row. Hold down the **Ctrl** key and press the **F8** key to select a row; then hold down the **Shift** key and press the **down arrow** key twice until three rows are highlighted.

21. With this entire range selected, press the **Alt** key, then the **E** key to access the **Edit** menu, and then the **E** (for Clear) key to clear all the data from that range of cells.

22. Use the arrow keys to move the cursor to the **Column C** cell of the second **Summ Teacher** row. Use the keyboard to type =Teacher and press the **Enter** key.

23. Use the arrow keys to move the cursor to the **Column D** cell in the same **Summ Teacher** row. Use the keyboard to type the formula =Count(Teacher) and press the **Enter** key. This formula tells Works to enter the total number of records (or students) for each distinct teacher name in this cell.

24. Use the arrow keys to move the cursor to the **Column B** cell of the **Summ Report** row. This line will define the end-of-report totals. Use the keyboard to type   Total Number of Students: in this cell. (First press the spacebar six times and then begin typing with the word Total. The six preceding spaces will help position the label within the report.) When you have finished, press the **Enter** key.

25. Use the arrow keys to move the cursor to the **Column D** cell of the **Summ Report** row and use the keyboard to type the formula =Count(Last Name) and press the **Enter** key.

The most difficult part of the report generation procedures is now complete. However, you'll add several document formatting features to the report before it is finished. To do so, follow these steps:

1. Press the **Alt** key and then the **P** key to access the **Print** menu.
2. Press the **M** (for Page Setup & **M**argins) key to change the left and right margins so that the document will fit on one page. Notice that the **Page Setup & Margins** dialog box appears on the screen.
3. Hold down the **Alt** key and press the **E** (for L**e**ft margin) key to position the cursor in the **Left margin** box.
4. Use the keyboard to type **.5** (for one-half inch) in the box, then press the **Tab** key to move the cursor to the **Right margin** box.
5. Use the keyboard to type **.5** in the **Right margin** box, then press the **Enter** key to accept those settings. Your document will now fit on a single page.

Now that the document will fit on the page correctly, the next step is to set appropriate headers and footers for the document. To do so, follow these steps:

1. Press the **Alt** key and then press the **P** key to access the **Print** menu.
2. Press the **H** (for **H**eaders & Footers) key to access the **Headers & Footers** dialog box. When the **Headers & Footers** dialog box appears on the screen, press the **Tab** key to enter the **Footer** prompt box.
3. Type **&cpage &p** and then press the **Enter** key. This footer code instructs Works to go to the center of the page (**&c**), print the word *page*, and follow that entry with the page number (**&p**). Therefore, Works will place a centered page number on the bottom of each page of the report.

If you would like to learn more about the control of headers and footers, you may want to use the Works on-line Help system to view other header and footer options. To access the Help feature, press the **F1** key, select the **Reports** options within the **Help Index**, and press the **Enter** key.

Your new database report is now complete. Before you preview or print the report, remember to save it on your Works **Data** disk and give the report a name. To name the report, follow these steps:

1. Press the **Alt** key and then press the **V** key to access the **View** menu.
2. Press the **R** key to access the **Reports** option.
3. Press the **Tab** key to move the cursor to the **Name** box and use the keyboard to type the new report name—**New List**.
4. Hold down the **Alt** key and press the **R** (for **R**ename) key to change the report's name to **New List**.
5. Hold down the **Alt** key and press the **D** (for **D**one) key to accept the report's new name.

Now that the report has been given a new name, you can save the modified **CLASSES.WDB** file on your Works **Data** disk. The new version of the file will now include the **New List** report that you just created.

Re-saving the Database File

The **New List** report form you created is still in the computer's memory, but it is not yet contained within the **CLASSES.WDB** file stored on your Works **Data** disk. You will now save your modified document on your Works **Data** disk, replacing the **CLASSES.WDB** file with the one currently in memory. This new version of the document includes any changes you've made since you last saved the file as well as the **New List** report form. To save the file, follow these steps:

1. Press the **Alt** key and then the **F** (for **F**ile) key (or use the mouse to point to the **File** command on the menu bar).
2. Press the **S** (for **S**ave) key to select the **Save** command (or press the mouse button, Drag the pointer down the options to highlight the **Save** choice, and release the mouse button). In a few moments, Works will store the improved version of the document on your Works **Data** disk.

Printing the New List Report

Your next task will be to print the information from your **New List** database report. To print the report (provided you are still in the **New List** report screen), follow these steps:

1. Press the **Alt** key and then press the **P** key to access the **Print** menu.
2. Press the **V** key to pre**v**iew the document. Notice that the **Print Preview** dialog box appears on the screen.
3. Hold down the **Alt** key and press the **P** key to **p**review the document on the screen.
4. If the document appears as you wish, press the **P** (for **P**rint) key to print the document on paper.

If you want to make changes before you print, press the **Esc** key to cancel the printing process and return to the database report. Make the changes that you wish within the database or the database report layer. When you have completed making the changes that you want, repeat the previous steps to complete printing the document. Remember, if you are using a 5.25 inch floppy disk drive system, you will have to exchange disks to access the print preview layer, but Works will tell you when to insert the **Accessories** disk.

Exiting Works

Once you have printed the report on paper and are confident that it has been stored on your Works **Data** disk, you can safely exit Works without worrying about losing the information in your document (if you made changes after previewing, re-save your document). To exit the program and shut down the computer, use the same steps that you have used in the preceding exercises. If you need additional help, consult the more detailed instructions presented in the **Exiting Works** section on pages 60–61.

If you want to continue working with the program now, follow these steps to close the current document, **CLASSES.WDB**, without exiting Works:

1. Press the **Alt** key and the **F** (for **F**ile) key.
2. Press the **C** key to select the **Close** command.

The current document, **CLASSES.WDB**, is no longer in the computer's memory, but Microsoft Works still is. You are now ready to begin the next section without having to restart Works.

Using the Database Glossary File

Orientation to the Glossary File

The glossary located in **Appendix B** is also on your Works **Data** disk as a database file entitled **GLOSSARY.WDB** (Figure 6.9). You can expand the glossary by adding your own terms, or update it by modifying or deleting any of the included terms. You can also search the database for specific definitions, or even print the entire glossary on paper.

Getting Started

Use the same procedures to start Works that you have used in the preceding exercises. If you need additional help, consult the more detailed instructions presented in the **Getting Started** section on pages 55–56. If you only closed your database document and did not exit Works at the end of the previous section, then you are ready to open the **GLOSSARY.WDB** file.

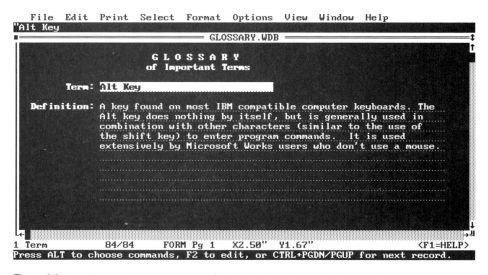

Figure 6.9 Database **GLOSSARY.WDB** file displaying the definition of the term **Alt Key**

Opening the GLOSSARY.WDB File

Once you have Works loaded into memory, you are ready to access the **GLOSSARY.WDB** file. The information contained in the **GLOSSARY.WDB** file can be manipulated in the same fashion as any Works database. To open the glossary file, follow these steps:

1. Press the **O** key to select the **Open Existing File** command (or use the mouse to highlight the **Open Existing File** choice and release the mouse button).
2. Hold down the **Alt** key and press the **I** (for D**i**rectories) key. When the blinking cursor appears in the **Directories** dialog box, press the **down arrow** key to highlight the letter of the disk drive containing your Works **Data** disk, and press the **Enter** key.
3. Hold down the **Alt** key and press the **F** (for **F**iles) key. When the blinking cursor appears in the **Files** dialog box, use the **down arrow** key to highlight the file **GLOSSARY.WDB**, and press the **Enter** key.
4. Works will copy the **GLOSSARY.WDB** file from the disk and place the copy in the computer's temporary memory. In a few moments, you'll see the document displayed in form view on the screen.

Querying in the GLOSSARY.WDB Document

To locate the meaning of any term in the glossary, use the same procedures you used to perform a query during the database exercises. Let's use the glossary to find the meaning of the term *Dialog Box.*

1. Press the **Alt** key, then the **V** key to access the **View** menu.
2. Press the **Q** (for **Q**uery) key.
3. Use the keyboard to type Dialog Box into the **Term** prompt box, then press the **F10** key to apply the query.

The definition of *Dialog Box* is now displayed on the screen. You can alter any of the definitions you wish by simply typing over the original definition. Now let's cancel the query so that you can page through the glossary. To do so, follow these steps:

1. Press the **Alt** key, then the **S** key to access the **Select** menu.
2. Press the **L** (for Show A**l**l Records) key.

This command selects (and makes available) all the records in the database. Now hold down the **Ctrl** key and press the **Page Up** and **Page Down** keys to navigate through the document.

Printing the GLOSSARY.WDB Document

If you want to print out a copy of the whole glossary, follow these steps:

1. Once the **GLOSSARY.WDB** document is open in the computer's memory, press the **Alt** key, and then press the **V** (for **V**iew) key.

2. Press the number **1** key to select the report entitled **GLOSSARY**. In a few moments, the glossary will be displayed on the screen.
3. Press the **Esc** key to display the report format.
4. Next, press the **Alt** key, and then press the **P** key to access the **Print** menu.
5. Finally, press the **P** key and then the **Enter** key to print the entire glossary.

When the document has finished printing, press the **F10** key to exit the report form and return to the form display. If you only want to print a portion of the glossary, first use the query process to select the records (or terms) that you want to have printed; then follow the same steps described above to print just that selection.

Amending the Glossary

You can easily add new terms to the glossary or alter existing entries. Since the glossary is a Works database file, you edit it just as you would any other database and then re-save the changes—replacing the earlier version of the file with your newly modified version. If you want to add new records (or terms) to the **GLOSSARY.WDB** file, follow these steps:

1. Once the document is open in the computer's memory, hold down the **Ctrl** key and press the **End** key to move the cursor to the end of the file.
2. Use the keyboard to type the new term, press the **Tab** key, and then enter the definition.
3. If you wish to add more terms, hold down the **Ctrl** key and press the **Page Down** (or **Pg Dn**) key to move the cursor to the next blank record and repeat the process until you have added all of the new terms you wish.

If you want to modify the existing information in one of the records in the **GLOSSARY.WDB** file, follow these steps:

1. Once the document is open in the computer's memory, hold down the **Ctrl** key and press the **Page Down** (or **Pg Dn**) key until the record you want to change is displayed on the screen.
2. If you want to change the term, use the keyboard now to type the new term, then press the **Enter** key to establish the new term name.
3. If you want to change the definition, first press the **Tab** key to position the cursor in the **Definition** box. Once the cursor is in the **Definition** box, use the keyboard to type the new definition, then press the **Enter** key to establish it.
4. If you wish to change more terms, hold down the **Ctrl** key and press the **Page Down** or **Page Up** keys to move the cursor to the appropriate record and repeat the process until you have made all of the changes you wish.

Re-saving the Amended Glossary

When you have finished adding records or altering the extant records, you will want to save the changes that you made. Your new version of the **GLOSSARY.WDB** file can replace the earlier version by following these steps:

1. Press the **Alt** key and then the **F** (for **F**ile) key (or use the mouse to point to the **File** command on the menu bar).
2. Press the **S** key to select the **Save** command (or press the mouse button, Drag the pointer down the options to highlight the **Save** choice, and release the mouse button). In a few moments, Works will store the improved version of the document on your Works **Data** disk.

Exiting Works

Once you are confident that the new version of the glossary has been stored on your Works **Data** disk, you can safely exit Works without worrying about losing the information in your file. To exit the program and shut down the computer, use the same steps that you have used in the preceding exercises. If you need additional help, consult the more detailed instructions presented in the **Exiting Works** section on pages 60–61.

Integrating Databases into the Instructional Process

Now that you are familiar with how the Microsoft Works database manager can help you organize and manipulate information, let's consider approaches for using databases instructionally. The Works database manager is ideally suited for effective instruction of students from elementary through college levels. The capabilities that databases offer for recognizing relationships by organizing and arranging information make databases appropriate in nearly all disciplines.

Most of the suggestions in this section can be used effectively with a single computer in a classroom, although some are more appropriate for a computer lab. The strategies can be enhanced by using a large monitor or an LCD with an overhead projector, but they can all be modified to suit the teacher, the equipment, the students, and each lesson's objective.

Conducting Class Surveys

Surveys are good activities to introduce your students to the world of databases. Students usually find surveys interesting and motivating. You might begin the school year by surveying your students on their favorite foods, pastimes, colors, movies, singers, songs, sports, books, etc. The surveys might also include questions about their least favorite subjects and activities. Additional survey questions can include names and ages of siblings, names and types of pets, personal motto, favorite quotations, bed time, hours slept per night, birth month and sign, musical instrument(s) played, parents' occupations, chores responsible for, and part-time jobs held (see the excerpt from a sample survey in Figure 6.10).

From the completed surveys, create a database file with a field name for each question (favorite food, etc.) and use it to introduce your students to the Works

Name

1) When is your birthday? _____

2) What are 2 of your favorite foods?
   a) _____
   b) _____

3) What are 2 of your favorite drinks?
   a) _____
   b) _____

4) What are 2 of your favorite books?
   a) _____
   b) _____

5) Who are 2 of your best friends?
   a) _____
   b) _____

6) What are 2 of your favorite movies?
   a) _____
   b) _____

7) What are 2 of your favorite songs?
   a) _____
   b) _____

8) What are 2 of your favorite school subjects?
   a) _____
   b) _____

9) What are 2 of your favorite sports?
   a) _____
   b) _____

10) What is your favorite color?_____

Figure 6.10 Interest survey

database manager. Using a large monitor or an LCD with an overhead projector, guide your students through database manipulations such as sorting, searching, and changing the screen from list to form display. Have students formulate search questions such as, "Which students list pizza as one of their favorite foods, have a pet dog, and are responsible for washing the dishes in their homes?" Then display the answer for all students to see and discuss.

Once students understand how a database works, create a list of questions for students to answer independently by accessing the database. The questions should be designed to require students to use all the different powers of the Works database, including sorting, searching, and querying. When they've completed the exercise, students can use the reporting powers to print out the answers. Students might then be interested in formulating additional questions for their classmates to answer, encouraging the students to explore the database file even further. You might decide to have the database file available for students to use throughout the first part of the school year.

As students learn to use the database, they also learn more about their classmates—often discovering they have more in common with other students than they had realized. In addition, the students are often initially more motivated to investigate information about their peers than they might be to examine information about more academic topics.

Related Activities

- Arrange your students into groups and have them design and conduct different survey questions for their classmates to answer. After the students have gathered the data, help them organize the information into a database file.
- Working in small groups, students can design and conduct surveys of the other classes or individuals in your school. After all groups have gathered the data, help them organize the information into a database file and compare the survey responses with those of their classmates.
- Arrange your students into teams and have them design and conduct surveys of the individuals in your community. After the students have gathered the survey data, help them organize the information into a database file and design sample questions for their classmates to answer that help compare the responses from the community with those from their classmates.

Creating Databases to Enhance Units of Study

Class projects and units of study provide an excellent vehicle for compiling instructional databases. All disciplines have a body of information associated with them that students must master. Part of this information is a collection of facts that you want students to learn and then use to recognize the trends and patterns characteristic of the discipline. In a study of the solar system, for instance, you want students to recognize and explain the relationships that exist in the arrangement of the planets. For example, the more distant a planet is from the sun, the longer its "year." Also, the time it takes a planet to rotate on its axis determines the length of the planet's "day." In a study of the United States, you might want students to recognize and explain patterns such as that areas in the eastern part of the country generally earned statehood before areas west of the Mississippi and that a state's population (not its size) directly affects its number of representatives to the United States Congress.

Units of study such as the solar system or the United States are ideally suited to the use of databases. Often patterns are difficult to see when information is presented in a static form such as a table in a textbook. If the same information is available in a dynamic form such as an electronic database file, the data can be manipulated so that the relationships are more discernible. Once your students are competent database users, they can use database powers to manipulate the information and discover the patterns or trends for themselves. This discovery experience often leads to a more complete and lasting understanding than by telling them the pattern and asking them to learn it.

The following activities can be implemented in many different ways. Commercial or teacher-made databases can be provided to students with guide questions for them to answer. As they manipulate the database files to answer your questions, students can identify the patterns or important concepts for themselves. This approach is probably the most effective one to adopt when you first start using databases instructionally.

A second, more powerful, approach involves having your students create actual database files with predetermined fields. Use this approach during a study of the solar system by assigning groups of students to gather specific data on each planet and having them insert the information into an already created (blank) database form. To encourage accuracy, have two groups (or individuals) responsible for separately gathering the data on each planet. Before the data are entered into the database file, have the two groups (or individuals) verify that their data are identical, resolving any inconsistencies before the information is entered. This approach can be used most effectively after your students have already had several opportunities to use databases instructionally.

In the third approach, your students design and create the database files themselves. This method is particularly effective as a whole class activity the first time and later as a small group activity. During your study of the Age of Exploration, for example, ask students to design a database that would help them understand and interpret the information they are studying. After they design the database (determining the fields and the type of data to include), the students can then use appropriate resources to gather the necessary data to complete their database, then enter the data into the file. Later, they can share their database file with the class, demonstrating how it can be used to interpret the information about exploration that they have included in the file. This approach is recommended only after your students have had considerable experience with the instructional use of databases.

These instructional strategies can all be used in any discipline and at nearly any grade level (excluding K–2). The following examples briefly suggest units of study that particularly lend themselves to the instructional use of databases, but they are included only to start you thinking. Many more ideas will occur to you (and your students) once you introduce them to the instructional uses of databases. For some of the suggested units, **templates** have been placed on your Works **Data** disk as possible starting points for generating new databases. (A template is like a blank file when you load it into memory—it does not contain any information. When you, or your students, enter information into the suggested fields, you can save the file using a new file name and maintain the original template to use again.) Add additional fields and delete unwanted fields by using the appropriate commands under the database manager's **Edit** command on the menu bar.

■ Solar System

Open the template, **PLANETS.WDB**. Organize your students into nine groups with each group responsible for two planets. Once the template is open in the computer's memory, you can print blank data-gathering sheets for your students' use by accessing the simple report form, **Data Sheet.** To print the blank data-gathering sheets, use the same procedures that you used when printing the **CLASSES.WDB** report form:

1. Press the **Alt** key, then press the **V** (for **V**iew) key.
2. Press the number **1** key to select the **Data Sheet** report form.
3. Press the **Enter** key several times to exit the report preview screen.
4. Press the **Alt** key, then press the **P** key to access the **Print** menu.
5. Press the **V** key to access the **Print Preview** dialog box.
6. Hold down the **Alt** key and press the **P** key to preview the report on the screen.
7. If the data sheet looks suitable, press the **P** key to print it on paper. If not, make whatever changes you want, then repeat the same procedures and print.

Distribute the printed data-gathering sheets to the students.

The students' task is to use the appropriate resources to find the data they need to complete the **Planets** database. Before they enter the information in the file, have one representative from each of the two groups responsible for each planet compare the groups' findings to ensure accuracy and consistency. When the database file is complete, have the students look for patterns such as the relationship between a planet's distance from the sun and the length of its "year," the relationship between the time it takes a planet to rotate on its axis and the length of its "day," and the relationship between a planet's distance from the sun and its surface temperature.

■ States

Open the template, **STATES.WDB**. Have your students complete this activity individually (with each individual responsible for two or three states—perhaps one state per week). Once the template is open in the computer's memory, you can print blank data-gathering sheets for your students' use by accessing the simple report form, **Data Sheet.** To print the blank data-gathering sheets, use the same procedures that you used when printing the **CLASSES.WDB** report form:

1. Press the **Alt** key, then press the **V** (for **View**) key.
2. Press the number **1** key to select the **Data Sheet** report form.
3. Press the **Enter** key several times to exit the report preview screen.
4. Press the **Alt** key, then press the **P** key to access the **Print** menu.
5. Press the **V** key to access the **Print Preview** dialog box.
6. Hold down the **Alt** key and press the **P** key to preview the report on the screen.
7. If the data sheet looks suitable, press the **P** key to print it on paper. If not, make whatever changes you want, then repeat the same procedures and print.

Distribute the printed data-gathering sheets to the students.

The students' task is to use the appropriate resources to find the data that they need to complete the **States** database. Before they enter the information in the file, the two individuals responsible for each state should compare their findings to ensure consistency. When the database file is complete, have the students look for patterns such as the relationship between geographical location and the year statehood was achieved, the relationship between geographical location and population rank order, and the relationship between population and the number of representatives to the United States Congress.

■ Minerals

Open the template, **MINERALS.WDB**. Arrange your students into groups with each group responsible for two minerals. Once the template is open in the computer's memory, you can print blank data-gathering sheets for your students' use by accessing the simple report form, **Data Sheet.** To print the blank data-gathering sheets, use the same procedures that you used when printing the **CLASSES.WDB** report form:

1. Press the **Alt** key, then press the **V** (for **View**) key.
2. Press the number **1** key to select the **Data Sheet** report form.
3. Press the **Enter** key several times to exit the report preview screen.
4. Press the **Alt** key, then press the **P** key to access the **Print** menu.
5. Press the **V** key to access the **Print Preview** dialog box.
6. Hold down the **Alt** key and press the **P** key to preview the report on the screen.
7. If the data sheet looks suitable, press the **P** key to print it on paper. If not, make whatever changes you want, then repeat the same procedures and print.

Distribute the printed data-gathering sheets to the students.

The students' task is to use the appropriate resources to find the data they need to complete the **Minerals** database. Before they enter the information in the file, the two individuals responsible for each mineral should compare their findings to ensure consistency. When the file is complete, this database will be especially useful for students conducting science experiments designed to determine the identity of a particular substance by its properties. Also, have the students use the database to look for patterns such as the relationship between a mineral's relative hardness and its specific gravity and the relationship between a mineral's class and its specific gravity.

■ **Presidents**

Open the template, **PRESIDES.WDB**. Have your students complete this activity individually (with each individual responsible for two or three presidents—perhaps one president per week). Once the template is open in the computer's memory, you can print blank data-gathering sheets for your students' use by accessing the simple report form, **Data Sheet.** To print the blank data-gathering sheets, use the same procedures that you used when printing the **CLASSES.WDB** report form:

1. Press the **Alt** key, then press the **V** (for **V**iew) key.
2. Press the number **1** key to select the **Data Sheet** report form.
3. Press the **Enter** key several times to exit the report preview screen.
4. Press the **Alt** key, then press the **P** key to access the **Print** menu.
5. Press the **V** key to access the **Print Preview** dialog box.
6. Hold down the **Alt** key and press the **P** key to preview the report on the screen.
7. If the data sheet looks suitable, press the **P** key to print it on paper. If not, make whatever changes you want, then repeat the same procedures and print.

Distribute the printed data-gathering sheets to the students.

The students' task is to use the appropriate resources to find the data that they need to complete the **Presidents** database. Before they enter the information in the file, the individuals responsible for each president should compare their findings to ensure consistency. When the database file is complete, have the students look for patterns such as the relationship between the state of birth and the president's political party and the relationship between presidential order and the state of birth.

■ **Holidays**

Open the template, **HOLIDAYS.WDB**. Arrange your students into groups with each group responsible for three or more holidays. Once the template is open in the computer's memory, you can print blank data-gathering sheets for your students' use by accessing the simple report form, **Data Sheet.** To print the blank data-gathering sheets, use the same procedures that you used when printing the **CLASSES.WDB** report form:

1. Press the **Alt** key, then press the **V** (for **V**iew) key.
2. Press the number **1** key to select the **Data Sheet** report form.
3. Press the **Enter** key several times to exit the report preview screen.
4. Press the **Alt** key, then press the **P** key to access the **Print** menu.
5. Press the **V** key to access the **Print Preview** dialog box.
6. Hold down the **Alt** key and press the **P** key to preview the report on the screen.
7. If the data sheet looks suitable, press the **P** key to print it on paper. If not, make whatever changes you want, then repeat the same procedures and print.

Distribute the printed data-gathering sheets to the students.

The students' task is to use the appropriate resources to find the data they need to complete the **Holidays** database. Before they enter the information in the file, have one representative from each of the two groups responsible for each holiday compare their findings to ensure consistency. When the database file is complete, have students look for patterns such as the relationship between the type of holiday and its country of origin and the relationship between the religious origin of the holiday and the countries where it is currently observed.

■ Suggestions for Databases

- Additional topics for creating science databases include dinosaurs, famous scientists, scientific inventions, trees, leaves, elements, advancements in computer technology, plants, animals, whales, gases, and micro-organisms.
- Other social studies databases might include events in local, state, American, and world history; the events of the American Civil War and the American Revolutionary War; accomplishments of community helpers, famous women, or inventors; facts about countries of the world; Native American tribes; transportation improvements; communication improvements; the original thirteen American Colonies; careers.
- Arts-related databases could include a library of novels, famous authors, and book reviews; plot elements and characters in a novel or short story; grammatical terminology; foreign vocabulary.
- Suggestions for health-related databases include caloric content of various foods, calorie-burning rates of various exercises, drugs, diseases, and careers in the health industry.
- Student-oriented databases include favorite sports, sports figures, movies, singers, songs, possessions, games, local amusements, toys, albums, television programs, and pastimes.

Related Activities

- After your students have created their own database files, have them demonstrate ways to use their files to other classes and grade levels.
- Have students generate sets of questions for their classmates to answer using the file. Rotate the groups so that they can explore the other databases and answer the others' questions.
- Save these database files and the sets of questions as valuable resources for following years. Consider sharing the files with other teachers and placing a copy in the media center or library for all students and teachers to access.

Guiding Brainstorming Sessions

Database managers can be used very effectively to guide your students in brainstorming sessions. We discussed brainstorming sessions in the integration section of the chapter on word processing. When you use a database manager to guide brainstorming sessions, you can store and access more information even faster.

The teaching techniques are similar to those discussed in the word processing integration section. The teacher's role is to record students' suggestions as they make them. When the time allotted for brainstorming ideas expires, the class reviews the suggestions and prioritizes or sequences them.

How can a database manager assist in this procedure? By running the Microsoft Works database manager in a computer connected to a large monitor or an LCD, the teacher (or a student with keyboarding skills) can quickly enter student responses. The facilitator can record the initial responses in a new database document with a single field named Suggestions or Ideas. Follow these steps to create a document:

1. Create a new database file.
2. Create a field in the form display by entering text followed by a colon (e.g., **Ideas:**).
3. Change from form to list display for easier viewing (by using the **View** command).
4. Change the width of the field to 30 characters (by using the **Format** command).

As students make suggestions, enter them into the column in the one field that you have created. The students will see the responses displayed as quickly as they are made. When the time comes to review and prioritize the suggestions, you can use the database features to facilitate and enhance the process. First, ask students to examine the ideas and suggest new categories (or fields) into which the responses can be organized. When the class agrees on several new categories into which to organize their data, add new fields named for those categories. After you add the new fields, resize them so that all the fields are visible on the screen.

Next, you can use the Works **Copy** and **Move** commands (under the **Edit** menu) to arrange the ideas into the appropriate fields. Once the data are placed into the appropriate categories, you can print a copy of the list. Now you may want to distribute copies of this list to groups of students and ask each group to determine the relative importance of the ideas in the separate categories.

Finally, you can ask the groups to share their rank-ordered lists with the entire class, reach a consensus on priorities, create one final list with additional copy and move procedures, and print out a master list for each student to keep with his or her materials. Alternatively, instead of copying and moving data entries, you can edit the entries (press the **F2** key to edit the current data entry) and place the numeral before each field entry that establishes its relative importance in that category. With this method, you can use the database sorting power to arrange the field entries into the proper order of importance. Using this approach, you may want to print out the database one field at a time so that each field maintains the correct sequence. In either case, once a final list is agreed upon by your students, you can print out a polished list and make copies for all the students just minutes after the brainstorming session ends. Remember, even if you don't have a large display device available, you can still use many of these same instructional procedures by modifying them to fit your classroom situation.

Related Activities

- Use an initial brainstorming session to come up with ideas for class rules that should be followed during the school year.
- Have students suggest ideas for projects or units that they would like to investigate during the school year.
- Students can suggest ideas for procedures that should be followed during subsequent brainstorming sessions.
- Rotate students in the role of brainstorming session guide after you have adequately modeled the procedures you expect. You can then take a seat with the class and offer brainstorming suggestions with the students.

Additional Activities

Educational Activities
Maintaining student records
Maintaining parent mailing lists
Maintaining class rosters
Maintaining classroom equipment inventories
Maintaining textbook inventories
Maintaining building inventories
Generating daily, weekly, or yearly schedules
Organizing information for instructional lessons
Maintaining lists of student birthdays, interests, pets, siblings, etc.
Organizing historical events
Teaching students research techniques
Maintaining lists of student readings

General Activities
Maintaining personal mailing lists
Maintaining inventories of personal belongings
Maintaining lists of personal books you've read and want to read
Cataloguing recipes
Maintaining lists of videos
Cataloguing slide, stamp, or coin collections
Maintaining lists of music albums, tapes, or CDs
Maintaining messages and your responses to them

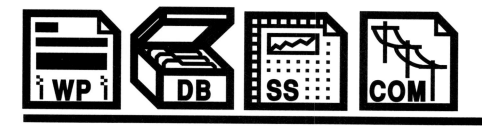

7 Focusing on Print Merging— A First Look at Data Integration

We have already compared the word processor to an enhanced typewriter and the database to an enhanced index card filing system. When we combine the power of the two applications, we have a powerful tool that can greatly increase professional productivity.

How can you use print merging in your classroom? As an educator, you are responsible for communicating to parents all school or class activities as well as their children's progress. Some of the typical parent communications you might send include opening day letters, Open House invitations, parent–teacher conference notifications, field trip announcements, invitations to special student performances, and report card cover letters. Print merging helps you accomplish these communication tasks in an efficient and personalized manner. Let's compare the process of handling a teacher's communication responsibilities using traditional means with the same process using the powers of print merging.

Imagine that, as a teacher, you would like to send a personalized letter welcoming students to your class and informing parents about necessary details for the first day of school. You also decide that, during this same first term, you would like to send similar letters to the parents of your students to announce Open House Night, to accompany progress monitors, to explain parent conference schedules, and to clarify major unit materials that you send home several times each quarter. Let's compare the traditional system of communication with the communication that uses print merging.

In the traditional manual system, you might create one standardized letter with blank spaces for the parents' names (or you could type twenty-five individual letters). Although you could use last year's document as a model, you would still need to type a new master letter with updated information. When you were finished, you would make a reproduction of the letter for each parent. In addition, to personalize each letter, you would have to write in, by hand, each parent's name and each child's name in the appropriate blank spaces. Alternatively, you could create a generic version of the letter with no personalized information. In either case, the reproductions would not be very attractive (or professional-looking), and they would require a significant amount of time to sign and address.

Contrast that process with the use of print merging. You can double the powers of word processors and database managers by combining your student database file with a single copy of the word-processed opening day letter. After spending a few minutes editing the letter to make it current and adding database **placeholders** (indicators placed in the word-processed document that tell Works where to include information from the database), you use print-merging powers to automatically produce twenty-five personalized copies of the letter. The printer takes some time to print out all the letters, but you are free to finish other chores while it works. When the letters are finished, each one includes the particular parent's name and complete address. In addition, each letter uses the child's name instead of the impersonal reference "your child" and includes the appropriate gender pronouns instead of "his/her," "he/she," and "him/her."

Instead of the laborious task of addressing all of the envelopes by hand, you can also use print merging to generate the mailing labels that you'll need during the year. Since your student records file already exists, you need only to create a new word-processed document with the necessary placeholders for the parents' names and addresses. You can use this same simple form for all the mailing labels you'll need throughout the year and for future student database files. You can then print out the class set of labels to stick on the envelopes—much quicker and more professional-looking than had you addressed the envelopes by hand.

The same process can be repeated for the term's other communication projects. Once the student database file is complete, you can reuse it for each communication task throughout the school year. For example, instead of laboriously handwriting each name and address on an awkward-looking Open House announcement, you can simply make minor changes to last year's letter and then print out individualized letters for the entire class. Such letters will be far more attractive and will be produced far more expeditiously than the hand-produced notices. Rather than spending evenings or even whole weekends preparing your professional communications, you can complete the chore in a much more professional manner in a much shorter time.

When you aggregate these product improvements and savings in time over the term, the increases in productivity are substantial. As you apply print-merging powers to your other communications during the year, the process becomes increasingly effective. When the time arrives for next year's parent conferences, field trip notices, and other announcements, you will have to spend only a short time preparing the communications. In this way, print merging offers educators an enormously powerful tool for increasing productivity.

An Introduction to Print Merging

As the preceding section demonstrates, print merging is a very useful application that combines (or merges) two other important computer applications—the word processor and the database manager. Print merging is one common example of **data integration**—that is, the incorporation of information from different applications such as word processors and database managers. Later in the text, you will be introduced to other instances of data integration involving word processing, spreadsheets, and charts. This chapter, however, will focus only on the print-merging process.

As you've already seen, print merging combines two separate applications. Therefore, when you print merge, you must have two files open in the computer's memory—in this case, a database file and a word-processed file. Once the two files are in RAM (either by creating new files or opening existing ones), you'll use the **Window** command on the menu bar to move between files.

The database file determines the type of information that will be included in the print-merged document and the number of documents that will be printed. The word processor establishes the format for the printout and the placement of the database information in the document. You use the database to determine the number of documents you wish to produce by selecting some or all of the records. Recall from the chapter on databases that Works provides searching and querying powers to select specific records that satisfy given criteria. For the opening day letter, a teacher would make sure to select the **Show All Records** choice in the database file.

In the word-processed letter, you must insert placeholders in the appropriate positions to guarantee that the information merged from the database file will be placed in the correct position. For example, you must position the cursor at the part in the letter where you would like the parents' names placed and insert a placeholder there. The placeholder tells the computer that the first letter it prints should have the parents' names from the first database record placed there, the second letter should have the parents' names from the second record, and so on.

Once you have inserted all the necessary placeholders in the word-processed document, you complete the print-merging process by printing from the word-processed document. Although you tell the computer that you want to print one copy, Works will print as many letters as you have records selected in your database file. One copy of the letter will be printed for each active record. If this concept seems somewhat confusing to you now, don't despair. You will work through a detailed example of this process in the following section.

In the next section you will learn to print merge a word-processed document with an existing database file, insert placeholders in appropriate places in a word-processed document, use database selecting powers to set the number of documents to print, and print out personalized documents.

Modifying a Word-Processed File for Print Merging

Orientation

In this exercise, you'll modify the **BET-LET.WPS** file that you created in Chapter 5. You will print merge the **BET-LET.WPS** file with the **SCHOOL.WDB** database. The **SCHOOL.WDB** file has more fields than your **STUDENT.WDB** file (such as Greeting Name and Custody Contact) and is therefore more suitable for illustrating the powers of print merging.

To begin, you'll need to have both the word-processed and the database documents in RAM; when you start Works, you'll open the database file first and then the word-processed document. You will add placeholders to the word-processed document where information will be inserted from the database file.

Getting Started

Use the same procedures to start Works that you have used in the preceding exercises. If you need additional help, consult the more detailed instructions presented in the **Getting Started** section on pages 55–56.

Opening the Database and Word-Processor Files

When you see the opening Works screen, open the **SCHOOL.WDB** file on your Works **Data** disk by following these steps:

1. Press the **O** key to select the **Open Existing File** command (or use the mouse to highlight the **Open Existing File** choice and release the mouse button).
2. Hold down the **Alt** key and press the **I** (for **D**irectories) key. When the blinking cursor appears in the **Directories** dialog box, press the **down arrow** key to highlight the letter of the disk drive containing your Works **Data** disk, and press the **Enter** key.
3. Hold down the **Alt** key and press the **F** (for **F**iles) key. When the blinking cursor appears in the **Files** dialog box, use the **down arrow** key to highlight the file **SCHOOL.WDB**, and press the **Enter** key.

4. Works will copy the **SCHOOL.WDB** file from the disk and place the copy in the computer's memory. In a few moments, you will see the document displayed on the screen.

Now open the file, **BET-LET.WPS**, which is also stored on your Works **Data** disk. To open that file, repeat a process similar to the one you just completed:

1. Press the **O** key to select the **Open Existing File** command.
2. Hold down the **Alt** key and press the **F** (for **F**iles) key. When the blinking cursor appears in the **Files** dialog box, use the **down arrow** key to highlight the file **BET-LET.WPS**, and press the **Enter** key.
3. Works will copy the **BET-LET.WPS** file from the disk and place the copy in the computer's memory. In a few moments, you will see your letter displayed on the screen.

Reformatting the Word-Processed Document

You will now insert database placeholders into this word-processed document so that, even though you only create a single copy of the letter, you'll be able to print twenty-five personalized copies. Each personalized letter will have the same basic text, but with different name and address information. You'll position the cursor to specify where the information from the database will be placed in the word-processed document.

First, however, you'll have to make two simple changes to the letter. If you followed the instructions in Chapter 5, the body of your letter is now double-spaced. Let's make the entire letter single-spaced so that it will fit easily on one page. To do so, follow these steps:

1. Press the **F8** key five times to highlight the entire document.
2. Press the **Alt** key and then the **T** key to access the **Format** menu.
3. Press the **S** (for **S**ingle-Space) key to make the entire letter single-spaced.

Next, you'll add an extra line between the date and the greeting. To add the additional line, use the arrow keys or the mouse to position the cursor to the left of the word *Dear* in the greeting and press the **Enter** key once. Press the **up arrow** key or use the mouse to position the cursor on the blank line that you just created. Now you are ready to begin adding the database placeholders to your letter.

Inserting Placeholders into BET-LET.WPS

You will use the **Insert Field** command in the **Edit** menu to add placeholders to your word-processed document. When you execute the **Insert Field** command, you will see the **Insert Field** dialog box (Figure 7.1).

Figure 7.1 **Insert Field** dialog box after the **SCHOOL.WDB** file has been selected

To issue the **Insert Field** command, follow these steps:

1. Press the **Alt** key and then the **E** key to access the **Edit** menu.
2. Press the **F** key to select the **Insert Field** option. The **SCHOOL.WDB** database document appears in the left box; the **Fields** box on the right is now blank. Since you have one database in RAM, the only choice you see in the left window is **SCHOOL.WDB**. Press the **down arrow** key once to highlight the **SCHOOL.WDB** database. In the **Fields** window, you can now see the fields contained in the **SCHOOL.WDB** database, including First Name, Last Name, and Street Address.
3. Hold down the **Alt** key and press the **F** key to position the cursor in the **Field** window. Now use the **down arrow** key to move the cursor down the list of fields until you highlight the Custody Contact field (or use the mouse with the up and down arrows on the scroll bar to the right of the **Fields** window). The Custody Contact field was designed for both traditional and nontraditional families (such as those with single parents) and contains the name of the custodial parent or guardian. This field is the first one you will merge for the inside address of your letter.
4. To select the Custody Contact field for merging, press the **Enter** key. In a moment, you'll notice that **<<Custody Contact>>** appears on the screen. This is the placeholder for the Custody Contact field data that will be merged from the records in the **SCHOOL.WDB** database (see Figure 7.2).

The cursor should still be to the right of the **<<Custody Contact>>** placeholder; if not, position it there. Press the **Enter** key to add another line. The cursor should now be back on the lefthand margin beneath the first placeholder. Again, issue the **Insert Field** command by following these steps:

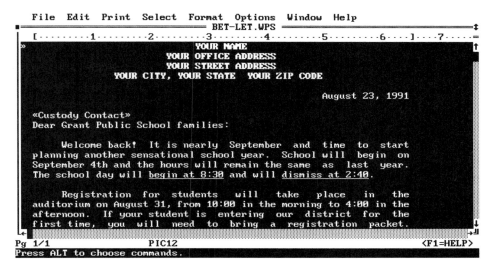

Figure 7.2 The **BET-LET.WPS** file with the Custody Contact placeholder inserted

1. Press the **Alt** key and then the **E** key to access the **Edit** menu.
2. Press the **F** key to select the **Insert Field** option.
3. Hold down the **Alt** key and press the **F** key to position the cursor in the **Field** window.
4. Use the **down arrow** key to move the cursor down the list of fields until you highlight the Street Address field; then press the **Enter** key.

The database placeholder **<<Street Address>>** should now appear beneath **<<Custody Contact>>** on your screen. If so, all is well. If not, repeat the above steps until it does appear.

Press the **Enter** key again to add another line. The cursor should now be back on the lefthand margin beneath the second placeholder. Once again, issue the **Insert Field** command by following these steps:

1. Press the **Alt** key and then the **E** key to access the **Edit** menu.
2. Press the **F** key to select the **Insert Field** option.
3. Hold down the **Alt** key and press the **F** key to position the cursor in the **Field** window.
4. Use the **down arrow** key to highlight the City field and press the **Enter** key.

The placeholder **<<City>>** should appear beneath the placeholder **<<Street Address>>** on your screen. Since you want the remainder of the address—state and ZIP code—on the same line, don't press the **Enter** key. Instead, press the **comma** (,) key and then the **space bar** one time to add a comma and a space after the **<<City>>** placeholder. Issue the **Insert Field** command again:

1. Press the **Alt** key and then the **E** key to access the **Edit** menu.
2. Press the **F** key to select the **Insert Field** option.

3. Hold down the **Alt** key and press the **F** key to position the cursor in the **Field** window.
4. Use the **down arrow** key to highlight the State field and press the **Enter** key.

The placeholder **<<State>>** should appear to the right of **<<City>>** on your screen. Press the **space bar** two times to separate **<<State>>** from the ZIP code and issue the **Insert Field** command again:

1. Press the **Alt** key and then the **E** key to access the **Edit** menu.
2. Press the **F** key to select the **Insert Field** option.
3. Hold down the **Alt** key and press the **F** key to position the cursor in the **Field** window.
4. Use the **down arrow** key to highlight the **Zip** field and press the **Enter** key.

The placeholder **<<Zip>>** should appear to the right of **<<State>>** on your screen. So far, so good. The inside address is complete.

Now let's personalize the greeting. First, press the **Enter** key to insert a blank line between the inside address and the greeting. Use the arrow keys or the mouse to position the cursor on the letter *G* in "Grant Public School families" and press the **Delete** (or **Del**) key repeatedly to remove all of that text. With the cursor to the right of *Dear* (but separated from it by one space) issue the **Insert Field** command again:

1. Press the **Alt** key and then the **E** key to access the **Edit** menu.
2. Press the **F** key to select the **Insert Field** option.
3. Hold down the **Alt** key and press the **F** key to position the cursor in the **Field** window.
4. Use the **down arrow** key to highlight the Greeting Name field and press the **Enter** key.

The placeholder **<<Greeting Name>>** should appear to the right of the word *Dear* on your screen. Add a comma after the words **<<Greeting Name>>** by pressing the **comma** (**,**) key. The greeting is now complete.

To learn how to insert placeholders within a paragraph, let's add one more placeholder, this time to the body of the letter. Use the arrow keys or the mouse to position the cursor on the letter *y* in the words *your child* in the second sentence of the second paragraph. Press the **Delete** (or **Del**) key repeatedly until the words *your child* are removed. With the cursor to the right of *If* (but separated from it by one space), issue the **Insert Field** command one last time:

1. Press the **Alt** key and then the **E** key to access the **Edit** menu.
2. Press the **F** key to select the **Insert Field** option.
3. Hold down the **Alt** key and press the **F** key to position the cursor in the **Field** window.
4. Use the **down arrow** key to highlight the First Name field and press the **Enter** key.

The placeholder **<<First Name>>** should appear to the right of the word *If* on your screen. You can make many other changes to the letter by inserting placeholders. Even though the placeholders from the **SCHOOL.WDB** database are now visible on the screen, only the personalized information will show up when you print the letter. We'll print out the documents on paper in the next section.

Saving the Word-Processed Document

It is always a good idea to save your work before you print. Be sure to change the name of the document so that it doesn't replace your original **BET-LET.WPS** file on your Works **Data** disk. To replace the name **BET-LET.WPS** with the name **PM-LET.WPS** (for **P**rint **M**erge **Let**ter), follow these steps:

1. Press the **Alt** key and then the **F** key to access the **File** menu.
2. Press the **A** key to select the **Save As** command.
3. Works suggests that you save the document using the name **BET-LET.WPS**.
4. Type the new name, PM-LET, and press the **Enter** key. Works will quickly store the letter you just typed on your Works **Data** disk under the name **PM-LET.WPS**. (Remember, Works adds the **.WPS** extension to your file name to show that it is a word-processed file.)

Exiting Works

When the computer has finished copying the **PM-LET.WPS** file to your Works **Data** disk, you can safely print or exit Works without worrying about losing the information in the file. Close the two files now; you will reopen them for the printing operation in the next section. This process will help you see that once a word-processed document has placeholders inserted, it can be printed at any time. To exit the program and shut down the computer, use the same steps that you have used in previous exercises. If you need additional help, consult the more detailed instructions presented in the **Exiting Works** section on pages 60–61.

Printing a Document with Print Merge

Orientation

Now you are ready to print copies of the word-processed document that you created in the previous exercise. You'll have to open the same two files that you used previously: **PM-LET.WPS** and **SCHOOL.WDB**. Rather than print all twenty-five letters, let's limit the number of active records in the database using the **Search** command. Since the **Insert Field** command produces one document for each *active record* in your database, you would print twenty-five letters in this situation—one for each record in the database—if you didn't limit the number of active records. To prevent this from happening, you'll first open the database file and limit the number of its active records. Then you'll open the word-processed document and print merge the two files.

Getting Started

Use the same procedures to start Works that you have used in the preceding exercises. If you need additional help, consult the more detailed instructions presented in the **Getting Started** section on pages 55–56.

Opening the SCHOOL.WDB Document

When you see the opening Works screen, open the file **SCHOOL.WDB**. To copy that file from your Works **Data** disk, follow these steps:

1. Press the **O** key to select the **Open Existing File** command.
2. Hold down the **Alt** key and press the **I** (for Directories) key. When the blinking cursor appears in the **Directories** dialog box, press the **down arrow** key to highlight the letter of the disk drive containing your Works **Data** disk, then press the **Enter** key.
3. Hold down the **Alt** key and press the **F** key. When the blinking cursor appears in the **Files** dialog box, use the **down arrow** key to highlight the file **SCHOOL.WDB**, and press the **Enter** key.
4. Works will copy the **SCHOOL.WDB** file from the disk and place the copy in the computer's memory. In a few moments, you will see the document displayed on the screen.

Selecting Records to Merge

Before you copy the word-processed file into memory for print merging, you will limit the number of active records. As you learned in the chapter on databases, you can select records by using either the Works searching powers or its querying powers. In this situation, since you have only one criterion to satisfy, you'll use the **Search** command to locate the students who have a 14219 ZIP code. To do so, follow these steps:

1. Press the **Alt** key and then the **S** key to access the **Select** menu.
2. Press the **S** key to **s**earch the database for particular records. Notice that the **Search** dialog box provides a place for you to enter the ZIP code.

3. Type **14219**.
4. Hold down the **Alt** key and press the **A** (for **A**ll) key to select all the records that match the 14219 ZIP code criterion.
5. Verify that a black dot appears to the left of the **All records** option and then press the **Enter** key to apply the search.

Notice that your screen will display four records—Bland, Dale, Kelly, and Phillips. Only four records contain the ZIP code 14219. Now when you print merge the file, you'll produce only four letters.

Opening the Word-Processed Document

Next you'll open the file **PM-LET.WPS** and copy it from your Works **Data** disk:

1. Press the **Alt** key and then press the **F** key to access the **File** menu.
2. Press the **O** key to select the **Open Existing File** command.
3. Hold down the **Alt** key and press the **F** key. When the blinking cursor appears in the **Files** dialog box, use the **down arrow** to highlight the file **PM-LET.WPS**. Press the **Enter** key.
4. Works will copy the **PM-LET.WPS** file from your Works **Data** disk and place the copy in the computer's memory. In a few moments, you will see your letter displayed on the screen.

Print Merging the Documents

Now you are ready for the printing process. This time you will not choose the **Print** command under the **Print** menu because the printer would then produce a copy of the letter exactly like the one displayed on the screen—placeholders and all. Instead, select the **Print Form Letters** command, also in the **Print** menu. Remember, the **Print Form Letters** command produces one document for each *active record* in your database—in this case, those records with the ZIP code 14219.

After checking to be certain that your printer is turned on and ready to print, follow these steps:

1. Press the **Alt** key, then the **P** key to access the **Print** menu.
2. Press the **F** key to access the **Print Form Letters** dialog box.
3. Press the **Enter** key to select the **SCHOOL.WDB** as the database with which to merge the letters.
4. Hold down the **Alt** key and press the **P** key to begin the printing process.

You now have four unique printed copies of your letter, and you have completed the print-merging exercises. You may exit Works and turn off your computer.

Exiting Works

This time, you will not bother saving your files because you did not make any changes that you want to preserve. When Works cautions you that you didn't save your files, therefore, use the **Tab** key to select the **No** option and continue exiting Works using the same steps that you have used in the preceding exercises. If you need additional help, consult the more detailed instructions presented in the **Exiting Works** section on pages 60–61.

Integrating Print Merging into the Instructional Process

Now that you are familiar with the power that print merging provides for helping you generate personalized standard documents, let's consider approaches for using print merging instructionally. In most cases, the Works print-merging powers are better suited for creating instructional materials for students than they are for students to use themselves. In this section, however, several activities are suggested in which students could use print merging for individual or class projects.

The following suggestions can all be used effectively with a single computer in a classroom, although they could also be conducted in a computer lab. Using a large monitor or an LCD with an overhead projector would help introduce a classroom of students to print merging, but they are not at all essential to any of these activities.

Creating Personalized Math Word Problems

Helping students develop effective skills for solving math word problems is one area of the curriculum in which we are generally not doing a very good job. This is so, at least partially, because our students have no "ownership" of the word problems they are usually asked to solve. Too often, students find math word problems both uninteresting and irrelevant to their lives.

You can use print merging to create unique math word problems personalized for each student. Students from grades three through eight have been very positive about the technique. Naturally, students who previously have hated math word problems will not suddenly love them, but many feel that the personal touch in the math word problems increases their interest in solving them. Students report that the word problems seem more pertinent to them because the problems involve their interests and their friends. See how the strategy works for you.

By combining a student interest database (like the one suggested in Chapter 6) with word-processed documents containing math word problems and database placeholders, you can print merge a document that includes unique word

> **Jennifer** walked to the library with **Nancy** and **Amy. She** needed to return 2 overdue library books. When the friends arrived at the library, they were told that the fine for **The Island of the Blue Dolphins** was $1.79 and the fine for **Prince Caspian** was $2.85. **Jennifer**'s mother had given **her** $10 to pay the fines. How much money should **Jennifer** get back from the librarian after paying the fine?

Figure 7.3 A sample of print merging to create a unique math word problem

problems for every student in your class. (Figure 7.3 shows the print-merged data in boldface to illustrate the process.) Once you create a set of problems that you like, you merely have to recreate the student interest database for each school year.

If you like the idea of using personalized math problems with your students but do not have the time to enter the problems into the word processor, you might ask your administrator for secretarial support. If that is not possible, print merge a letter explaining the project to your students' parents and asking for parent volunteers to assist with the project. Often, skilled and willing parents are happy to help with their children's educational experience.

If you have success personalizing your students' math problems, consider extending the practice to major tests, selected review or practice sheets, or the weekly spelling list. However, if the technique is used too often, it could easily become counterproductive, so apply it sparingly.

Student Requests for Project Information

Some school projects require students to obtain information from sources other than libraries, texts, and encyclopedias. These projects can provide excellent vehicles for introducing students to more "adult world" resources, such as chambers of commerce, state tourist bureaus, corporate public relations offices, government agencies, and museums. Frequently, letters with the same text must be sent to several different sources of information. The powers of print merging can help with these projects.

Teach your students the print-merging process and help them create one carefully edited version of their letter requesting information. Once they have created one polished document, you can supply (or they can create) a simple mailing address database of potential sources. With a little planning, the students can produce multiple letters with no extra effort. You can save your database file as a resource for next year's project. Sample topics for this activity include mining, states, nuclear energy, solar energy, agriculture, authors' lives, careers, the lives of movie actors and actresses, manufacturing, national government, the television industry, and the transportation industry.

Student Invitations

Students often participate in plays, talent shows, or other special events and want to invite relatives and friends. You might have each student create a personal database with the names and addresses of his or her relatives and close friends. This database file can be used many times throughout the school year. For special events, ask each student to create a simple invitation to send to those individuals he or she would like to invite.

Related Activities

- If you have a utility program such as Brøderbund's Print Shop or New Print Shop, have your students create their own stationery—with a multicolored letterhead if you have a printer that supports color—and let them print out enough copies for all the special occasions during the year.
- Activities for which this exercise might apply include class or school plays, unit reports, musicals, recitals, talent shows, sports events, craft shows, and art shows.

Student Holiday Letters

To encourage writing skills, you might have students write periodic newsletters to relatives and friends about their lives. This activity could be used several times during the year—at Thanksgiving, Christmas, or Hanukkah, for example. Again, the students can create one carefully edited letter, and then print merge multiple copies.

Additional Activities

Educational Activities

Creating lists of mailing labels for professional correspondence
Creating personalized beginning-of-the-year letters
Creating personalized Open House Night letters
Creating personalized progress monitors
Creating personalized parent conference letters
Creating personalized report card cover letters
Creating personalized field trip announcements
Creating personalized parent volunteer requests
Creating personalized end-of-unit summary letters
Creating personalized invitations to special student performances
Creating personalized end-of-the-year letters

General Activities

Creating personalized holiday letters
Creating personalized home business mailings
Creating personalized newsletters to your friends
Creating personalized letters announcing the significant events in your life

8 Focusing on Spreadsheets

We have compared a word-processing program to a greatly extended electric typewriter and a database manager to an enhanced electronic index card system. Similarly, a computerized spreadsheet program can be thought of as an improved, electronic accountant's ledger. Using a spreadsheet, you can easily take care of all of your number-crunching chores by storing and manipulating numbers quickly and easily.

Like a ledger, a spreadsheet is divided into **rows** and **columns** that create a grid or table on the screen. At the intersections of rows and columns are **cells** that can store numeric data (used in calculations), text data (for labelling the spreadsheet), or mathematical formulas.

The spreadsheet's power to manipulate mathematical formulas can be a useful tool for educators when doing one of their number-crunching chores: calculating grades. This section will demonstrate how an electronic spreadsheet program can help you determine grades.

Even when handled efficiently, determining grades is always problematic. You must decide not only how many of each type of assignment you require, but also what value to place on each. You must also establish each assignment's relative portion of the total grade. Finally, you must determine what grade each student deserves on each assignment.

The scope of the task can be exhausting with a class of twenty-five students and six different subjects (or one subject for six classes of students). And grading can seem like your life's work when you consider anomalies like missing assignments, late work, incomplete projects, resubmitted work, new students, departing students, and unexpected requests for status reports and grade analysis reports. Electronic spreadsheets won't grade the papers for you (or make all of your students turn in their assignments on time), but the programs will take much of the unpleasantness out of calculating grades.

To help you see the advantages of the electronic spreadsheet over a gradebook and a calculator, imagine providing percentage grades in five subjects for your class of twenty-five students. Each semester, in addition to filling out report cards, you are asked to provide your principal with six separate grade lists, one for each subject area you teach. Your principal wants each subject list to have your students' grades arranged in descending order and to include statistics such as the class averages and the high and low grades in each subject.

In this imaginary scenario, you also have several students whose parents want to have their children's grades reported to them every two weeks in addition to the progress monitor you like to send out to all parents halfway through the marking period. It sounds like you have a lot of work ahead of you.

Let's compare two different procedures for satisfying these requests—one using a gradebook and a calculator, the other using an electronic spreadsheet. At the beginning of the term, you set up your gradebook by entering the students' names, planning the number of assignments you'll require, and deciding how many points each assignment will be worth. You enter all that information into the gradebook, but you can't do any other preparations until students turn in their work.

The initial process with an electronic spreadsheet will be a little more time-consuming than with a traditional gradebook the first time you set up a spreadsheet. First, you'll type the names of all your students into the spreadsheet, enter the number of assignments, and determine a point system. In addition, you'll enter formulas into the spreadsheet that will automatically calculate grades each time you enter students' scores.

The spreadsheet already has the necessary calculations designed for you. You only have to enter the correct command into the appropriate location, and the program will determine averages, high and low scores, totals, and many other calculations. The spreadsheet can also copy a formula from one location to many others. Therefore, once you establish the correct grading formulas for one student, you can copy them for the rest of the class in a matter of seconds. The same is true for the class statistics. You can establish the formula for one subject and then copy it for all the others. Even with these time-savers, setting up the electronic grading spreadsheet will probably take an hour or so longer than the gradebook. Once you've set up the spreadsheet, however, the time-saving features will become apparent.

To produce the biweekly reports for the concerned parents with the manual system, you would have to get out your gradebook and use your calculator to determine each student's grade every two weeks. Once you noted the grades, you'd probably compose short notes for each parent (or use an unattractive mimeograph form) listing the current grades. With each request, you would have to go through the entire process from scratch.

Using the spreadsheet, you need only to select the portion of the sheet containing each student's pre-calculated grades, copy it to a word-processed document explaining the system to parents, and print it out. The same word-processed document personalized with appropriate grading data for each child could be sent to all parents. Two weeks later, the document could be reprinted with new grades and calculated data. Advantage: spreadsheets!

Using a gradebook and calculator to calculate grades and prepare mid-term progress monitors for all your students would take up an afternoon (or even a whole weekend). Once the grades are calculated, you must record the grades on individual progress monitor sheets and send them to parents with an accompanying note. When you prepared the final term report cards, you would have to revise those calculations completely.

Preparing your progress monitors is much simpler with a spreadsheet. Because the current grades are already available on the spreadsheet, you only need to print them out and photocopy them onto the progress monitors. Better still, you can copy them into word-processed versions of the progress monitors and use the print-merging powers you learned in the last chapter to produce personalized monitors for each parent. The entire process will take less than an hour, and every parent will have a signed, personalized copy of the progress monitor. Again—advantage: spreadsheets!

Determining final term grades for multiple subjects is very complex with the calculator and gradebook approach. You would carefully compute each student's average for all six subjects, record the score in your gradebook, and then transcribe the number onto the report card. To fulfill your principal's request for class lists, you would have to go through the gradebooks and list students in numerical order by grade for mathematics, reading, science, and the other three subjects. Once the lists were complete, you would have to type them and compute the class statistics. Performing these tasks would fill up valuable evenings and weekends at the end of each semester.

What about using a spreadsheet to help you with grading? As soon as you enter the last scores for each student, the computer determines the final averages. You then print out a master grade sheet, alphabetically listing your students with all their grades. Finally, you use the spreadsheet's sorting powers to arrange the students according to their scores in each subject and print out a copy of each list—including the class average in that subject and the maximum and minimum scores. After an hour's work, you are ready for a weekend filled with well-deserved fun and relaxation.

If you apply the time-saving features of spreadsheets to the many grading periods in your professional life, you will experience the advantages of using an electronic spreadsheet. The increase in your time management will be dramatic when spreadsheet powers are applied to other number-crunching tasks, like handling field trip expenses, balancing your checkbook, and managing your personal budget.

An Introduction to Spreadsheets

As we mentioned earlier, a spreadsheet, like a ledger, is divided into **rows** and **columns** creating a grid or table on the screen. The individual element at the intersection of a row and a column is a **cell**. Each cell in a spreadsheet can store information: **numeric** data, **text** data, or mathematical **formulas**.

You can format and reformat data once they have been entered into the spreadsheet. Formatting options include justification, style, and (in the case of numeric data) numeric form. Any entry can be aligned at the left, right, or center of its cell. An entry can also be displayed in boldfaced, underlined, or italic characters. You can also vary the font and size of the characters in the spreadsheet, but note that your choice affects the entire spreadsheet.

Numeric data, the most common type of spreadsheet data, are used for calculations and can be displayed as percentages, dates (in several different formats), scientific notation, or currency. You can specify the number of decimal places to display. It is important to note that if you format a cell with a value of 1.234 to display one decimal digit, the resulting display will be **1.2**. However, if you multiplied that cell by the number 5, the result would be **6.17**, not **6**. Although the spreadsheet does not display all of the significant digits, it maintains them and uses them in all calculations you perform.

To clarify the meaning of the numbers, you create labels with **text** entries. Text in the spreadsheet can be manipulated in much the same way as it would be with the word processor. However, because the basic element in a spreadsheet is a cell instead of a line of text, powers such as word wrap are not available.

The most important elements in a spreadsheet are the **formulas**, which offer users the power to create mathematical expressions that perform computations on cell values and deposit the results in different cells. For example, the spreadsheet can add a column of numbers (such as monthly budget items) and then place the sum in a new cell labelled **TOTAL**. This power is enhanced by the existence of predefined formulas, called **functions**, which perform the most common mathematical calculations. Spreadsheets include many built-in functions, including **avg**, **sum**, **max**, and **min**. Microsoft Works has more than sixty functions.

Formulas can be reproduced **relative** to their location in the spreadsheet. This means that each newly created formula will perform calculations in cells with relative positions in the spreadsheet. A simple example will help illustrate this concept. Imagine a yearly budget in which each month's expense items are listed in consecutive columns. At the bottom of the January column, you have a **TOTAL** cell, where you want the spreadsheet to display the sum of all the expenses for the month of January. At the bottom of the next column, you want a formula that will sum all the expenses for February. The next column should sum the expenses for March, and so on. With spreadsheets this process is easy because once you have created the January formula, you can copy it to all the other columns (months) in that row; each formula will be translated to cells of the same position in the next column. The ability to copy relative to position is one of a spreadsheet's most important powers.

In addition to having formatting control over individual cells, you can also format columns and rows individually or in groups. You can modify column widths to display more or fewer characters or alter both the order of columns and the sequence of rows. You can also move, remove, or simply clear rows and columns of their data.

In the next section, you will master the Microsoft Works spreadsheet. You will learn to create a spreadsheet, format an existing spreadsheet, build formulas, use functions, copy formulas across rows and columns, and print out a spreadsheet.

Creating and Saving a New Spreadsheet File

Orientation

This exercise is designed to help you become better acquainted with electronic spreadsheets, often the most difficult productivity application for novices to understand. People with a background in accounting and a familiarity with ledgers can grasp the concepts of spreadsheets far more rapidly than individuals without this background. Nonetheless, anyone who manipulates numbers in some part of their professional lives will find that electronic spreadsheets are tools with many time-saving applications.

This exercise will introduce you to the spreadsheet display and commands by showing you how to create a simple spreadsheet to compute your monthly expense budget. First, you will need to open a new Microsoft Works spreadsheet file.

Getting Started

Use the same procedures to start Works that you have used in the preceding exercises. If you need additional help, consult the more detailed instructions presented in the **Getting Started** section on pages 55–56.

Creating a New Spreadsheet Document

When you see the opening Works screen, create a new spreadsheet file by following these steps:

1. Press the **N** (for Create **N**ew File) key to start a new document.
2. Press the **S** (for **S**preadsheet) key to open a new spreadsheet document.

Works quickly copies the spreadsheet program into RAM. In a few moments, you will see a new spreadsheet document displayed on the screen, ready for you to enter your data. Notice in Figure 8.1 that a spreadsheet document is a table of blank cells divided into columns (marked with letters) and rows (marked with numbers). You can move the cursor from cell to cell by using the mouse or with the usual cursor movement keys, the **Tab** key or the arrow keys.

Your first spreadsheet will be a simple budget for a six-month period. To begin, do the following:

1. Position the cursor in cell **A6**. Placing the cursor in cell **A6** will leave some blank rows at the top of the spreadsheet for budget headings you'll add later.
2. Type **Expense Item** and press the **Tab** key once. Notice that the words **Expense Item** appear in cell **A6** and the cursor is now in cell **B6**. Use the **left arrow** key (or the mouse) to move the cursor back to cell **A6**. The contents of cell **A6**, Expense Item, appear on the display line below the menu bar. Notice that the words do not quite fit into the cell because the width of each column is set automatically to accommodate nine digits (as well as a + or − sign). With the column width set for 10, only seven columns (**A** through **G**) can fit on the screen.

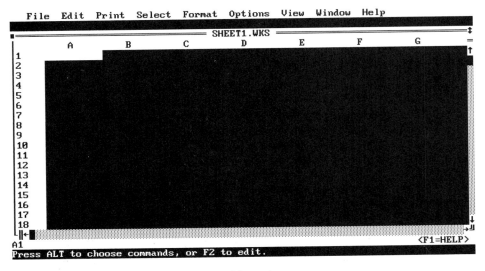

Figure 8.1 Opening screen of a new spreadsheet document

Modifying Column Width in a Spreadsheet

You eventually will need eight columns (one for the expense items, six for the months, and one for the average expenses). To see your entire budget on the screen at one time, let's first widen column **A** to fifteen characters by following these steps:

1. Press the **Alt** key and then the **T** (for Forma**t**) key to access the **Format** menu.
2. Press the **W** (for Column **W**idth) key to change the field width (Figure 8.2).
3. Replace the current field width of **10**, displayed in the dialog box, by typing **15** and pressing the **Enter** key to accept that value.

Next, you'll reduce the widths of columns **B** through **G** to six characters—enough to accommodate any of your budget figures. You'll change the width of the next six columns in one step by using the **F8** key, the **Shift** key, and the **right arrow** key. To do this, follow these steps:

1. Use the arrow keys or the mouse to position the cursor in column **B**, then hold down the **Shift** key and press the **F8** key. This process will highlight the entire column **B**.
2. Hold down the **Shift** key and press the **right arrow** key five times to highlight the columns from **B** through **G**.
3. With these six columns selected, press the **Alt** key, then press the **T** key to access the **Format** menu.
4. Press the **W** (for Column **W**idth) key to change the field width.
5. Replace the current field width of **10**, displayed in the dialog box, by typing **6**. Press the **Enter** key to accept that value.

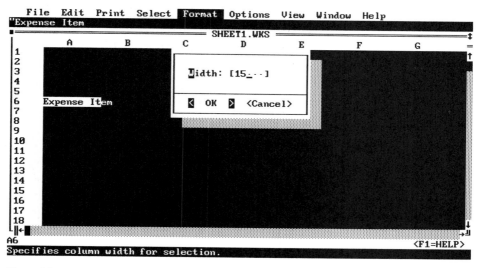

Figure 8.2 Column Width dialog box with width of 15 characters indicated

Finally, to ensure that column **H** is wide enough to display the average data for the six-month period, let's first increase the width of column **H** to fifteen characters. To make column **H** fifteen characters wide, follow these steps:

1. Use the arrow keys or the mouse to position the cursor in column **H**, then hold down the **Shift** key and press the **F8** key to highlight column **H**.
2. Press the **Alt** key, then press the **T** key to access the **Format** menu.
3. Press the **W** (for Column **W**idth) key to change the width of the field.
4. Replace the current field width of **10**, displayed in the dialog box, by typing **15**. Press the **Enter** key to accept that value.

You should now be able to see all eight columns, **A** through **H**, on the screen. If you can, you are ready to enter the budget data into your spreadsheet. If you cannot see all eight columns on the screen, either open a new spreadsheet document and repeat the preceding steps, or reread the instructions to identify the source of the problem.

Entering the Labels into the Spreadsheet

Use the arrow keys or the mouse to position the cursor in cell **B6**. Type Jan into the cell and press the **Enter** key. Now you'll use the Works **Fill Series** command to enter the names of the next five months. To do so, follow these steps:

1. With the cursor positioned in cell **B6**, hold down the **Shift** key and press the **right arrow** key five times to highlight cells **B6** to **G6**.
2. Press the **Alt** key, then press the **E** key to access the **Edit** menu.
3. Press the **L** key to apply the **Fill Series** command.
4. Select the **Month** option displayed in the **Units** dialog box (Figure 8.3) by pressing the **M** (for **M**onth) key and then pressing the **Enter** key.

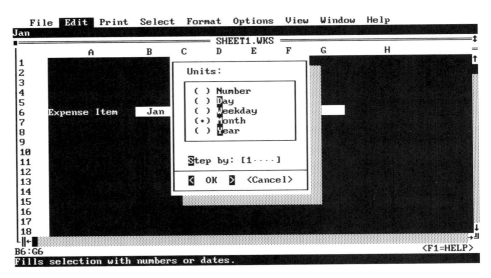

Figure 8.3 Fill Series Units dialog box

Now you'll see the names of all six months, **Jan** through **Jun**, displayed on your screen. To finish the column headings on your budget, follow this step:

5. Use the arrow keys or the mouse to position the cursor in cell **H6**, type **Average**, and press **Enter**.

Now let's enter the names of your expense items. Use the arrow keys or the mouse to position the cursor in cell **A7** and follow these steps:

1. Type Rent and press the **down arrow** key.
2. The cursor has automatically moved down to cell **A8**. Type Food and press the **down arrow** key again.
3. Type Clothing and press the **down arrow** key.
4. Type Utilities and press the **down arrow** key.
5. Type Transport and press the **down arrow** key.
6. Type Miscellaneous and press the **down arrow** key.
7. Type Total and press the **down arrow** key.

The cursor should be in cell **A14**. You have finished entering the labels for your spreadsheet document and can now enter your data.

Entering the Data into the Spreadsheet

Let's assume that your rent is $400 each month. We'll use the Works **Fill Right** command to duplicate the rent amounts for the six-month period. To do so, follow these steps:

1. Position the cursor in cell **B7**. Enter 400 (do not enter the dollar sign) in cell **B7** and press the **right arrow** key.
2. Position the cursor in cell **B7**, hold down the **Shift** key and press the **right arrow** key five times to highlight cells **B7** to **G7**.
3. Press the **Alt** key and then press the **E** key to access the **Edit** menu.
4. Press the **R** key to apply the **Fill Right** command.

In a moment, Works places (or fills) the number 400 in cells **C7** through **G7**. Inspect the spreadsheet so far. Note that the labels (such as Expense Item or Rent) have automatically aligned to the left in the cells. The values (that is, numbers like 400) automatically align to the right. You'll adjust the column displays when you've finished entering the numbers.

For the next step, have the cursor positioned in cell **B8**, the first cell in your food row. Let's imagine that your food costs fluctuate between $150 and $225 per month. Follow these steps to enter your food costs for the six-month period:

1. Type 175 in cell **B8** and press the **right arrow** key.
2. Type 190 in cell **C8** and press the **right arrow** key.
3. Type 225 in cell **D8** and press the **right arrow** key.
4. Type 180 in cell **E8** and press the **right arrow** key.
5. Type 210 in cell **F8** and press the **right arrow** key.
6. Type 200 in cell **G8** and press the **right arrow** key.

If you make a mistake, move the cursor into the cell with the error, retype the number correctly, and then press the **Enter** key. The incorrect entry—whether number or text—will be replaced by the new entry as soon as you press the **Enter** key.

Position the cursor in cell **B9**, the first cell in your clothing row. Your clothing costs fluctuate between $40 and $70 per month. Now enter your clothing costs.

1. Type **55** in cell **B9** and press the **right arrow** key.
2. Using the same procedure, continue across the row, entering these values in the next 5 cells: **45** (in **C9**), **60** (in **D9**), **40** (in **E9**), **70** (in **F9**), and **50** (in **G9**).

Position the cursor in cell **B10**. The cost of your utilities fluctuates between $30 and $105 per month. To continue:

1. With the cursor in cell **B10**, enter **95**. Press the **right arrow** key.
2. Continue across the row, entering these values in the cells **C10** to **G10**: **105** (in **C10**), **85**, **60**, **45**, and **30**.

Position the cursor in cell **B11**. Your transportation costs vary between $25 and $75 per month. To enter those costs:

1. With the cursor in cell **B11**, enter **75**. Press the **right arrow** key.
2. Continue across the row, entering these values in cells **C11** to **G11**: **45** (in **C11**), **65**, **75**, **25**, and **45**.

To enter the last row of budget figures, position the cursor in cell **B12**. Your miscellaneous costs vary between $50 and $205 per month. To enter those costs:

1. Type **65** in cell **B12** and press the **right arrow** key.
2. Enter these values in the cells **C12** to **G12**: **95** (in **C12**), **50**, **155**, **205**, and **85**.

Entering Formulas into a Spreadsheet

Now it's time to enter the first formulas into your spreadsheet. Position the cursor in cell **B13**, the TOTAL cell for the month of January. In this cell, you'll create a formula that will add the values in cells **B7** through **B12** and display the total amount here. The symbol that Microsoft Works uses to begin a formula or computation is the equal (=) sign (the key to the left of the **Backspace** key on the keyboard). To instruct cell **B13** to total the expenses for January and display the result:

1. Type **=sum(B7:B12)** exactly as it is shown here, and press the **Enter** key. If you make a typing mistake, press the **Enter** key, move the cursor back to cell **B13**, and retype the formula. If all is well, the value 865 should be displayed in cell **B13**, and the cursor should be in cell **B14.**
2. Position the cursor in cell **B13**. Notice that the value 865 is shown in cell **B13** and the formula =sum(B7:B12) is shown on the **Display Line** (beneath the **File** and **Edit** commands on the menu bar). The cell displays the results of the

calculation; the **Display Line** shows the formula that was used to produce that result.

Copying Formulas Across a Spreadsheet Row

To complete the calculations for the remainder of the six-month period, we'll use the spreadsheet's ability to copy a formula from one cell to another, relative to its new position. For example, the formula in cell **B13**, =sum(B7:B12), should be very similar to the formula in cell **C13,** except that it should add the cells in column **C** instead of column **B**. Therefore, the formula in cell **C13** should read =sum(C7:C12). Similarly, the formula in cell **D13** should read =sum(D7:D12); the formula in cell **E13** should read =sum(E7:E12); the formula in cell **F13** should read =sum(F7:F12); and the formula in cell **G13** should read =sum(G7:G12).

You could enter the different formulas by hand, of course, but let's use the computer's power to facilitate the process:

1. Use the arrow keys or the mouse to position the cursor in cell **B13**. This is the **source** cell—that is, the original from which you will make your copies. Hold down the **Shift** key and press the **right arrow** key five times to highlight all the **target** cells (**C13** through **G13**). Be certain that all the cells from **B13** to **G13** are highlighted before you continue. If not, press an arrow key to cancel the highlighting, then position the cursor in cell **B13** and try again.
2. To replicate the formulas—that is, copy the formulas relative to their new positions in the subsequent columns—press the **Alt** key and then press the **E** key to access the **Edit** menu.
3. Press the **R** key to apply the **Fill Right** command.

In a moment, Works replicates a relative formula from cell **B13** into cells **C13** through **G13**. The **Fill Right** command has instructed Works to fill the source formula to all the highlighted target cells to the right. Check your screen to see if the operation was successful. If not, repeat the previous steps.

Copying Formulas Down a Spreadsheet Column

Next, let's use the spreadsheet to calculate a six-month average for each expense. The copying procedure is almost the same as before. This time, however, you'll fill the formula down instead of to the right.

1. Use the arrow keys or the mouse to position the cursor in cell **H7**. In this cell, you'll enter a formula to average your six monthly rent bills (clearly, the formula will be more useful in the other rows with fluctuating costs). Type =AVG(B7:G7) and press the **Return** key. You should see the resulting average, 400, displayed in cell **H7** when you finish.

2. Use the arrow keys or the mouse to position the cursor in cell **H7**. In this case, cell **H7** is the source cell. Hold down the **Shift** key and press the **down arrow** key six times to highlight cells **H7** to **H13**. Cells **H8** to **H13** are the target cells. (Although all cells from **H7** to **H13** are highlighted, cell **H7** is the source cell.)

3. To replicate the formulas down the column, press the **Alt** key, then the **E** key to access the **Edit** menu.

4. Press the **F** key to apply the **Fill Down** command.

In a moment, Works replicates the relative formulas into the cells **H8** through **H13**. The **Fill Down** command has instructed Works to fill the formula from the source cell to all the highlighted target cells below it. Check your screen to see if the operation was successful. (If not, repeat the previous steps.) Notice that now you have strange numbers displayed in some cells (numbers such as 196.66666667 and 53.33333333). These numbers are the result of the division process carried out by the **average** function. The figures are accurate representations of the division operation, but they display more digits than you need to see.

Setting Cell Attributes in a Spreadsheet

At any point in this process, you may format numbers and text in the spreadsheet. Your spreadsheet will display numbers with a dollar sign but no decimal places. Later, we can enhance the headings by aligning them in the center of their cells. To format the values, follow these steps:

1. Highlight all the cells in the spreadsheet that contain numbers. If the numbers in column **H** are still highlighted from the previous operation, hold down the **Shift** key, then press the **left arrow** key six times to highlight all the numerical cells. Alternatively, you could position the cursor in cell **H7**, hold down the **Shift** key and press the **left arrow** key six times; with the **Shift** key still held down, press the **down arrow** key six times to highlight all the numerical cells.

2. To control the manner in which the numbers in these cells are displayed, access the **Format** command. Press the **Alt** key; then press the **T** key to access the **Format** menu.

3. Press the **U** (for Currency) key to assign a currency display for the numbers selected.

4. Replace the suggested 2 decimal digits displayed in the dialog box by typing **0**. Press the **Enter** key. The cells are displayed in currency format, preceded by a dollar sign ($) and without decimal places.

Now let's improve the appearance of your column heading labels by aligning them in the center of their cells and choosing a boldface style.

1. Position the cursor on cell **H6**. Hold down the **Shift** key, then press the **left arrow** key seven times to highlight cells **H6** through **A6**.

2. Press the **Alt** key, then the **T** key to access the **Format** menu.

3. Press the **S** key to access the **Style** menu.
4. Press the **C** key to center the text in the cells (notice that a dot (•) appears to the left of the **Center** option).
5. Press the **B** key to boldface the text in the cells (notice that an **X** appears to the left of the **Bold** option).
6. Press the **Enter** key to apply the command. The labels are now centered and displayed in bold type.

Adding Headings in a Spreadsheet

Finally, let's place a heading at the top of your budget. Position the cursor in cell **C3** and type 1991 **Budget Summary for** *Your Name* (enter your own name). Press the **Tab** key. Note that the label extends across four cells (**C3** through **F3**) because they are empty. If there were text in cell **D3**, it would block out a portion of the heading from view. The heading is *contained* in one cell (**C3**) but *displayed* in four. You can only change or enhance the heading from the cell that contains it. To demonstrate this, try to make the heading boldface type with the cursor in cell **D3**:

1. Press the **Alt** key, then press the **T** key to access the **Format** menu.
2. Press the **S** key to access the **Style** menu.
3. Press the **B** (for **B**old) key to boldface the text in the cells (notice that an **X** appears to the left of the **Bold** option).
4. Press the **Enter** key to apply the command.

The heading is *not* displayed in bold type. Now use the **left arrow** key to position the cursor in the cell that contains the heading, cell **C3**, and repeat the procedures:

1. Press the **Alt** key, then press the **T** key to access the **Format** menu.
2. Press the **S** key to access the **Style** menu.
3. Press the **B** (for **B**old) key to boldface the text in the cells (notice that an **X** appears to the left of the **Bold** option).
4. Press the **Enter** key to apply the command.

The heading *is* now displayed in bold type.

Saving a Spreadsheet

Your budget is complete, but you haven't saved it yet. Since this is a new spreadsheet document, Microsoft Works is still calling it **SHEET1.WKS**. To save the document, follow these steps:

1. Press the **Alt** key and then the **F** (for **F**ile) key.
2. Press the **A** key to select the **Save As** command. Note the **Save file as** dialog box displayed on the screen. Works suggests that you save the document using the name, **SHEET1.WKS**, on the active disk.

3. Regardless of which system you use (floppy disk or hard disk drive), you must instruct Works to save the file on your Works **Data** disk. Hold the **Alt** key and press the **I** (for D**i**rectories) key. When you see the blinking cursor in the **Directories** dialog box, press the **down arrow** key until you highlight the letter of the disk drive containing your Works **Data** disk (the **[-A-]** drive if you are using a *hard disk drive system,* or the **[-B-]** drive if you are using a *dual floppy disk system*) and press the **Enter** key. Notice the **Directory of** line in the dialog box now shows that the active directory is the location of your Works **Data** disk.

4. Type the name for your file, BUDGET, and press the **Enter** key. Works will quickly store your spreadsheet on your Works **Data** disk under the name, **BUDGET.WKS**. Recall that Works adds the **.WKS** extension to your file name to indicate that it is a spreadsheet file.

Exiting Works

Once you have printed your spreadsheet document and are confident that it has been stored on your Works **Data** disk under the name **BUDGET.WKS**, you can safely exit Works without worrying about losing the information in your file. To exit the program and shut down the computer, use the same steps that you have used in previous exercises. If you need additional help, consult the more detailed instructions presented in the **Exiting Works** section on pages 60–61.

If you want to continue working with the program now, follow these steps to close the current document without exiting Works:

1. Press the **Alt** key and the **F** (for **F**ile) key.
2. Press the **C** key to select the **Close** command.

The current document is no longer in the computer's memory, but Microsoft Works still is. You are now ready to begin the next section without having to restart Works.

Enhancing and Printing an Existing Spreadsheet

Getting Started

In this exercise, you will complete a simple gradebook by entering the necessary formulas into an existing spreadsheet and then printing out the finished product. The gradebook is already stored on your Works **Data** disk with the name, **GRADES.WKS**. The gradebook data include the students' names and their scores on the term's tests. You'll add formulas to calculate the students' total scores for the term and their final grades. You'll also create some statistical data, such as the average, high, and low grades for each test. First, let's copy the incomplete gradebook file into RAM from your Works **Data** disk.

Use the same procedures to start Works that you have used in previous exercises. If you need additional help, consult the more detailed instructions presented in the **Getting Started** section on pages 55–56. If you only closed the document in the previous section and did not exit Works, then you are ready to open the next file.

Opening the Existing Spreadsheet File

When you see the opening Works screen, open the file, **GRADES.WKS**. To copy that file from your Works **Data** disk into the computer's memory, follow these steps:

1. Press the **O** key to select the **Open Existing File** command (or use the mouse to highlight the **Open Existing File** choice and release the mouse button).
2. Hold down the **Alt** key and press the **I** (for D**i**rectories) key. When the blinking cursor appears in the **Directories** dialog box, press the **down arrow** key to highlight the letter of the disk drive containing your Works **Data** disk, and press the **Enter** key.
3. Hold down the **Alt** key and press the **F** (for **F**iles) key. When the blinking cursor appears in the **Files** dialog box, use the **down arrow** key to highlight the file, **GRADES.WKS**, and press the **Enter** key.
4. Works will copy the **GRADES.WKS** file from the disk and place the copy in the computer's temporary memory (RAM).

In a few moments, you should see the spreadsheet file displayed on the screen. So far, the gradebook looks like Figure 8.4.

```
 File  Edit  Print  Select  Format  Options  View  Window  Help
=VLOOKUP(H7,H$35:I$39,1)
                          ====== GRADES.WKS ======
      A            B        C    D    E    F    G    H      I     J
1
2             SPRING 1991       Grade Sheet for Section 107
3     ===================================================================
4                          Test Scores (%)              Avg.  Final
5     Last Name    First Name  #1   #2   #3   #4   #5   (%)   Grade
6     ===================================================================
7     Allen        Paul        95   90   95   75   85               0
8     Anderson     Jane        90   85   95   80   60
9     Blanchard    Jim         80   75   75   80   85
10    Bland        Fred        60   60   65   65   70
11    Casey        Oliver      70   80   80   85   80
12    Cooper       George      60   60   55   85   90
13    Cooper       Jessie      95   80   60   55   45
14    Craft        Doug        70   70   70   60   85
15    Dale         Sally       40   50   60   69   45
16    Dunlop       James       80   80   90   90   80
17    Grant        Bill        75   90   60   45   60
18    Johnson      Sarah       70   70   60   80   85
I7                                                        <F1=HELP>
Press ALT to choose commands, or F2 to edit.
```

Figure 8.4 GRADES.WKS spreadsheet file

Inserting Functions into a Spreadsheet

Notice on the opening screen that the students' scores and names have been entered. The column headings are already formatted, the statistical data at the bottom of the spreadsheet are set to be boldfaced, and all the numerical data are set to display no decimal digits. In the previous exercises, you used the **Format** menu to specify similar style features. In this exercise, you will complete the necessary formulas to compute the final grades and statistical data required for the gradebook, then print out the resulting spreadsheet.

To begin, let's complete the statistical data at the bottom of the spreadsheet. Use the arrow keys or the mouse to position the cursor in cell **C35**. In cell **C35**, place a formula that calculates the average for the students' scores on their first test. This time, instead of typing the cell designations into the formula, you'll use the Microsoft Works **point mode** to complete the task. Point mode is a powerful tool that allows users to insert selected cell ranges into functions simply by highlighting the first and last cells in the range. When you create the formula, you enter the appropriate function until you reach the point where the cell range belongs (for example, **C7:C31**), then you use the arrow keys or the mouse to select the range of the cells that you want to average and apply the function. To use the point mode, follow these steps (very carefully and exactly):

1. With the cursor still in cell **C35**, type =avg(
2. Use the **up arrow** key or the mouse to position the cursor in cell **C31**. Notice that the formula on the **Display Line** now reads =avg(C31.
3. With the cursor in cell **C31**, press the **colon** (:) key to fix cell **C31** as the last cell in the range.
4. Use the **up arrow** key to move the cursor to cell **C7**—the first cell in the range—and press the **right parenthesis** key ( )) to indicate the end of the range.
5. Press the **Enter** key to calculate the formula.

The formula on the **Display Line** now reads =avg(C7:C31) and the cells in this range are no longer highlighted. Note that the correct average, 76, is rounded to the nearest integer or whole number and displayed in cell **C35**.

Now position the cursor in cell **C36** where you want to place a formula that calculates the lowest score on the first test. You'll use the same technique to enter this formula:

1. Type =min(
2. Use the **up arrow** key or the mouse to position the cursor in cell **C31**. Notice that the formula on the **Display Line** now reads =min(C31.
3. With the cursor in cell **C31**, press the colon (:) key to fix cell **C31** as the last cell in the range.
4. Use the **up arrow** key to move the cursor to cell **C7** and press the **right parenthesis** key ( )) to fix it as the first cell in the range.
5. Press the **Enter** key to enter the formula into cell **C36**.

The formula in cell **C36** now reads =min(C7:C31) and the cells in this range are no longer highlighted. Note that the correct minimum score of 40 is displayed in cell **C36** and the cursor is in cell **C37**. Here you'll place a formula that calculates the highest score on the first assignment. You'll use the same technique to enter this formula:

1. Type =max(
2. Use the **up arrow** key or the mouse to position the cursor in cell **C31**. Notice that the formula on the **Display Line** now reads =max(C31.
3. With the cursor in cell **C31**, press the **colon** (:) key to fix cell **C31** as the last cell in the range.
4. Use the **up arrow** key to move the cursor to cell **C7** and press the **right parenthesis** key (**)**) to indicate the end of the range.

The formula in the **Display Line** should now read =max(C7:C31). That is the correct formula, so press the **Enter** key to record it into the cell. Note the correct maximum score, 100, is now displayed in cell **C37**.

Copying Formulas Across a Row in a Spreadsheet

The next step is to replicate, or copy, those formulas you entered for the first test to the other four tests.

1. Position the cursor in cell **C35**, hold down the **Shift** key, and press the **down arrow** key to highlight cells **C35**, **C36**, and **C37**. These are the source cells for the copying you'll do.
2. With the **Shift** key still held down, press the **right arrow** key four times until you reach column **G**. This operation will highlight the range—the cells in rows **35**, **36**, and **37** from column **C** through column **G**.
3. To copy the formulas from the source cells to the target cells in the range, press the **Alt** key, then the **E** key to access the **Edit** menu.
4. Press the **R** (for **R**ight) key to copy the formulas from the source to the target cells.

Inserting More Formulas in a Spreadsheet

From the test statistics, let's calculate the students' totals and final grades. You'll want to place a formula in cell **H7** that will calculate each student's average test score. Use the point mode again by following these steps:

1. Position the cursor in cell **H7** and type =avg(
2. Use the **left arrow** key or the mouse to position the cursor in cell **C7**. Notice that the formula on the **Display Line** now reads =avg(C7.
3. With the cursor in cell **C7**, press the **colon** (:) key to fix cell **C7** as the beginning cell in the range.

4. Use the **right arrow** key to move the cursor to cell **G7**—the final cell in the range—and press the **right parenthesis** key (**)**) to indicate the end of the range.

The formula on the **Display Line** now reads =avg(C7:G7). That is the correct formula, so press the **Enter** key to place the function into cell **H7**. Note that the correct average for Paul Allen—88, rounded to the nearest integer or whole number—is now displayed in cell **H7**. To replicate the formula for the other twenty-four students, follow these steps:

1. With the cursor in cell **H7**, use the **Shift** and **down arrow** keys or the mouse to highlight the cells from **H7** to **H31**.
2. Press the **Alt** key, then the **E** key to access the **Edit** menu.
3. Press the **F** (for **F**ill Down) key to copy the formulas from the source to the target cells.
4. Press any arrow key to deselect the highlighted text.

Using the VLOOKUP Function

Now for the final grades. Using the Microsoft Works **VLOOKUP** function, you can assign to each student the numerical equivalent of a letter grade: 0 = F, 1 = D, 2 = C, 3 = B, and 4 = A. Imagine you have a grading scale that assigns a 0 (or F) to any point total less than 60. Progressively, a score between 60 and 70 earns a 1 (or D); a score between 70 and 80 earns a 2 (or C); a score between 80 and 90 earns a 3 (or B); and a score greater than 90 earns a 4 (or A). Therefore, if a student's total is 87, he or she will receive a 3 (or B), whereas, if the score is 68, he or she will receive a 1 (or D). A vertical table of that grading scale has been entered into your spreadsheet in cells **H35** through **I39** (see Table 8.1). Use the arrow keys or the mouse to move to those cells and inspect the grading table.

Now position the cursor in cell **I7**. Examine the **VLOOKUP** formula in cell **I7** shown on the **Display Line**:

=VLOOKUP(H7,H$35:I$39,1)

This formula has already been entered into your spreadsheet to eliminate any typing confusion. The syntax (or command structure) of the **VLOOKUP** function is:

=VLOOKUP (reference cell, comparison range, offset)

Table 8.1 The grading scale

Table Range	Number Score	Letter Score
Below 60	0	F
60 to 69	1	D
70 to 79	2	C
80 to 89	3	B
Over 90	4	A

The reference cell represents the situation to be tested—in this case, the student's average. The comparison range represents the table containing the cutoff points for each category—in this case, the scale of cutoff points for the average scores (0, 60, 70, 80, 90). The offset specifies the column in which the function's results are listed—in this case, the number grades (0, 1, 2, 3, 4).

The =VLOOKUP(H7,H$35:I$39,1) formula is in cell **I7**. If that formula were written in English, it would read something like this: "Look at cell **H7** (Paul Allen's average) and compare the number you find there with the list of numbers in cells **H35** through **H39**. As soon as you find a number greater than the one you're comparing (the student's average), stop and return to the preceding number—the last number the average exceeded. Locate the cell to the right of that number (in column **I**), take the digit that you find in that cell (from column **I**) and display it in cell **I7**." If that still doesn't sound like English, perhaps a concrete example will help. Let's examine the workings of the particular formula in cell **H7**.

The **VLOOKUP** function finds Paul Allen's average of 88 in cell **H7**. The function compares 88 to the numbers in cells **H35** through **H39** and discovers that 88 is larger than any number until it reaches 90. It goes back to the previous number, 80 (the last number it exceeds), looks to the right of the 80, and finds the digit 3. It then displays the number 3 in cell **H7**. Therefore, when you look for Paul Allen's grade, you will see the number 3 (representing a **B**) displayed there.

Absolute and Relative Cell Reference

The dollar signs that precede the row numbers in the formula say that the rows they reference are not **relative**, but **absolute** references. You learned about relative references in the last exercise when you copied formulas from one cell to another. The format of the formulas stayed the same, but the rows and columns the formulas referenced were relative to (or dependent on) their position in the rows and columns of the spreadsheet. All of the formulas you have copied so far have included relative references. However, in the case of the grades, the same standard (or scale) must apply for all the students; the grading scale, therefore, represents an absolute reference.

No dollar signs appear before cell **H7** in the formula because each student's average is relative to the row it is in (the student who earned the average). However, since the grading scale is consistent for all the students, none of the rows influences the position of the grading scale. Therefore, the dollar signs preceding the row numbers in the range indicate that they do not change with position.

Copying More Formulas Down a Column

Now you can copy the formula in cell **I7** into the other cells in the column. To replicate this formula for the other twenty-four students, follow these steps:

1. Use the arrow keys or the mouse to position the cursor in cell **I7**. This cell is the source cell for the copying you'll do.
2. Hold down the **Shift** key and press the **down arrow** key until you reach row **31**. The complete range should include the cells in column **I** from row **7** through row **31**.
3. With the range still highlighted, press the **Alt** key, then the **E** key to access the **Edit** menu.
4. Press the **F** (for **F**ill Down) key to copy the formulas from the source to the target cells.
5. Press any arrow key to deselect the highlighted text.

Note that the displays in the cells in columns **H** and **I** are now correct.

Portrait and Landscape Orientations in a Spreadsheet

Your spreadsheet should now be complete and ready for printing. It will fit easily on a single page, but often spreadsheets are too wide to fit onto a sheet of paper. One option is to print the spreadsheet in several sections with the **portrait** orientation, but a better option is to print the entire spreadsheet in **landscape** orientation. A page with the portrait orientation is 8.5 inches wide and 11 inches high. With landscape orientation, the page is simply rotated ninety degrees so that it is 11 inches wide and 8.5 inches high.

To utilize these different orientations fully, you must have either a wide-carriage or laser printer available. However, even without a printer, you can use the Works print preview capabilities to view the two different orientations on the screen even if you cannot print them on paper. To change the orientation of the page, follow these steps:

1. Press the **Alt** key and then the **P** key to access the **Print** menu.
2. Press the **M** (for Page Setup & Margins) key to change the page width and length. Notice that the **Page Setup & Margins** dialog box appears on the screen.
3. Hold down the **Alt** key and press the **L** (for Page **l**ength) key to position the cursor in the **Page length** box.
4. Type **8.5** (for eight and one-half inches) in the box, then press the **Tab** key to move the cursor to the **Page width** box.
5. Type **11** (for eleven inches) in the **Page width** box, then press the **Enter** key to accept those settings. Your document will now be rotated ninety degrees.

The next procedure is to inspect the spreadsheet on the screen. To preview the document, follow these steps:

1. Press the **Alt** key, then press the **P** key to access the **Print** menu.
2. Press the **V** (for Preview) key to preview the document on the screen. Notice that the **Print Preview** dialog box appears on the screen.
3. Hold down the **Alt** key and press the **P** (for **P**review) key to preview the document on the screen.

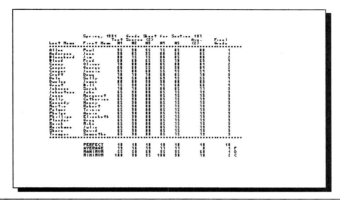

Page 1   Press PgUp or PgDn for
   Spring, 1991 Grade Sheet f...   previous or next page.
                          Press P to print.
                          Press ESC to cancel.

Figure 8.5 GRADES.WKS spreadsheet in print preview display of the landscape orientation

4. Notice that the document—shown in the Greeking display (Figure 8.5)—appears to be rotated ninety degrees.

If you have a wide-carriage or laser printer available, you may want to print the document in the landscape orientation. To do so, simply press the **P** (for **P**rint) key. If you do not have the necessary printer, press the **Esc** key to cancel the printing process and return to your document. Let's reset the page settings to the portrait orientation in preparation for printing the spreadsheet. To change the page orientation again, follow these steps:

1. Press the **Alt** key and then press the **P** key to access the **Print** menu.
2. Press the **M** (for Page Setup & **M**argins) key to change the page width and length. Notice that the **Page Setup & Margins** dialog box appears on the screen.
3. Hold down the **Alt** key and press the **L** (for Page **l**ength) key to position the cursor in the **Page length** box.
4. Type **11** (for eleven inches) in the box, then press the **Tab** key to move the cursor to the **Page width** box.
5. Type **8.5** (for eight and one-half inches) in the **Page width** box, then press the **Enter** key to accept those settings. Your document will now be printed in the standard portrait orientation.

To preview the document in portrait orientation, follow these steps:

1. Press the **Alt** key, then press the **P** key to access the **Print** menu.
2. Press the **V** (for Pre**v**iew) key to preview the document on the screen. Notice that the **Print Preview** dialog box appears on the screen.

3. Hold down the **Alt** key and press the **P** (for Preview) key to preview the document on the screen.
4. Notice that the document appears in portrait orientation.

It is always a good practice to save a document on your data disk before you print it. So let's cancel the printing process to save the spreadsheet. Press the **Esc** key to cancel the print preview and return to your document. Remember, if you are using a 5.25 inch floppy disk drive system, you will have to exchange disks to access the print preview layer. Works will prompt you to insert the **Accessories** disk.

Saving the Spreadsheet

Because you used an existing spreadsheet file for this exercise, it already has a name, **GRADES.WKS**. To preserve the original file, you can create a new file name for your changed file by following these steps:

1. Press the **Alt** key and then the **F** (for **F**ile) key (or use the mouse to point to the **File** command on the menu bar).
2. Press the **A** key to select the **Save As** command (or press the mouse button, Drag the pointer down the options on the pull down menu until you highlight the **Save As** choice, and release the mouse button). Works suggests that you save the document on the active disk using the name, **GRADES.WKS**.
3. Type a new file name, MY-GRADE, and press the **Enter** key. Works will quickly store the letter you just typed on your Works **Data** disk under the name, **MY-GRADE.WKS**.

Printing the Spreadsheet

Now that the file has been safely stored on your Works **Data** disk, you can print the document. The document fits easily on a page, so you do not have to change the margins or any other settings. First, make certain that your printer is turned on and ready to print. To print the document in portrait orientation, follow these steps:

1. Press the **Alt** key and then press the **P** key to access the **Print** menu.
2. Press the **P** key to access the **Print** dialog box.
3. Hold down the **Alt** key and press the **P** key once more to print the document on paper.

You already have saved the changes made to this document; when the printing is complete, you can exit Works.

Exiting Works

Once you have printed your document and have stored the **MY-GRADE.WKS** file on your Works **Data** disk, you can safely exit Works without losing the information in your file. To exit the program and shut down the computer, use the same steps that you have used in previous exercises. If you need additional help, consult the more detailed instructions presented in the **Exiting Works** section on pages 60–61.

Integrating Spreadsheets into the Instructional Process

Now that you are familiar with the power of the Microsoft Works spreadsheet, let's examine approaches for using spreadsheets in the classroom. Before you have students create spreadsheets, familiarize them with using electronic calculators so they understand the calculating functions of the spreadsheet. Next, have them enter information into partially completed spreadsheets with formulas already in place (either the examples included on your Works **Data** disk or ones that you prepare for them). Once they see spreadsheets work, they will be eager to learn how to build their own spreadsheets for school and personal applications.

The following suggestions can all be used effectively with a single computer in the classroom or in a computer lab. A large monitor or an LCD with an overhead projector would help to introduce a classroom of students to spreadsheets, but they are not essential to any of these activities. The first activities— **Multiplication Table**, **Magic Square**, and **Baseball Statistics**—are supported with template files on your Works **Data** disk. They should prove to be a fun and effective way to introduce students to spreadsheets.

Multiplication Table

One of the files on your Works **Data** disk is a template called **MULTIPLY.WKS**. This file has formulas already included for students to use and inspect. In addition, portions of the spreadsheet have been protected so that students do not accidentally lose data, formulas, or instructions. (Incidentally, to remove the cell protection, use the mouse to choose the **Protect Data** command in the **Options** menu.)

The spreadsheet (as shown in Figure 8.6) displays a ten-by-ten multiplication table. The instructions in the spreadsheet ask students to change the numbers in the two cells (**A2** and **B1**) that determine the range of the multiplication factors. If students follow the on-screen instructions and replace the ones with tens, the multiplication table will display the products of the numbers between ten and twenty. Have your students experiment with other numbers, including decimals and integers. Explain that if they enter very large numbers, the spreadsheet columns will not be wide enough to display them and they will see a string of number signs (######) instead. This is the spreadsheet's way of telling them the resulting products are too large to display with the current column widths. If they want to use large numbers and verify the correct results, explain the procedure for increasing the column widths.

```
    File   Edit   Print   Select   Format   Options   View   Window   Help
1
                                    MULTIPLY.WKS
       A      B      C      D      E      F      G      H      I      J      K
 1            1      2      3      4      5      6      7      8      9      10
 2      1     1      2      3      4      5      6      7      8      9      10
 3      2     2      4      6      8      10     12     14     16     18     20
 4      3     3      6      9      12     15     18     21     24     27     30
 5      4     4      8      12     16     20     24     28     32     36     40
 6      5     5      10     15     20     25     30     35     40     45     50
 7      6     6      12     18     24     30     36     42     48     54     60
 8      7     7      14     21     28     35     42     49     56     63     70
 9      8     8      16     24     32     40     48     56     64     72     80
10      9     9      18     27     36     45     54     63     72     81     90
11      10    10     20     30     40     50     60     70     80     90     100
12
13          Replace the digits in cells B1 and A2 to create a new
14                      multiplication table:
15
16          For instance, change the 1's in cells A2 and B1 to 10's,
17                      and see what happens.
18
B1                                                              <F1=HELP>
Press ALT to choose commands, or F2 to edit.
```

Figure 8.6 **MULTIPLY.WKS** spreadsheet

After they have explored the calculating powers of the spreadsheet for several minutes, the students can inspect the cells containing formulas. Discuss the syntax of formulas in Microsoft Works—for instance, formulas must begin with an equal sign (=)—and help them interpret the purpose of the different formulas. In particular, explain the difference between what is displayed on the screen in a cell, the value that cell's formula produces, and what is visible on the display line, the formula for the active cell (the cell in which the cursor is positioned). Have them save their files under a new name using their initials, such as **TABLE-ES.WKS**, when they have finished exploring.

Related Activities

- Have your students modify the spreadsheet to create an additional table for younger brothers and sisters.
- Ask your students to modify the spreadsheet to create a subtraction table and to explain the negative numbers that will result.
- Challenge your students to modify the spreadsheet to create a division table in which the quotient (or missing factor) is displayed with differing (two, three, or four) decimal places.

Magic Square

The **MAGIC.WKS** template on your Works **Data** disk also has formulas already included for students to use and inspect. Again, portions of the spreadsheet have been protected so that students do not accidentally lose data, formulas, or instructions. (Remember, to remove the cell protection, choose the **Protect Data** command in the **Options** menu.)

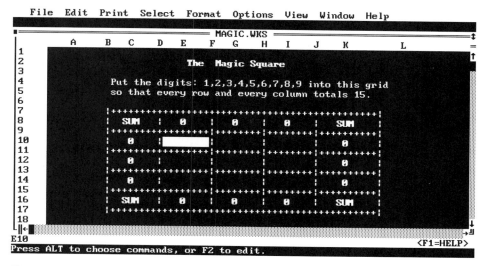

Figure 8.7 The **MAGIC.WKS** screen display

The spreadsheet displays a magic square grid (Figure 8.7). Notice that the appearance of this spreadsheet is different from the others in two ways: it is displayed with much larger characters (size 14), and the characteristic grid marks around each cell are not displayed. These style enhancements make the spreadsheet easier for younger students to read. The on-screen instructions ask students to enter the digits 1, 2, 3, 4, 5, 6, 7, 8, and 9 into the magic square grid. The nine appropriate cells for entering these digits are **E10, E12, E14, G10, G12, G14, I10, I12,** and **I14**. Challenge your students to use each of the digits only one time and still have all twelve **SUM** figures (actually, only six unique sums) equal fifteen. The problem can be solved, of course.

Have your students experiment by trying numbers and inspecting the resulting sums. If someone finds a solution, verify that none of the digits has been used twice. Challenge your students to find more than one solution to the puzzle.

After they have explored the calculating powers of the spreadsheet for several minutes, have students inspect the cells containing formulas. Discuss the syntax of formulas in Works and help students interpret the purposes of the different formulas. Reinforce the difference between what is displayed on the screen in a cell and what is visible on the **Display Line** for the active cell. If some students solve the puzzle, have them save their solutions under new file names, like **MAGIC-MM.WKS**, when they have finished exploring.

Related Activity

- Challenge your students to modify the spreadsheet to create a four-by-four or two-by-two magic square in which selected digits can be entered only one time. Help them determine what new **SUM** total should replace fifteen (or if any should).

Baseball Statistics

Another template on your Works **Data** disk is a file called **STATS.WKS**. This file also has already included formulas for students to use and has protected areas so that students do not accidentally lose data. (Again, you can remove the cell protection by choosing the **Protect Data** command.)

The spreadsheet (shown in Figure 8.8) displays a table designed to calculate baseball statistics, including batting averages and on-base percentages. The instructions on the screen ask students to enter the names of players in column **B** and each player's statistics (times at bat, hits, and walks) in columns **C** through **E**. If students follow the instructions, the statistics table will display the batting averages and on-base percentages for any players they enter—themselves, their friends, or their major league idols. (Explain to students that the *ERROR* messages in the cells in columns **F** and **G** are the result of missing data in the cells in columns **C**, **D**, and **E**. Once numbers are entered into those cells, the correct batting averages and on-base percentages will appear in the cells in columns **F** and **G**.)

Have your students enter as many players as they want. If they enter more than twenty-five or thirty players, show them how to copy the formulas down to additional cells. After they have explored the spreadsheet for several minutes, you might have them inspect and interpret the syntax of the formulas. Again, reinforce the difference between what is displayed on the screen in a cell and what is shown on the **Display Line**. Have them save their files under a new name, such as **STATS-TM.WKS**, when they are finished exploring.

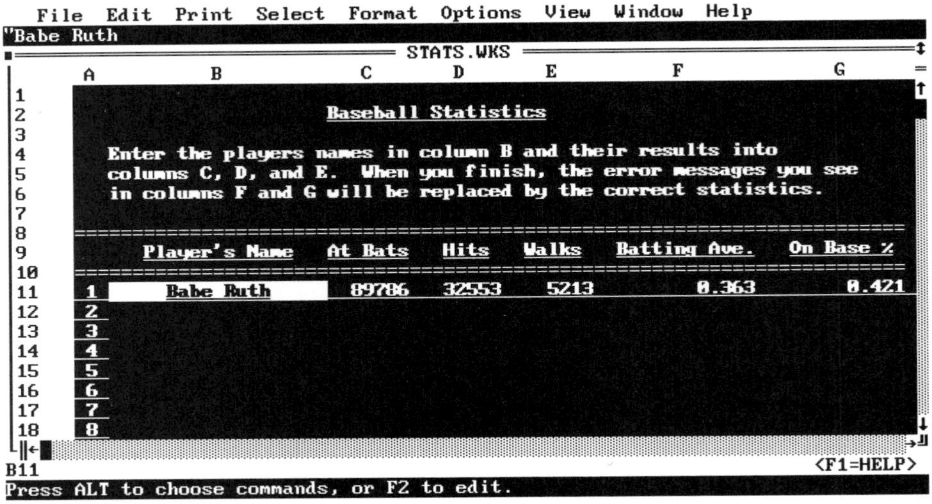

Figure 8.8 The **STATS.WKS** screen display

Related Activities

- Have your students create a "stats sheet" for basketball that includes percentages for field goals and free throws, as well as the average points, rebounds, and assists per game.
- Students might want to create a "stats sheet" for football that includes the quarterback's pass completion percentage, as well as the average yards rushing, average yards passing, and average points per game—for and against the team.
- Additional sports topics to consider include track, hockey, soccer, tennis, swimming, and cross-country running.

Guess My Rule

One of the files on your Works **Data** disk is a template called **GUESS.WKS**. This template is an interesting tool for exploring numerical relationships that works best with either a large monitor or an LCD with an overhead projector. The activity can be performed without a display screen, but it may not work as effectively (see the final comment in the **Related Activities** section below).

The spreadsheet contains an electronic version of the old "function game" (Figure 8.9). To begin the game, the teacher thinks of a function, or series of operations, to perform on any number that the students suggest. The number of operations that can be performed on the suggested number should be announced to the class (and probably limited to one or two operations at first).

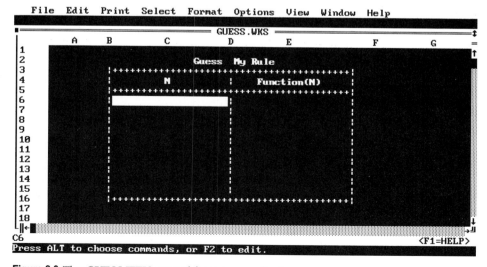

Figure 8.9 The **GUESS.WKS** spreadsheet screen display

After deciding on a function, the teacher tells the class to suggest a number (N) "to put into the function machine" (or similar age-appropriate words—this game can engage the interest of students from elementary school through college, depending on the complexity of the functions). After a student suggests a number, the teacher tells the class what "comes out of the function machine" as an answer. The challenge of the game is for the students to determine what rule the teacher or the function machine is using to produce the answers. The student who correctly guesses the rule or the function then assumes the role of the teacher in deciding the function for the next round.

For example, imagine that the function is: "You multiply the suggested number (N) by three and then subtract three from that product to get an answer." With this function in the "machine," if a student suggests the number 6, the result would be 15, because six multiplied by three equals eighteen, and eighteen minus three equals fifteen. Similarly, if a student offers the number 1, the function would result in 0, because three multiplied by one equals three, and three minus three equals zero.

With the **GUESS.WKS** spreadsheet, the teacher enters the function, or formula, into cell **E6** and then copies it quickly down column **E**. In the example just discussed, the following formula would be entered in cell **E6**: =C6*3-3. When the formula is complete and copied down the column, the teacher asks students to suggest possible numbers. As soon as the numbers are entered into the cells in column **C**, the correct response is displayed in the adjacent cell in column **E**. When a student guesses the correct function or rule, he or she creates the next function, or formula, entering and copying it down the spreadsheet column with the teacher's assistance.

Related Activities

- With each new game, open a new version of the **GUESS.WKS** file. Since it is a template file, it will open ready to use in a few seconds.
- Include more complex rules after students become adept at determining the patterns. Include operations such as squaring and cubing, and finding square roots and reciprocals. Also include, when appropriate, fractions, decimals, integers, and different bases, such as binary, octal, or hexadecimal.
- If no full-class display devices are available, hand students paper copies of the grid and have them follow on paper while the student rule-maker uses the computer's spreadsheet to help determine the correct responses.

Helping Students Manage Their Budgets

Young people are often inexperienced at managing money from allowances, part-time jobs, or whatever. This activity shows them how they can use spreadsheets to organize their finances. Begin with a brainstorming session to determine your students' most common sources of income and types of expenditure. Agree on some standard terminology for the category labels (clothing, school supplies, and entertainment, for example), then build a template file for your students to use later. Using this system, you will have put the formulas into the appropriate cells so that the students can simply enter the numbers and see the results displayed.

Alternatively, you could demonstrate to the students how to insert formulas into cells and have them design their own budget files. With either approach, have the students maintain the files throughout the year so they can observe their own spending patterns over time, calculate monthly averages, determine semi-annual figures, or anticipate the need to reduce their spending in one category (e.g., the movies) so they can have additional funds available for another category (e.g., cassette tapes).

Related Activity

- Demonstrate financial modeling by asking "what if" questions. For instance, if students decrease the amount of money they spend on movies or increase the amount they spend on clothes, what will the result be on their overall financial state?

Helping Students Manage Their Spending Money

This activity shows students how they can use spreadsheets to keep track of how they spend their money. One of the files on your Works **Data** disk is a template called **SPEND.WKS**, with formulas already included for students to use. Using this template, students can simply enter their incomes and expenditures, and the spreadsheet will automatically update and display a current balance for them. This file can be used to introduce students to the banking system—especially the procedures necessary to maintain an accurate checking account balance. Have students save their files under a new name, such as **SPEND-TM.WKS**, once they have entered their own data.

By updating their files once a week throughout the year, students can observe their own spending patterns over time and understand both the importance of financial planning and the meaning of negative numbers (if they have to borrow money from family or friends to cover their expenses).

Related Activity

- Demonstrate how to change the **SPEND.WKS** spreadsheet file into an accurate checking or savings account balancing tool.

Helping Students Anticipate Their Grades

This activity is especially useful with high school students who are concerned about the effect a test score may have on their class grade or the effect that the grade in a particular course may have on their cumulative grade-point average (GPA). Demonstrate to the students the procedure for creating a new spreadsheet. Discuss the necessary column headings and help them enter the appropriate formulas in the correct cells. (If you have a letter grading system, also help them translate letter grades to numerical equivalents.)

To demonstrate the spreadsheet's modeling power, have the students enter their "worst case" grade predictions into the proper cells. Then ask them to determine the effect poor grades would have on their cumulative GPA. Next, have them change each grade to a score they can use as a goal to see what GPA those grades produce. Students can use this tool to set goals, track progress, formulate strategies, and perhaps mitigate any overly drastic reactions to one poor score, or any overly optimistic expectation attached to one good result.

Related Activity

- Show your students how to maintain their grades for your class (or all of their classes, if you teach in a self-contained elementary school classroom) and have them record the scores for each test and assignment as it is returned so that they know how they stand in the class.

Additional Activities

Educational Activities
Preparing your class budget
Handling any club or special group budgets you sponsor
Handling a class store account
Calculating field trip expenses
Giving statistical analyses of your students' standardized test scores
Providing statistical analyses of your grading results
Coordinating class purchases
Maintaining book club or special function money
Generating any information you want to have in a table format
Helping students with financial management using simple budgets

General Activities
Managing your personal budget
Handling your personal investments
Preparing your income tax returns
Helping to schedule your loan repayments
Helping you plan for retirement
Overseeing your savings account
Balancing your checking account

9 Focusing on Charting

We have compared some of the other computer productivity tools in Works to typewriters, index card systems, and ledgers. To what can we compare a charting program? We might say that using a charting program is like having a skilled electronic draftsman who will generate graphs in whatever form you request based on the data you provide. If you change your mind and want, say, a pie chart instead of a bar chart, the draftsman will have to return to the drawing board and create a new chart.

An electronic charting program can also produce graphs or charts based on your data; even better, it will draw directly from spreadsheet data. You enter the information you want charted into a spreadsheet, specify the type of graph representation you want to have drawn, and then instruct the charting program to create the graphic form you select—bar, line, or pie, for example (Figure 9.1). The programs even allow you to switch the display from one graphic form to another without having to reenter the data. How can charting programs enhance the productivity of an educator? Let's use another short scenario to illustrate some of the possibilities that using a charting program provides.

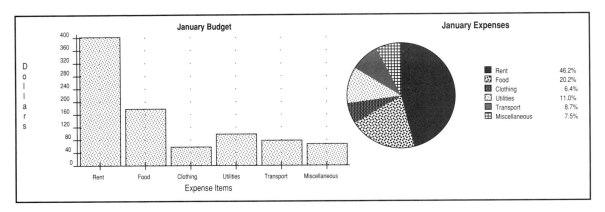

Figure 9.1 Typical bar chart and pie chart

Imagine that you are a classroom teacher with a demanding principal. For a special presentation to parents, your principal requests that you supply graphs comparing your students' academic performances that term with those from a previous term on a series of standardized tests that you administered. For each student, the principal wants a bar graph with four bars. The first bar shows each student's score from last term; the second bar shows the grade-level average score for that year; the third bar shows the student's score this term; and the last bar shows the grade-level average for this year. It's a good method for charting student progress, but requires a lot of work from the teachers involved.

Let's examine the traditional approach to satisfy the principal's request. With a calculator, each teacher computes the class average and adjusts these data by class size to determine the grade-level average. The teachers obtain the scores computed last term (in a similar time-consuming manner) and produce twenty-five bar graphs by hand. Even though the teachers create a blank master bar graph from a stencil, the process takes a great deal of time, and the resulting graphs do not have a very professional appearance.

Contrast that method with a computerized approach to creating the graphs. Because you and your colleagues use computers to handle many of your professional chores, you already maintain the standardized test results in a spreadsheet. You can access the grade-level average easily and perform any additional analyses of the data that your principal sometimes requests. Once the average is computed, you merely select the portion of the spreadsheet that you want graphed and print out the twenty-five bar graphs.

Your team of teachers might decide on a consistent color scheme for your grade level to make the graphs more appealing and easier to read. If you have a printer with color capability, you can change the black printer ribbon for a color ribbon before you print and produce twenty-five multicolored graphs—all in far less time than the traditional approach to creating graphs.

Expand this scenario to include many other productivity tasks: creating pie graphs to depict class or schoolwide demographic data, producing line or bar graphs to show daily attendance figures, generating pie graphs to illustrate class or club budgets, or making bar graphs to illustrate grade distributions in a class, at a grade level, or on a schoolwide basis. If you consider the potential of charting programs for instruction, their utility is even greater: graphing the results from student-conducted surveys; familiarizing students with the advantages and disadvantages of the different graphic forms by displaying the same data set with various graph styles; and representing sports statistics with the appropriate graphic forms.

When you combine the instructional applications of charting programs with the productivity powers they provide, the advantages of charting programs are clear. The unique power to visualize instantly the same data set in different graphic forms is reason enough to use the programs. When you add the many other features we haven't discussed yet, the advantages of using charting programs are even greater.

An Introduction to Charting

In Microsoft Works, the charting program is an **overlay** (a program-within-a-program) that operates within the spreadsheet. When you create a chart within a spreadsheet file and then save the spreadsheet, you save that chart and any other charts that you may have produced with the data in that same file. If you want to make a chart based on new data, you create a new spreadsheet file as you learned to do in the last chapter. Once you have entered the data you want graphed, you command the charting program to draw the graph. The program automatically produces a bar graph of the data you highlighted, so you must specify a line, pie, or other graphic form for your chart.

Graphs typically have **titles** and **legends** that help people understand or interpret them. The title appears at the top of the chart and may include a subtitle for clarification. Legends appear at different places, depending on the type of graph (beneath a bar graph or to the right of a pie graph); they further clarify the data illustrated by the graph.

Charts are classified into two major categories—**pie** and **series** charts. Pie or circle charts are used to represent the parts of a whole; they show the relationship between different elements that combine to produce an aggregate figure, such as expense items in a total budget or student ethnic origins in a classroom. Pie graphs are comprised of segments or sections, the size of which represents a given percent of the whole pie. Each segment can be labeled with its corresponding percentage and distinguished from the other segments by different colors or fill patterns. Segments can be further distinguished or emphasized by exploding them from the pie. An **exploded** segment is separated from the circle to draw special attention to it. The **legend** in a pie chart is boxed with each segment identified by a label, its pattern, and its corresponding percentage.

Series charts, which include bar, line, stacked bar, and combination bar and line, are used to illustrate sequences of data that can be compared with some common metric or scale (Figure 9.2). A line chart shows change over time; a bar

Figure 9.2 Different chart types available in Microsoft Works

or stacked bar chart compares similar items with a common scale; a combination bar and line chart combines the two. A series chart has a horizontal **X-axis** and a vertical **Y-axis**. Each axis and individual bar can have a label that further explains its data. Also, the Y-axis scale can be adjusted to show the data in the way you think is best.

In a vertical bar graph, the X-axis lists the series and the Y-axis shows the scale against which the series is measured. For example, in a budget bar graph, the budget items (rent, food, etc.) would be listed and labeled along the X-axis, while the dollar amounts would be placed on the Y-axis. The bar above each budget item would represent the dollar amount allocated to that item.

In some cases, only one chart type can possibly display the data, but more often, several different graphic forms can represent the same data. Generally, however, one type of graph can present a specific message with a given set of data more persuasively. Using the charting program to redraw the same data in different forms will help you determine which form is best for the data.

In the next section, you will learn to create a bar graph from existing spreadsheet data, to change a bar graph into a pie or line graph, to add and change the titles and legends on a chart, to specify the fill patterns and colors for individual bars or pie wedges, and to print out charts in landscape and portrait orientations.

Creating and Saving a Chart in a Spreadsheet File

Orientation

In this exercise you will become acquainted with the Microsoft Works charting features. Because Works uses spreadsheet data for the charts it generates, you must create the spreadsheet with the data you want to graph before you create a chart. All of the charts that you generate are part of the spreadsheet file you create; when you save the spreadsheet, you save your charts with it.

In this section, you will create a simple pie chart to display the ethnic distribution of the students in your school. The exercise will introduce you to the charting screen and commands. First, however, you need to open a new Microsoft Works spreadsheet file.

Getting Started

Use the same procedures to start Works that you have used in the preceding exercises. If you need additional help, consult the detailed instructions presented in the **Getting Started** section on pages 55–56.

Creating a New Chart

When you see the opening Works screen, create a new spreadsheet document to contain your chart by following these steps:

1. Press the **N** (for Create **N**ew File) key to start a new document.
2. Press the **S** (for **S**preadsheet) key to open a new spreadsheet document.

In a few moments, Works copies the spreadsheet program into memory and displays a blinking cursor to indicate you can now work. Because you'll need only two columns for the chart you're going to create, you can make the columns wide enough to fit your categories easily. To make column **A** 20 characters wide, follow these steps:

1. Position the cursor in cell **A2**.
2. Press the **Alt** key, then press the **T** key to access the **Format** menu.
3. Press the **W** (for Column **W**idth) key to change the field width.
4. Replace the current field width of **10**, displayed in the dialog box, by typing 20 and pressing the **Enter** key to accept that value.

Beginning with cell **A2**, enter the data shown in Table 9.1. To do so, follow these steps:

1. Type Western European into cell **A2**.
2. Press the **right arrow** key to move to cell **B2**, and type 376.
3. Position the cursor in cell **A3**, type Eastern European, then press the **right arrow** key.

Continue entering all the data in the table. When you have finished, you'll use this data to generate a pie chart.

Table 9.1 Data for pie chart on ethnic distribution

Row #s	Column A	Column B
1		
2	Western European	376
3	Eastern European	216
4	African	168
5	Hispanic	64
6	East Asian	85
7	Middle Eastern	32

Creating a New Pie Chart

After you have entered the data for your chart, you must select the data that you want to graph. To do so, follow these steps:

1. Use the arrow keys or the mouse to place the cursor in cell **A2**.
2. Hold down the **Shift** key and press the **down arrow** key five times to highlight all the ethnic categories.
3. With the **Shift** key still held down, press the **right arrow** key to extend the highlighting to include all the numeric data.

All the information that you want to chart is now selected. To draw the chart, follow these steps:

1. Press the **Alt** key, then press the **V** key to access the **View** menu.
2. Press the **N** (for **N**ew Chart) key to create a new chart.

If you are using a *floppy disk drive system,* you will have to exchange disks to access the graphics layer of the program. Works will prompt you to insert the **Accessories** disk. If you are using a *hard disk drive system,* you will not have to exchange any disks.

As soon as you are in the graphics layer, you will see a bar chart of your data appear on the screen. The chart lacks a title and other features, so you will need to improve the chart later. Now press the **Esc** key to return to the screen display. Note that Works places the word **Chart** on the line at the bottom of the screen indicating that you are in chart layer, not the spreadsheet. Notice also that the charting menu bar is different from the spreadsheet menu bar—for instance, there are no **Edit** or **Select** menus, but there is a **Data** menu. In the chart layer, you can manipulate the charts you create from spreadsheet data. Whenever you want to return to the spreadsheet, press the **F10** key.

First, let's change the bar graph to a pie chart. To do so, follow these steps:

1. Press the **Alt** key, then the **T** key to access the **Format** menu.
2. Press the **P** (for **P**ie) key to select a pie chart.

If you are using a monochrome computer system, you will want to follow these steps to make the charts look better on the screen:

1. Press the **Alt** key, then the **O** key to access the **Options** menu.
2. Press the **F** (for **F**ormat for B&W) key to select the black and white screen setting that uses patterns in place of colors.

Next, let's add a title to the chart:

1. Press the **Alt** key and then press the **D** key to access the **Data** menu.
2. Press the **T** (for **T**itles) key to enter the chart titles you want.
3. When the **Chart Titles** dialog box appears, type Ethnic Demographic Distribution.
4. Press the **Tab** key to enter the **Subtitles** box and type Grant Public School, 1991.
5. Press the **Enter** key to exit the **Chart Titles** dialog box.

Let's see what the chart looks like as a pie chart. To draw the chart, follow these steps:

1. Press the **Alt** key and press the **V** key to access the **View** menu.
2. Press the **1** (for Chart**1**) key to display a pie chart for the same data you graphed as a bar chart a few moments ago (see Figure 9.3).

Inspect the pie chart you just created. Note that each ethnic category name is accompanied by its percentage of the school population. Although the screen font may truncate some of the category names (such as Western European 40%), the labels should be complete when they are printed on paper. If you want to reassure yourself that the labels will be printed, you can use the print preview capability to view the chart as it will look on paper.

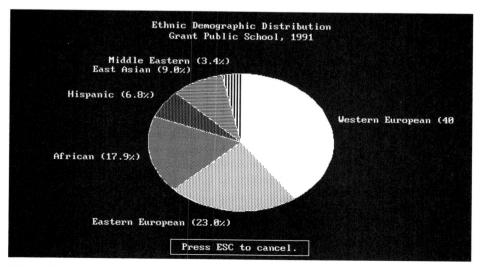

Figure 9.3 Pie chart of Ethnic Demographic Distribution

If the chart looks satisfactory, press the **F10** key. This keystroke returns you to the spreadsheet. If you wish to change the spreadsheet data, you can do that now and then have Works redraw the chart.

Redrawing the Pie Chart with Changed Data

Let's imagine that the new school year brought a sudden influx of East Asian students into your school, changing their number from 85 to 137. You wish to generate a new chart reflecting the updated student demographics at your school.

1. Position the cursor in cell **B6** (where the number 85 is presently displayed).
2. Type the number **137** to replace the 85. Press the **Enter** key.
3. Press the **Alt** key, then the **V** key to access the **View** menu.
4. Press the **1** (for Chart**1**) key to redraw the chart with the new data.

Notice how the pie chart and the corresponding percentages have changed to reflect the new number of East Asian students (see Figure 9.4). The percentage rose from 9.0% to 13.8%, while the other ethnic group percentages declined accordingly.

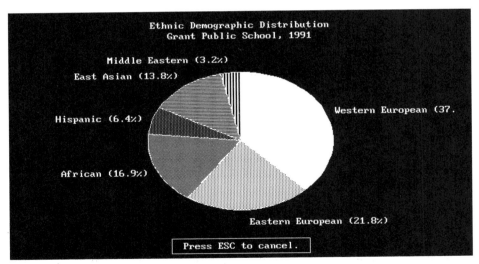

Figure 9.4 Pie chart of Ethnic Demographic Distribution, reflecting the increase in the number of East Asian students

Saving a Chart within a Spreadsheet File

If your chart looks good, press the **F10** key to return to the spreadsheet. Now let's save the chart as part of a spreadsheet file and then exit Works. To store the document on your Works **Data** disk under the name **ETHNIC**, follow these steps:

1. Press the **Alt** key and then the **F** (for **F**ile) key.
2. Press the **A** key to select the **Save As** command.
3. Works suggests that you save the document on the active disk using the name **SHEET1.WKS**.
4. Hold down the **Alt** key and press the **I** (for **D**irectories) key. When you see the blinking cursor in the **Directories** dialog box, press the **down arrow** key until you highlight the letter of the disk drive containing your Works **Data** disk, then press the **Enter** key. Notice that the **Directory of** line in the dialog box now shows that the active directory is the drive holding your Works **Data** disk.
5. Type the name for your file, ETHNIC, and press the **Enter** key. Works will quickly store your spreadsheet and chart on your Works **Data** disk under the name **ETHNIC.WKS**. (Remember, Works adds the **.WKS** extension to your file name to show that it is a spreadsheet file.)

The pie chart of your students' ethnic distribution is now saved within the **ETHNIC.WKS** spreadsheet file. When you want to access the chart again, you must first open the spreadsheet file, then open the chart.

Exiting Works

You can now safely exit Works without worrying about losing the information in your file. To exit the program and shut down the computer, use the same steps that you have used in the preceding exercises. If you need additional help, consult the more detailed instructions presented in the **Exiting Works** section on pages 60–61.

Enhancing and Printing Charts from Existing Spreadsheets

Orientation

In this exercise, you'll use the gradebook spreadsheet that you completed in an earlier exercise. You'll enhance the data presentation by creating several different graphs to communicate student progress to parents. The spreadsheet file you'll use, **MY-GRADE.WKS**, is stored on your Works **Data** disk. You'll open the file, create and print the charts, resave the spreadsheet and the charts using a new name, **MY-CHART**, and then exit Works. This file will include the charts you create as well as the spreadsheet data already saved in the file, **MY-GRADE.WKS**.

You will generate two series charts in this exercise. The first will be a bar graph comparing an individual student's test scores and term averages with the class averages in the same categories. The second bar chart will compare an individual student's test results with three statistics: the class average, the maximum, and the minimum scores. Both of the charts visually convey students' progress to their parents.

Getting Started

For this exercise, open an existing file, **MY-GRADE.WKS**, instead of creating a new one. Use the same procedures to start Works that you have used in the preceding exercises. If you need additional help, consult the more detailed instructions presented in the **Getting Started** section on pages 55–56.

Opening an Existing Spreadsheet File

When you see the opening Works screen, open the file **MY-GRADE.WKS**:

1. Press the **O** key to select the **Open Existing File** command.
2. Hold down the **Alt** key and press the **I** (for D**i**rectories) key. When the blinking cursor appears in the **Directories** dialog box, press the **down arrow** key to highlight the letter of the disk drive containing your Works **Data** disk, then press the **Enter** key.
3. Hold down the **Alt** key and press the **F** (for **F**iles) key. When the blinking cursor appears in the **Files** dialog box, use the **down arrow** key to highlight **MY-GRADE.WKS**, then press the **Enter** key.
4. Works will copy the **MY-GRADE.WKS** file from the disk into the computer's temporary memory. In a few moments, you will see the document displayed on the screen.

Modifying the Spreadsheet

To simplify the charting process, the first thing you'll do is eliminate column **A**, which lists the students' last names. Works will only take labels from one column, so you'll use the first names for this chart. To eliminate the column, follow these steps:

1. Position the cursor in any cell in column **A**, hold down the **Shift** key, and press the **F8** key to select the whole column.
2. Press the **Alt** key, then press the **E** key to access the **Edit** menu.
3. Press the **D** (for **D**elete Row/Column) key to delete the column that you selected.

Column **A** disappears, but all of the remaining data is recalculated and the spreadsheet is still intact. You already have the information saved, so deleting this column for the charting process will not actually lose any data; the data will still be available in their original form on your Works **Data** disk in the file **MY-GRADE.WKS**. If you were to save this document now without renaming it, however, the original file would be replaced by this version and the last name data would be lost. To prevent this from happening, you will rename the file later using the **Save as** command. For now, let's create the first chart.

Rearranging the Spreadsheet Data

You'll create a chart for Paul Allen, displaying two bars for each of the term's five tests. The first bar will display the class average scores, and the second bar will represent Paul's test results. The finished chart will offer a graphic comparison of his performance with the average results for the entire class. Although Paul performed very well during the term, he did not quite manage to maintain an **A** average. Perhaps a chart showing that his results are well above average will reassure his parents that he is doing well.

The first step in creating this chart is to rearrange the existing data to facilitate the charting process. You have already stored this file on your Works **Data** disk; the manipulations you'll perform on your file, therefore, will not destroy the information you already have in your file. However, remember *not* to resave this document after the changes have been effected until you change the file name, or the modified version of the document will replace the original version that you wanted to preserve.

Begin the data manipulation process by positioning the cursor in cell **A7**. You will move Paul Allen's information from the alphabetical list to a blank section at the bottom of the spreadsheet. To relocate Paul's data, follow these steps:

1. Hold down the **Shift** key and press the **right arrow** key five times to highlight the row **7** data from columns **A** through **F**.
2. Press the **Alt** key, then press the **E** key to access the **Edit** menu.
3. Press the **C** (for **C**opy) key to place a copy of the selected data in another part of the spreadsheet.
4. Position the cursor in cell **A43** and press the **Enter** key to insert the data into the new spreadsheet location.

Next, let's place the class average statistics in row **A44** below Paul's data:

1. Position the cursor in cell **A35**.
2. Hold down the **Shift** key and press the **right arrow** key five times to highlight the **Row 35** data in columns **A** through **F**.
3. Press the **Alt** key, then press the **E** key to access the **Edit** menu.
4. Press the **S** (for Copy **S**pecial) key to apply the **Copy Special** command.

You cannot use the **Copy** command in this situation because these cells contain formulas that would be incorrect when copied to new locations. Instead of calculating the average for cells **B7** through **B31**, the relocated formulas would calculate averages relative to their new positions in row **A44**—that is, cells **B17** through **B41**. By using the **Copy Special** command, however, you can copy only the values—that is, the figures you see displayed in the cells.

5. Use the arrow keys or the mouse to position the cursor in cell **A44** and press the **Enter** key to move the data into the new spreadsheet location.
6. When the **Copy Special** dialog box appears on the screen, press the **Enter** key to select the **Values only** option.

The necessary data are now in the correct places, ready for you to create the bar graph.

Creating the Bar Chart

Now that you have ordered the data you can select the data that you want to chart by following these steps:

1. Use the arrow keys or the mouse to place the cursor in cell **A43**.
2. Hold down the **Shift** key and press the **right arrow** key five times to highlight all of Paul's data.
3. With the **Shift** key still held down, extend the highlighting to include the AVERAGE data by pressing the **down arrow** key.

All the information that you want to chart is now selected. To draw the chart, follow these steps:

1. Press the **Alt** key, then press the **V** key to access the **View** menu.
2. Press the **N** (for **N**ew Chart) key to create a new chart.

Remember, if you are using a *floppy disk drive system,* you will have to exchange disks to access the graphics layer of the program. Works will prompt you to insert the **Accessories** disk. If you are using a *hard disk drive system,* you will not have to exchange any disks.

In a few moments, the chart will appear on the screen. The bar chart lacks a title and other features. You'll need to enhance the chart, so press the **Esc** key to return to the screen display. Note that Works places the word **Chart** on the line at the bottom of the screen to inform you that you are in the chart overlay, not the spreadsheet. From the charting menu bar that is now displayed, you can manipulate the charts you create from spreadsheet data. Whenever you want to return to the spreadsheet, press the **F10** key.

If you are using a monochrome computer system, you will want to follow these steps to make the charts look better on the screen:

1. Press the **Alt** key, then press the **O** (for **O**ptions) key to access the **Options** menu.
2. Press the **F** (for **F**ormat for B&W) key to select the black and white screen setting that uses patterns in place of colors.

Let's change the scale of the Y-axis so that the comparison between Paul's scores and the class average is more discernable. To rescale the Y-axis, follow these steps:

1. Press the **Alt** key, then the **O** key to access the **Options** menu.
2. Press the **Y** (for **Y**-axis) key to select a new scale for the axis.
3. When the **Y-axis** dialog box appears, type **50** for the new minimum, press the **Tab** key, then type **100** to set the maximum. Press the **Enter** key.

Next, let's add titles for the chart and the axes. To add titles:

1. Press the **Alt** key, then press the **D** (for **D**ata) key to access the **Data** menu.
2. Press the **T** (for **T**itles) key to enter the chart titles you want.

When the **Chart Titles** dialog box appears, type the appropriate titles for the chart by following these steps:

1. With the cursor in the **Chart title** box, type Paul's Scores vs. the Average to title the chart.
2. Press the **Tab** key twice to enter the **X-axis** box and type Tests.
3. Press the **Tab** key again to enter the **Y-axis** box and type Percent Scores.
4. Press the **Enter** key to exit the **Chart Titles** dialog box.

Now let's add labels for the bars along the X-axis. The bars represent tests 1 through 5 placed along the top of the spreadsheet. To add labels, follow these steps:

1. Position the cursor in cell **B5**, hold down the **Shift** key, then press the **right arrow** key four times to highlight cells **B5** through **F5**.
2. Press the **Alt** key, then press the **D** key to access the **Data** menu.
3. Press the **X** (for **X**-Series) key to instruct Works that the highlighted cells contain the X-axis labels.

Let's add two additional enhancements to the chart, a border and grid lines. To add a border, follow these steps:

1. Press the **Alt** key, then press the **O** key to access the **Options** menu.
2. Press the **B** (for **B**order) key to place a border around the entire bar graph.

To add grid lines along the X-axis, follow these steps:

1. Press the **Alt** key, then press the **O** key to access the **Options** menu.
2. Press the **X** key to access the **X-axis** dialog box. Press the spacebar to select the **Grid lines** option (verify that an **X** appears to the left of the **Grid lines** option).
3. Press the **Enter** key to accept that option.

Let's select fonts for printing so that the titles and legends you placed on the chart will print in appropriate sizes:

1. Press the **Alt** key, then press the **T** key to access the **Format** menu.
2. Press the **F** (for Title **F**ont) key to change the font of the chart's title.
3. Use the **down arrow** key or the mouse to select from the **Fonts** box a font that displays a size near 30 in the **Sizes** box. Your font choices depend on the printer you installed with the Works **Setup** disk, but Bold Modern B is one common font. If the Bold Modern B choice is available, use the **down arrow** key to highlight it.
4. Press the **Tab** key to move the cursor to the **Sizes** box, then use the **down arrow** key to highlight **32** (or a similar size). Press the **Enter** key to establish those font settings for the chart title.

Finally, let's select the printer fonts for the legends you placed on the chart so they will also print appropriately. To select the fonts, follow these steps:

1. Press the **Alt** key, then the **T** key to access the **Format** menu.
2. Press the **O** (for **O**ther Font) key to change the font of the chart's legends.
3. Use the **down arrow** key or the mouse to highlight the Bold Modern B font (or a similar selection) in the **Fonts** box.
4. Press the **Tab** key to move the cursor to the **Sizes** box, then use the **down arrow** key to highlight **24** (or a similar size). Press the **Enter** key to establish those settings for the chart legends.

Viewing the Bar Chart

Let's see what the chart looks like at this point. To draw the chart, follow these steps:

1. Press the **Alt** key, then the **V** key to access the **View** menu
2. Press the **1** (for **Chart1**) key to redraw the chart (Figure 9.5).

If the chart looks fine, press the **Esc** key to return to your data so that you can print the chart.

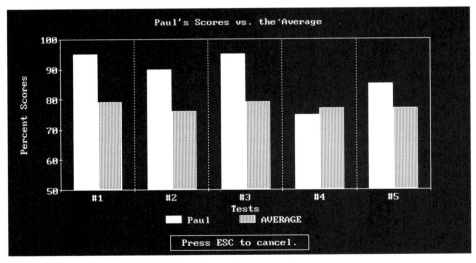

Figure 9.5 A bar chart illustrating Paul's academic standing

Printing the Bar Chart

The chart shows that Paul performed well above the class average on all but the fourth test. Both he and his parents can be pleased with his performance. Let's print a copy of the chart on paper to send home with Paul. In the next chapter, you'll learn to use data integration and the word processor to enhance your printing of charts. For the moment, however, you can easily print a copy of your chart by using the commands available under the **Print** menu. To print the chart, follow these steps:

1. Press the **Alt** key, then press the **P** key to access the **Print** menu.
2. Press the **V** key to preview the document on the screen. Notice that the **Print Preview** dialog box appears on the screen.
3. Hold down the **Alt** key and press the **P** key to **p**review the document on the screen.
4. If the chart appears as you wish, press the **P** (for **P**rint) key to print the document on paper.

If you want to make changes before you print, press the **Esc** key to cancel the printing process and return to the document. When you have finished making the changes that you wish, repeat the previous steps to print the document.

When you have finished printing the chart, press the **F10** key to exit the charting overlay and return to the spreadsheet. Don't worry; your chart is still available within the spreadsheet and will be stored on your data disk later when you save the spreadsheet file.

Creating a More Complex Bar Chart

Now that your first chart is complete and printed, you'll create a slightly more complicated bar graph. You'll use this chart, which will feature four bars for each test score, to communicate Sally Dale's continued poor progress to her parents. Although Sally has average ability, she scored poorly on all her tests and will receive a failing mark for the term. You want to make certain that she and her parents are aware that her performance is one of the lowest in her class. You'll create a bar chart that visually conveys her academic standing compared to the other students in her class.

The first bar on the graph will represent the highest score on the test, the second bar will depict the class average score, the third bar will show Sally's test score, and the fourth bar will represent the lowest score on the test. The finished chart will offer a graphic comparison of Sally's performance and the class statistics.

The first step will be to manipulate the spreadsheet data so that the class statistics are arranged in the following sequence: high score, average score, individual student's score, and low score. To accomplish this task:

1. Position the cursor in cell **A15**.
2. Prepare to copy Sally's data down to the bottom of the spreadsheet by holding down the **Shift** key and pressing the **right arrow** key five times to highlight the row **15** data from columns **A** through **F**.
3. Press the **Alt** key, then press the **E** key to access the **Edit** menu.
4. Press the **C** (for **C**opy) key to place a copy of the selected data in another part of the spreadsheet.

5. Position the cursor in cell **A50** and press the **Enter** key to insert the data into the new spreadsheet location.

Next we'll manipulate the class statistics so they are grouped with Sally's data. To accomplish this task:

1. Position the cursor in cell **A37**.
2. Prepare to copy the HIGH SCORE statistics to row **A48** by holding down the **Shift** key and pressing the **right arrow** key five times to highlight the **Row 37** data from columns **A** through **F**.
3. Press the **Alt** key, then the **E** key to access the **Edit** menu.
4. Press the **S** key to apply the **Copy Special** command.

(Remember, you cannot use the **Copy** command in this situation because these cells contain formulas that would be incorrect when copied to new locations.)

5. Position the cursor in cell **A48** and press the **Enter** key to move the data into the new spreadsheet location.
6. When the **Copy Special** dialog box appears on the screen, press the **Enter** key to select the **Values only** option.

Now move the AVERAGE statistics to row **A49**. To move the row of statistics, follow these steps:

1. Position the cursor in cell **A35**, hold down the **Shift** key, and press the **right arrow** key five times to highlight the **Row 35** data from columns **A** through **F**.
2. Press the **Alt** key, then the **E** key to access the **Edit** menu.
3. Press the **S** key to apply the **Copy Special** command.
4. Position the cursor in cell **A49** and press the **Enter** key to move the data into the new spreadsheet location.
5. When the **Copy Special** dialog box appears on the screen, press the **Enter** key to select the **Values only** option.

To move the LOW SCORE statistics to row **A51**, follow these steps:

1. Position the cursor in cell **A36**, hold down the **Shift** key, and press the **right arrow** key five times to highlight the **Row 36** data in columns **A** through **F**.
2. Press the **Alt** key, then press the **E** key to access the **Edit** menu.
3. Press the **S** key to apply the **Copy Special** command.
4. Position the cursor in cell **A51** and press the **Enter** key to move the data into the new spreadsheet location.
5. When the **Copy Special** dialog box appears on the screen, press the **Enter** key to select the **Values only** option.

The necessary data are now correctly placed for creating the bar graph.

Drawing the Bar Chart

The data indicate that Sally's test results are well below average; frequently, they are among the lowest scores in the class. Sally needs to improve her academic performance. Using the chart as a more visual representation of her performance may help make the message more explicit to both Sally and her parents.

You decide to draw and print the chart for the conference with Sally's parents. You already have ordered the data, so you can now select the data that you want to chart. Follow these steps:

1. Use the arrow keys or the mouse to place the cursor in cell **A48**.
2. Hold down the **Shift** key and press the **right arrow** key five times to highlight all of the highest scores.
3. With the **Shift** key still held down, extend the highlighting by pressing the **down arrow** key three times to include all of the remaining data.

The information that you want to chart is now selected. To draw the chart, follow these steps:

1. Press the **Alt** key, then the **V** key to access the **View** menu.
2. Press the **N** (for **N**ew Chart) key to create a new chart.

Remember, if you are using a floppy disk drive system, you will have to exchange disks to access the graphics layer of the program. Works will prompt you to insert the **Accessories** disk.

In a few moments the chart will appear on the screen. Again, you'll need to enhance it, so press the **Esc** key to return to the screen display. Works placed the word **Chart** on the line at the bottom of the screen to inform you that you are in the chart layer, not the spreadsheet.

If you are using a monochrome computer system, follow these steps to make the charts look better on the screen:

1. Press the **Alt** key, then the **O** key to access the **Options** menu.
2. Press the **F** (for **F**ormat for B&W) key to select the screen setting for the black and white display that uses patterns in place of colors.

Let's add titles for the chart and the axes. To add titles, follow these steps:

1. Press the **Alt** key, then press the **D** key to access the **Data** menu.
2. Press the **T** (for **T**itles) key to enter the chart titles you want.

When the **Chart Titles** dialog box appears, type the appropriate titles for the chart by following these steps:

1. With the cursor in the **Chart title** box, type Sally's Scores vs. the Class to title the chart.
2. Press the **Tab** key twice to enter the **X-axis** box and type Tests.
3. Press the **Tab** key again to enter the **Y-axis** box and type Percent Scores.
4. Press the **Enter** key to exit the **Chart Titles** dialog box.

Now let's add labels for the bars along the X-axis. The bars represent tests 1 through 5 placed along the top of the spreadsheet. To add labels, follow these steps:

1. Position the cursor in cell **B5**, hold down the **Shift** key, and press the **right arrow** key four times to highlight cells **B5** through **F5**.

2. Press the **Alt** key, then press the **D** key to access the **Data** menu.
3. Press the **X** (for **X**-Series) key to tell Works that the highlighted cells contain the X-axis labels.

Let's add a border and grid lines to the chart. To add the border, follow these steps:

1. Press the **Alt** key, then press the **O** key to access the **Options** menu.
2. Press the **B** (for **B**order) key to place a border around the entire bar graph.

To add the grid lines along the X-axis, follow these steps:

1. Press the **Alt** key, then press the **O** key to access the **Options** menu.
2. Press the **X** key to access the **X-axis** dialog box. Press the spacebar to select the **Grid lines** option (verify that an **X** appears to the left of the **Grid lines** option).
3. Press the **Enter** key to accept that option.

Now let's change the pattern on the bars themselves to make Sally's bar more discernable. To change the bar patterns, you'll use the **Data Format** dialog box (Figure 9.6). To make the change, follow these steps:

1. Press the **Alt** key, then the **T** key to access the **Format** menu.
2. Press the **D** key to access the **Data Format** menu.
3. Let's change the **1st Y** series pattern, the HIGH SCORE bar, to one using a series of Xs. Hold down the **Alt** key and press the **P** (for **P**atterns) key. Use the **down arrow** key to scroll down the pattern choices until you highlight the **XX**.

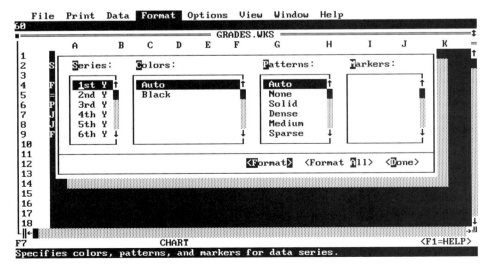

Figure 9.6 Data Format dialog box

4. Hold down the **Alt** key and press the **F** (for **F**ormat) key to apply the formatting change on the first bar—that is, to make the bar's pattern filled with Xs.
5. To make Sally's bar more recognizable, change the **3rd Y** series pattern to solid black. Hold down the **Alt** key, press the **S** (for **S**eries) key, and use the **down arrow** key to highlight the **3rd Y** option.
6. Hold down the **Alt** key and press the **O** (for C**o**lors) key, then use the **down arrow** key to highlight **Black**.
7. Press the **Tab** key to move the cursor to the **Patterns** box and use the **down arrow** key to highlight the **Solid** option.
8. Hold down the **Alt** key and press the **F** (for **F**ormat) key to apply the formatting change on the second bar—that is, make the bar's pattern solid black.
9. Hold down the **Alt** key and press the **D** (for **D**one) key to exit the **Data Format** dialog box.

Let's select fonts so that the titles and legends you placed on the chart will print in appropriate sizes. To select the fonts, follow these steps:

1. Press the **Alt** key, then press the **T** key to access the **Format** menu.
2. Press the **F** (for Title **F**ont) key to change the font of the chart's title.
3. Use the **down arrow** key or the mouse to select a font from the **Fonts** box with a size near 30 as shown in the **Sizes** box. Again, your font options depend on the printer you installed with the Works **Setup** disk, so use the **down arrow** key to highlight the same font you used in the last exercise.
4. Press the **Tab** key to move the cursor to the **Sizes** box, then use the **down arrow** key to highlight **32** (or a similar size). Press the **Enter** key to establish those font settings for the chart title.

Finally, to ensure that the legends will also print appropriately, let's select the printer fonts for the legends you placed on the chart. To select the fonts, follow these steps:

1. Press the **Alt** key, then the **T** key to access the **Format** menu.
2. Press the **O** (for **O**ther Font) key to change the font of the chart's legends.
3. Use the **down arrow** key or the mouse to highlight the same font you used for the title font.
4. Press the **Tab** key to move the cursor to the **Sizes** box, then use the **down arrow** key to highlight **24** (or a similar size). Press the **Enter** key to establish those font settings for the chart legends.

Viewing the Bar Chart

Let's see how the chart looks at this point. To draw the chart, follow these steps:

1. Press the **Alt** key, then press the **V** key to access the **View** menu.
2. Press the **2** (for Chart**2**) key to redraw the chart (Figure 9.7).

If the chart looks fine, press the **Esc** key to return to your data so that you can save the chart before you print it on paper.

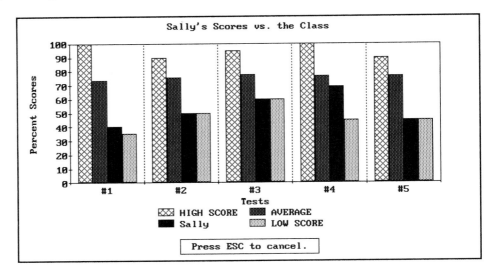

Figure 9.7 The reformatted bar chart illustrating Sally's academic standing

Saving the Charts in a Spreadsheet File

Before you print a document, you should always save it on your Works **Data** disk. To preserve the **MY-GRADE.WKS** file in its original form, you now want to save the changes you made to the document by using a new file name, **MY-CHART.WKS.** To do so, follow these steps:

1. Press the **Alt** key, then the **F** (for **F**ile) key.
2. Press the **A** key to select the **Save As** command.
3. Works suggests that you save the document on your Works **Data** disk using the name **MY-GRADE.WKS**.
4. Type the name MY-CHART, and press the **Enter** key. Works will quickly store the document on your Works **Data** disk under the name **MY-CHART.WKS**.

Printing the Bar Chart

Next, let's print a copy of the chart on paper to send home to Sally's parents. To print the chart, follow these steps:

1. Press the **Alt** key, then press the **P** key to access the **Print** menu.
2. Press the **V** key to preview the document on the screen. Notice that the **Print Preview** dialog box appears on the screen.
3. Hold down the **Alt** key and press the **P** key to **p**review the document on the screen.
4. If the chart appears as you wish, press the **P** (for **P**rint) key to print the document on paper.

If you want to make changes before you print, press the **Esc** key to cancel the printing process and return to the document. Make the changes that you wish, then repeat the previous steps to print the document.

When you have finished printing the chart, press the **F10** key to exit the charting overlay and return to the spreadsheet. Don't worry: your chart is still available within the spreadsheet and will be stored on your data disk when you save the spreadsheet file.

Exiting Works

You can safely exit Works without losing the data in your file. To exit the program and shut down the computer, follow the same steps that you have used in previous exercises. If you need additional help, consult the more detailed instructions presented in the **Exiting Works** section on pages 60–61.

Integrating Charts into the Instructional Process

Now that you are familiar with the Microsoft Works charting procedures, let's examine approaches for using these charting capabilities in the classroom. Before introducing your students to the Works charting program, have them complete several graphing exercises by hand. Have students interpret commercially available or teacher-prepared graphs and charts you generate for them from surveys or other class projects. This experience will help them understand the advantages of a program such as Works. Additionally, these concrete experiences will ensure that your students have a firm foundation in graphing data. After doing these preliminary procedural exercises, students can use the powers of the software to concentrate on understanding the concepts behind graphing without worrying about the straightness of their lines. Provide students with simple spreadsheet templates, such as those on your Works **Data** disk (or similar files of your creation). Finally, have them create their own charts to present projects of their own design to their classmates.

The following suggestions can be used effectively with a single computer in a classroom or in a computer lab with many machines. A large monitor or an LCD with an overhead projector would be beneficial when introducing a classroom of students to charting software, but they are not at all essential to any of these activities. The first activity, **The Survey Charter**, uses a template file stored on your Works **Data** disk.

The Survey Charter

The file **CHARTER.WKS** has charts already established for students to use and inspect. In addition, the spreadsheet has been formatted to display data in a

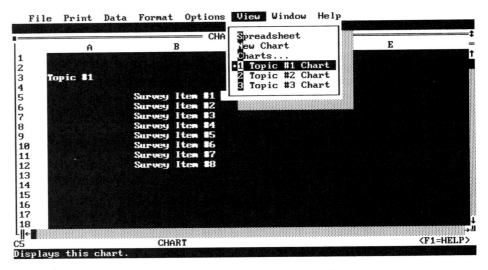

Figure 9.8 CHARTER.WKS document displaying the **Topic #1 Chart** choice under the **View** menu

simple format for easy examination and interpretation. Once you open the file, you'll see that the spreadsheet displays a tally sheet to record and chart the results of three different survey topics with eight or fewer categories in each survey. To use the spreadsheet, students should first replace the labels on the screen (**Item #1, Item #2**, etc.) with the categories from a survey that they have conducted. Next, they should enter the numbers for each category in the cell to the right of the category name (column **C**). They can ignore any categories they don't use because these default names (**Survey Item #1, Survey Item #2**, etc.) will not appear on the chart when printed. If students want to take out unnecessary item numbers, they can position the cursor inside the cell and remove them with the **Backspace** key.

When the students have completed entering the data into the spreadsheet, instruct them to select the **1 Topic #1** choice under the **View** command on the menu bar (see Figure 9.8); their survey information will quickly be displayed in pie graph form.

The students will notice that the title for the chart is now **You Name It #1**, probably not an appropriate chart title for their survey information. Instruct them to use the **Titles** option under the **Data** command on the menu bar to enter their own title. They can then display their chart with its title using the **View** command. Recommend that the students use the **Format** command on the menu bar to change from pie chart format to other chart styles until they find the type of chart that best displays their survey data.

If your students have a second survey to chart, have them move to rows **11** through **20** where a second tally sheet has been established. They should follow the same procedures to build the chart as they used to create the first one. If they would like to create a third chart, have them scroll down to rows **23** through **30**, where another tally sheet exists.

After your students have finished formatting their data, help them print the charts on paper to be included in reports or displayed on the bulletin board. Finally, have them save their files under a new name, such as **CHART-JB.WKS**, when they have finished printing.

Related Activities

- Assign each of your students to select a topic of interest and conduct a class survey using data sheets printed out from the **CHARTER.WKS** file. Ask students to limit the possible responses to eight categories (help them modify the file if they want to include more categories). When the results have been gathered, have each student chart the graphs, print them on paper, and display them on a bulletin board as A Profile of the Class (or other age-appropriate wording).
- Challenge your students to conduct the same surveys they used for the previous charting project, but this time have them survey students from another class or grade level. After they gather and chart the results, display the graphs on a bulletin board. Use the charts to discuss the similarities and differences between peers.
- Encourage your students to survey their parents using the same topics of interest used in the other survey projects. After they gather and chart the results, display the graphs on a bulletin board and discuss the similarities and differences between different generations.
- Create (or challenge your students to create) a file similar to the **CHARTER.WKS** file for a class of younger students, who can then enter data and generate a variety of series charts (line, bar, stacked bar, or combination bar/line).
- Survey topics suitable for charts on student favorites include colors, pastimes, books, sports, foods, movies, television shows, seasons, activities, vacation sites, songs, entertainers, school subjects, singers, and holidays.
- Survey topics for student least favorites include sports, foods, chores, colors, school subjects, pastimes, movies, holidays, television shows, seasons, activities, pet peeves, and singers.
- Survey topics on more educationally important subjects include attitudes; community, school, or social issues; political party preferences; presidential election results; educational and/or career expectations; state populations or areas; and the number of state representatives.

Graphing the Weather

The weather is an ideal topic for graphing exercises. Weather happens every day, so the graphing exercises can be integrated into the science curriculum as an on-going project in which all students can take part. Charting the weather can also help students recognize and discover important weather phenomena on their own, instead of trying to memorize textbook information for a test. Once your students have been introduced to the Works charting capabilities, they can maintain accurate weather data to chart on a daily, weekly, monthly, or seasonal basis.

You might assign a rotating group of students to gather data on a daily basis, including the temperature at a set time in the morning and the afternoon, the rainfall for a twenty-four hour period, the barometric pressure at a predetermined time in the morning and the afternoon, and possibly the wind velocity. These data can be recorded and maintained with paper and pencil, then charted using Works (as line or bar charts) at periodic intervals appropriate to your instructional plans.

Related Activities

- Have students gather non-numerical weather data such as predominant cloud type or general weather descriptors ("cloudy" or "fine"). Use the data to develop monthly pie or bar charts showing the most common weather patterns in your area.
- After students have gathered rainfall and barometer readings, have them use the data to develop a line chart with two series. Challenge them to discover any relationships that may exist between barometric pressure changes and rainfall, for example.
- Assign students to develop a line chart that compares the average daily temperatures in your area with three other selected regions of the world. The average temperatures of Jakarta (Indonesia), Yellow Knife (Northern Territories, Canada), and Cape Town (South Africa) offer a good comparison.

Additional Activities

Educational Activities

You can use the Microsoft Works charting powers to graph:

Your students' demographic data each year
Your students' socio-economic data each year
One student's performance compared to the class average
One student's performance compared to last term
The distribution of your grades each term
Your students' standardized test results each year
Your students' standardized test results over time
Students' survey results on topics of interest

Field trip expenses
Sport statistics
Class and school budgetary distributions
Individual student's scores over the period of a year
World economic data to help students compare the living standards in different countries

General Activities

For your personal use you can also graph your:

Yearly budget to compare it with other years
Personal budget to see the distribution of your monthly or yearly expenses
Daily weight to document effects of a diet
Daily caloric intake to monitor your nutrition

10   Focusing on Spreadsheets, Charts, and Word Processing—A Second Look at Data Integration

In the chapter on print merging, we combined the powers of databases and word processors. We demonstrated that when the two programs are merged, they provide a new tool for increasing your professional productivity. In this chapter, we look at another example of integrating data between applications—in this case, spreadsheets, charting, and word processing.

We compared the word processor to an enhanced typewriter, the spreadsheet to an enhanced accountant's ledger, and the charting program to a skilled draftsman. When combined by data integration, the applications merge calculated data tables and graphic forms, like pie or bar graphs, into word-processed documents such as reports or grant proposals. Each application performs that part of the task for which it is best suited.

How can you use this form of data integration in your professional life? As an educator, you are sometimes asked to produce annual reports for your administrators or to submit grant proposals. On other occasions, you might produce summary statements for the student groups you sponsor or for professional organizations to which you belong. Tasks like these are greatly simplified by data integration. Another scenario will illustrate how this integration of data can be useful for educators. Let's contrast report generation using traditional means with the same process using data integration.

Your administrator has asked you to compile a summary report at the end of the semester that includes student attendance figures, semester grades in each subject or class you teach, student demographic data, and standardized test results. Some of the data, including the student grades and the standardized test results, display best in table form. Demographic data, grade distributions, and daily attendance figures look best in graphic form. The administrator expects the tables and charts to be included on the appropriate pages of the report, not placed as addenda.

If you generate the report using typewriters, rulers, scissors, tape, and photocopy machines, the task will be daunting and the result disappointing. The report itself will have to be typed, leaving spaces in the body of the text for the requested tables and charts. Each chart and table will have to be manually constructed to fit its space in the report. Each table will need carefully aligned columns and ruled lines done by hand.

Creating the charts is even more labor intensive. The information must be compiled. In the case of grade distributions, the number of each grade will have to be determined and then illustrated with a pie chart. Daily student attendance figures for the first eighteen weeks of school must be compiled and represented on a line graph. A mistake in any chart or table would mean starting over or whiting out the error. Clearly, both alternatives are time-consuming, prone to mishaps, and may not result in attractive or professional products when completed.

After all the tables and charts are completed, they need to be individually taped into the appropriate parts of the report and photocopied. The photocopy machine transforms your "cut and pasted" report into a tape-less product that can be sent to the administrator. Although the photocopy machine does a good job with the reproductions, there are some telltale tape lines around the tables and charts. The task is finished, but the report is not the masterpiece that all your efforts deserve.

If you did the same task with an integrated productivity package like Microsoft Works, you would still have to enter the body of the report, but the word-processed features we discussed earlier would enhance its appearance. Next, you would open the spreadsheet file you use to maintain your student attendance. After you selected the appropriate data in the file, the charting program would draw the line graph you needed. Next, you would copy the chart, place it into the correct part of the word-processed document, and resize it so that all the details are easily readable.

For tables such as the standardized test results, you would open the spreadsheet file and select the data you wished to include in the report. You would then copy the data and insert the copy into the correct section of the report. You would repeat the same process for each of the other charts and tables that you needed to include in your report. In some cases, you might even reformat the spreadsheet data to fit more appropriately into the word-processed document.

The entire process would take a fraction of the time required by the traditional approach, and the finished product would look far more professional. Extend this productivity advantage over many tasks and many semesters to see the reasons for adopting the data integration approach.

A Further Introduction to Data Integration

As the preceding section demonstrated, data integration combines word-processed documents, spreadsheets, and charts. However, many data integration variations are possible with Microsoft Works. Information can be passed from database to spreadsheet (for enhanced calculating powers), spreadsheet to database (for enhanced sorting and searching powers), and any application to the communications program (for exchanging files with remote users). This section focuses only on the process of integrating spreadsheet data and charts into a word-processed document, but the process for the other data integration situations is quite similar.

Whereas print merging involved combined database and word-processed documents, this section examines merging spreadsheet data and charts with word-processed documents. The steps to bring about this data integration are different from those used in the print-merging process. In each instance, we must have two or more files open in the computer's memory—a word-processed document where the data or chart will be placed, and a spreadsheet file where the data or chart originated.

Let's first discuss the process for integrating spreadsheet data into a word-processed document. First you'll select the portion of the spreadsheet that contains the data you want to insert into the word-processed document. Next, you'll execute a **Copy** command to place a copy of the data into the **clipboard**. The **clipboard** is an area in the computer's memory where information can be stored temporarily. Each time you copy (or move) data, it is placed temporarily in the clipboard, and whatever had previously been in the clipboard is removed. The spreadsheet data you highlight will be stored in the clipboard until you replace it (by copying or moving other data) or turn off the computer.

The next step in the integration process is to use the **Window** command to switch to the word-processed document. When you are working with the word-processed document, move the cursor to the place in the document where you want to paste the spreadsheet data and press the **Enter** key. Pressing the **Enter** key inserts a copy of whatever text or graphic you have in the clipboard at the cursor's position. The spreadsheet data you copied will now be a part of the word-processed document.

You may need to reformat the inserted data by changing the tab settings or using other format commands. If you copy data that are too wide to fit across your word-processed document with the margins you have set, the data will wrap around to the next line. As you experiment with data integration, it is a good idea to copy and reformat small portions of your spreadsheets. Later, you can explore more advanced methods to move larger spreadsheet sections into your documents.

Copying charts into word-processed documents is similar to integrating database information for print merging. You must first create, label, and format the charts you want in a spreadsheet file. Once the charts are completed to your satisfaction, you can use the **Window** command to switch to the word-processed document, move the cursor to the position in the document where you want to place the chart, and execute an **Insert Chart** (instead of an **Insert Field**) command.

After the chart is inserted into the document, you can resize it to fit. By using the **Indents & Spacing** command available under the **Format** menu, you'll be able to adjust the height and width of the chart as appropriate to your document.

In the next section, you will learn to insert a data table from an existing spreadsheet file into a word-processed document; to format the table with appropriate commands once it is placed in the word-processed document; to copy a chart (in either landscape or portrait orientation) into a word-processed document; to adjust the height and width of the chart after it is in the document; and to print out word-processed documents that contain data integrated from spreadsheets and charting programs.

Combining Spreadsheet Data with Word-Processed Documents

Orientation

In this exercise, you will create a simple word-processed document to use with the **MY-GRADE.WKS** spreadsheet file that you completed in an earlier chapter. You'll improve the document by adding spreadsheet data to it—the type of grading information used to communicate student progress to parents.

The spreadsheet file you'll use, **MY-GRADE.WKS**, should still be stored on your Works **Data** disk. First you'll open the spreadsheet file, then create a new word-processed document. When the new document is complete, you'll copy the spreadsheet data into it. Finally, you'll print the word-processed document, including the integrated spreadsheet data, and then save the new file before you exit Works.

Getting Started

Use the same procedures to start Works that you have used in the preceding exercises. If you need additional help, consult the more detailed instructions presented in the **Getting Started** section on pages 55–56.

Opening the Necessary Files

When you see the opening Works screen, open the file **MY-GRADE.WKS**. To copy the file from your Works **Data** disk, follow these steps:

1. Press the **O** key to select the **Open Existing File** command.
2. Hold down the **Alt** key and press the **I** (for Directories) key. When the blinking cursor appears in the **Directories** dialog box, press the **down arrow** key to highlight the letter of the disk drive containing your Works **Data** disk, then press the **Enter** key.
3. Hold down the **Alt** key and press the **F** (for **F**iles) key. When the blinking cursor appears in the **Files** dialog box, use the **down arrow** key to highlight **MY-GRADE.WKS**, then press the **Enter** key.
4. Works will copy the file from the disk and place the copy in the computer's temporary memory.

Soon you will see the familiar spreadsheet document displayed on the screen. Next you'll open a new word-processed document, so follow these steps:

1. Press the **Alt** key, then the **F** key to access the **File** menu.
2. Press the **N** (for Create **N**ew File) key to start a new document.
3. Press the **W** (for **W**ord Processor) key to open a new word-processed document.

In a few moments, Works copies the word-processing program into memory, opens a new document, and displays a blinking cursor to indicate that you can now begin entering text.

Creating the Progress Monitor

For this exercise, you'll create a simple "lack of" progress monitor you might send home to parents whose children are doing poorly in your class. You'd like to send home this type of monitor early in the term (say, after the first two tests have been completed and marked), in time for parental intervention to prevent the child from failing the term. You hope that you would mail out only a few of these monitors each term.

With only a few progress monitors to print, you don't need to use the print-merging powers you learned in Chapter 7. Nonetheless, a personalized letter may make a greater impact on parents than the report alone. Because only a few students need this progress monitor, you can enter the appropriate inside address and greeting information for the monitors on each word-processed letter, then use the Works data integration powers to complete the documents.

First, type the text that appears in Figure 10.1. This is the monitor you'll send to the parents of George Cooper. To personalize the letter, substitute the appropriate information for the words in all capital letters (such as YOUR NAME). When you've entered the text, use the **Alt** key or the mouse and the menu bar commands—or their keyboard equivalents—to format the document: boldfacing; right, center, and full justification; and single- and double-spacing. (Consult the exercise in Chapter 5 on formatting a word-processed document if you need help with any of these procedures.)

Be certain to place an extra carriage return after the sentence ending with the phrase, ". . . George will receive a failing grade." When you get to the end of the

YOUR NAME
YOUR OFFICE ADDRESS
YOUR STREET ADDRESS
YOUR CITY, YOUR STATE YOUR ZIP CODE

October 23, 1991

Mr. & Mrs. William Cooper
400 Grant Rd.
Buffalo, NY 14222

Dear Mr. & Mrs. Cooper:
    I am sending this progress monitor to alert you to concerns that I have about George's academic development in my class this year. I hope that by communicating with you at this point in the term, you can work with George to improve his results before it is too late in the marking period to remedy the situation.
    Below, I have included figures representing George's results on this semester's first two tests. In addition, I have listed some class statistics including the average, maximum, and minimum scores for each assignment. The class statistics may help you assess George's performance compared with that of his classmates. As you can see from the scores below, if his academic performance continues as it is now, George will receive a failing grade.

    I hope that you share my concern about George's performance and will do everything you can to help him improve his work over the remainder of the semester. Please feel free to call me at YOUR NUMBER between 2:45 and 3:45 any school day to discuss George's work with me.

Sincerely Yours,

YOUR NAME

Figure 10.1 The progress monitor

sentence, place the extra line in the document by pressing the **Enter** key twice instead of once. You will use that additional space when you copy selected spreadsheet data into the word-processed progress monitor.

Copying the Spreadsheet Data

Once you have finished entering the text and formatting the letter, you will insert the spreadsheet data from the file **MY-GRADES.WKS**. Access the spreadsheet file by following these steps:

1. Press the **Alt** key, then press the **W** key to access the **Window** menu.
2. Press the **2** (for **2 MY-GRADES.WKS**) key to choose the spreadsheet file. In a few moments, you'll see the spreadsheet screen display.

The information you want to copy to the word-processed document is separated into three different sections of the spreadsheet—the column headings, George's scores, and the class statistics. You could copy the data to the progress monitor one section at a time, or you could reassemble the data in the spreadsheet as a single section and then copy that section to the word-processed document. Although either technique will work, let's use the latter method.

1. Position the cursor in cell **A3**. Hold down the **Shift** key, press the **right arrow** key three times, then press the **down arrow** key three times to highlight the column headings—the range of cells from **A3** through **D6**.
2. To copy the data, press the **Alt** key, then the **E** key to access the **Edit** menu.
3. Press the **C** (for **C**opy) key to copy the selected data.
4. Position the cursor in cell **A55**, then press the **Enter** key to insert the copied data.
5. Position the cursor in cell **A12**. Hold down the **Shift** key, then press the **right arrow** key three times to highlight George's test scores—the range of cells from **A12** through **D12**.
6. To copy the data, press the **Alt** key, then the **E** key to access the **Edit** menu, then the **C** key to copy the selected data.
7. Position the cursor in cell **A59**, then press the **Enter** key to insert the copy of George's scores into row **59**.
8. Now position the cursor in cell **A35**. Hold down the **Shift** key, press the **right arrow** key three times, then press the **down arrow** key two times to highlight the class statistics—the range of cells from **A35** through **D37**.
9. To copy the data, press the **Alt** key, then the **E** key to access the **Edit** menu, then the **S** key to apply the **Copy Special** command.

(Remember, you cannot use the **Copy** command in this situation because these cells contain formulas that would be incorrect when copied to new locations.)

10. Position the cursor in cell **A60**, then press the **Enter** key to move the data into the new spreadsheet location.
11. When the **Copy Special** dialog box appears on the screen, select the **Values only** option by pressing the **Enter** key. This will insert the copy of the class statistics into rows **60** through **62**.

You've now assembled the block of data that you want to copy to the progress monitor. To select the data for copying:

1. Position the cursor in cell **A55**. Hold down the **Shift** key, press the **right arrow** key three times, then press the **down arrow** key seven times to highlight the range of cells from **A55** through **D62**.
2. Press the **Alt** key, then the **E** key to access the **Edit** menu.
3. Press the **C** (for **C**opy) key to copy the selected data.

The block of data that you have copied is now temporarily stored in the clipboard portion of the computer's memory.

Inserting Spreadsheet Data into the Progress Monitor

For the next step, you'll return to the word-processed document using the **Window** menu and paste the data into the appropriate position. To access the word-processed document, follow these steps:

1. Press the **Alt** key, then the **W** key to access the **Window** menu.
2. Press the **1** (for **1 WORD1.WPS**) key. In a few moments, the document will appear on the screen.
3. Position the cursor on the blank line after the phrase ". . . George will receive a failing grade." This is where you want to insert the copied data.
4. To insert the data, press the **Enter** key one time.

The copied information will quickly appear in the document, with each column of data separated by tabs.

In transferring the data, Works has included extra spaces in the lines of equal signs (=). These spaces correspond to the spreadsheet columns but serve no function in the word-processed document. Position the cursor on the spaces, and use the **Delete** (or **Del**) key to remove them; continue to remove the excess equal signs so that the rows align with the other columns of data.

A few more enhancements will finish off your progress monitor. First, let's emphasize the integrated data with boldface type. To do so, follow these steps:

1. Position the cursor below the HIGH SCORE row.
2. Hold down the **Shift** key, then press the **up arrow** key eight times, until the highlighting includes all of the data copied from the spreadsheet.
3. Hold down the **Control** (**Ctrl**) key and press the **B** (for **B**old) key so that the information appears in boldface type.

Now let's position the integrated data in the center of the word-processed document:

1. Make sure that all the data integrated from the spreadsheet document are still highlighted. If the data are still selected, continue with the next step. If not, repeat step 2 above to select it, then continue with this procedure.
2. Hold down the **Control** (**Ctrl**) key and press the **C** (for **C**enter) key to center the information.

The integrated data is now included in the "lack of progress" monitor, and the document is complete. Before you print it, however, let's continue the careful practice of saving the document to avoid losing information.

Saving the Progress Monitor

Because you made no changes to your spreadsheet file, **MY-GRADE.WKS**, you don't need to resave it. However, you do need to store the new word-processed document on your Works **Data** disk before you exit Works. You can use the same procedures you always use to save a file, but this time use the name **MY-INTEG** to store the report.

To store the file on your Works **Data** disk, follow these steps:

1. Press the **Alt** key and then the **F** (for **F**ile) key.
2. Press the **A** key to select the **Save As** command. Works suggests that you save the document using the name **WORD1.WKS** on the active disk.
3. Type the name for your file, MY-INTEG, and press the **Enter** key. Works will quickly store the file on your Works **Data** disk under the name **MY-INTEG.WPS**. (Recall that Works adds the **.WPS** extension to your file name to show that it is a word-processed file.)

Printing the Progress Monitor

Now that the document is stored on your data disk, you can safely print the finished product without worrying about losing data. To print the progress monitor, follow these steps:

1. Press the **Alt** key, then the **P** key to access the **Print** menu.
2. To change the left and right margins so that the document will fit easily on one page, press the **M** (for Page Setup & **M**argins) key. Notice that the **Page Setup & Margins** dialog box appears on the screen.
3. Hold down the **Alt** key, then press the **E** (for L**e**ft margin) key to position the cursor in the **Left margin** box.
4. Type .5 (for one-half an inch) in the box, then press the **Tab** key to move the cursor to the **Right margin** box.
5. Type .5 in the **Right margin** box, then press the **Enter** key to accept those settings.

Your next step is to preview the document on the computer screen before you print it on paper. Follow these steps:

1. Press the **Alt** key, then the **P** key to access the **Print** menu.
2. Press the **V** key to preview the document on the screen. Notice that the **Print Preview** dialog box appears on the screen.

3. Hold down the **Alt** key, then press the **P** (for **P**review) key to preview the document on the screen.
4. If the document appears as you wish, press the **P** (for **P**rint) key to print the document on paper.

If you want to make changes before you print, press the **Esc** key to cancel the printing process. Make whatever changes you wish to improve your progress monitor, then finish printing the document.

Creating Additional Progress Monitors

You spent a considerable amount of time producing a single copy of the progress monitor. However, once the first monitor is complete, making progress monitors for other students becomes much easier. You'll need to change only the inside address, the greeting, the student's name, and the student's spreadsheet data. You can create and print each additional progress monitor in only a few minutes, simply by entering the individualized data.

One final but important point: if you want to issue a progress monitor for each student—reporting both good and bad news—you could use data integration techniques to simplify the task. Once the spreadsheet data is available, you simply would add the same number of fields to your student records database as you have scores in your spreadsheet (assignments, totals, and grades). Next, you would copy all of the students' data from the spreadsheet into the student records database. Once the data are available, you can add print-merging placeholders to your word-processed progress monitors and print out a class set. This process is easy to complete and valuable to parents who will learn about their children's performances, whether the news is good or bad.

Exiting Works

You can safely exit Works without losing the information in your file. To exit the program and shut down the computer, use the same steps that you have used in the preceding exercises. If you need additional help, consult the more detailed instructions presented in the **Exiting Works** section on pages 60–61.

Combining Charts with Word-Processed Documents

Orientation

In this exercise, you'll use the **ETHNIC.WKS** spreadsheet file that you used to create a pie graph in Chapter 9 on charting. You'll add that pie chart to a report on student demographics for your administrators. The spreadsheet file,

ETHNIC.WKS, should still be stored on your Works **Data** disk. You'll open the spreadsheet file, then create a word-processed cover letter to accompany a grant proposal.

When you complete the letter, you'll add a pie chart placeholder to the document, save it using the name **CHAR-INT**, print out the finished word-processed product, and then exit Works. When the finished letter is stored on your Works **Data** disk, it will contain the pie chart placeholder, in addition to the text you will enter with the keyboard.

Getting Started

You have already created the file **ETHNIC.WKS**, so you'll open that existing file first, then create a new word-processed document. Use the same procedures to start Works that you have used in the preceding exercises. If you need additional help, consult the more detailed instructions presented in the **Getting Started** section on pages 55–56.

Opening the Necessary Files

When you see the opening Works screen, open the file **ETHNIC.WKS**. To copy the file into the computer's memory from your Works **Data** disk, follow these steps:

1. Press the **O** key to select the **Open Existing File** command.
2. Hold down the **Alt** key, and press the **I** (for Directories) key. When the blinking cursor appears in the **Directories** dialog box, press the **down arrow** key to highlight the letter of the disk drive containing your Works **Data** disk, then press the **Enter** key.
3. Hold down the **Alt** key and press the **F** (for Files) key. When the blinking cursor appears in the **Files** dialog box, use the **down arrow** key to highlight **ETHNIC.WKS**, then press the **Enter** key.
4. Works will copy the file from the disk and place the copy in the computer's temporary memory. In a few moments, you will see the familiar spreadsheet document appear on the screen.

Next you'll open a new word-processed document, so follow these steps:

1. Press the **Alt** key and then the **F** key to access the **File** menu.
2. Press the **N** (for Create **N**ew File) key to start a new document.
3. Press the **W** (for **W**ord Processor) key to open a new word-processor document.

In a few moments, Works copies the word processor into memory and displays the opening screen of a new document. The blinking cursor indicates that you can now begin to enter text.

Creating the Proposal Cover Letter

Now use the keyboard to enter the text in Figure 10.2. This is a cover letter for a grant proposal you want to submit to your superintendent. Substitute the appropriate information for the words in all capital letters (such as YOUR NAME) to personalize the letter. When you've entered the text, use the **Alt** key or the mouse and the menu bar commands (or their keyboard equivalents) to add the indicated formatting to the document, including boldfacing; right, center, and full justification; and single- and double-spacing. (Consult Chapter 5 on formatting a word-processed document if you need help with any of the procedures.)

In addition, be certain to place an extra carriage return after the sentence ending with the phrase ". . . to help with the project if the grant is funded." Place the extra line in the document by pressing the **Enter** key twice instead of once at the end of the sentence. You will use that additional space in the document when you place the selected pie chart into the word-processed letter.

Inserting the Chart into the Cover Letter

Now let's insert the chart placeholder into the appropriate section of the proposal letter. Use the arrow keys or the mouse to place the cursor on the blank line after the second paragraph (the one ending ". . . if the grant is funded"). You can insert the chart placeholder in this portion of your letter by following these steps:

1. Press the **Alt** key, then press the **E** key to access the **Edit** menu.
2. Press the **I** (for **I**nsert Chart) key to insert a chart placeholder in the document position that you have selected.

In a few moments, the **Insert Chart** dialog box will appear on the screen (see Figure 10.3). In the **Spreadsheets** box, there is only one spreadsheet selection

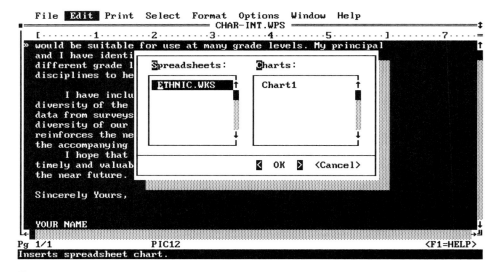

Figure 10.3 Insert Chart dialog box

YOUR NAME
YOUR OFFICE ADDRESS
YOUR STREET ADDRESS
YOUR CITY, YOUR STATE YOUR ZIP CODE

June 7, 1991

Dr. Francis Graceson
Superintendent of Grant Public Schools
47 Hunter Avenue
Placeville, NY 14216

Dear Dr. Graceson:

I am writing this cover letter to accompany my response to your call for grant proposals designed to generate classroom activities that enhance multi-cultural appreciation. I implemented a series of global community activities with my class at Grant Public School this year; all were well-received by the students and judged to be very successful by my principal. She suggested that I submit this grant proposal because she wants to see the activities adopted by many more classes next year.

I hope to modify and expand the activities this summer so that they would be suitable for use at many grade levels. My principal and I have identified teachers with experience from different grade levels and expertise in different disciplines to help with the project if the grant is funded.

I have included this pie chart to illustrate the ethnic diversity of the students in our school. We obtained this data from surveys conducted last month. The great ethnic diversity of our students, conveyed by the pie chart, reinforces the need for activities such as those detailed in the accompanying report.

I hope that you will agree that this proposal is both timely and valuable. I look forward to hearing from you in the near future.

Sincerely Yours,

YOUR NAME

Figure 10.2 Cover letter for a grant proposal

available, **ETHNICS.WKS**, because you have only one spreadsheet document open now. Press the **down arrow** key one time to highlight the **ETHNICS.WKS** spreadsheet, and notice that the **Chart1** option appears in the **Charts** box. **Chart1** is the pie chart containing the ethnic distribution data that you will include in your proposal letter.

To insert a chart placeholder at this position in the document, follow these steps:

1. Press the **Tab** key once to position the cursor in the **Charts** box.
2. Press the **down arrow** key once to highlight the **Chart1** option.
3. Press the **Enter** key to insert that chart in the proposal letter.

In a few moments, the chart placeholders will appear on the screen. To view the actual chart, you have to either print the document on paper or use the print preview capability to inspect the document's appearance on the screen (in the familiar Greeking display).

Sizing and Positioning the Chart

The next procedure is to establish the height and width of the chart. Let's make the chart smaller so it doesn't dominate the letter. To adjust the size of the chart, you will use the **Indents & Spacing** command in the **Format** menu. First, select the chart placeholder for resizing:

1. Position the cursor on the asterisk (*) to the left of the placeholder.
2. With the cursor on the asterisk, hold down the **Shift** key and press the **right arrow** key to highlight the placeholder.

When the placeholder has been selected, you can change the chart's size and positioning. To modify the chart's proportions, follow these steps:

1. Press the **Alt** key, then press the **T** key to access the **Format** menu.
2. Press the **A** (for Indents & Sp**a**cing) key to access the **Indents & Spacing** dialog box (Figure 10.4).

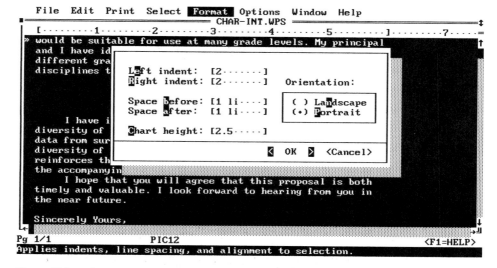

Figure 10.4 **Indents & Spacing** dialog box after data have been entered

3. Type **2** (for two inches) to represent the new left indent, then press the **Tab** key to move to the **Right Indent** box.
4. Type **2** (for two inches) to represent the new right indent, then press the **Tab** key three times to move to the **Chart Height** box.
5. Type **2.5** (for two and one-half inches) to represent the new height of the chart, then press the **Enter** key.

The resized chart should now fit into the proposal letter without being too overpowering. The chart's message is easily visible, but the body of the letter still occupies the dominant portion of the proposal letter. Now that the letter is complete, let's save the finished product before printing it on paper.

Saving the Letter

Now you know how to include either charts or spreadsheet data in your word-processed documents and print out the finished products. Since you made no changes to your spreadsheet file, **ETHNIC.WKS**, you do not need to resave it. However, you do need to store the new word-processed document containing the pie chart on your Works **Data** disk before you exit Works.

You can use the same procedures you always use to save a new file. This time, use the name **CHAR-INT** to store the report by following these steps:

1. Press the **Alt** key and then the **F** (for **F**ile) key.
2. Press the **A** key to select the **Save As** command. Works suggests that you save the document using the name **WORD1.WPS** on the active disk.
3. Type **CHAR-INT** to name your file and press the **Enter** key. Works will quickly store the file on your Works **Data** disk under the name **CHAR-INT.WPS**.

Printing the Letter

Now that the document is stored on your Works **Data** disk, you can safely print it on paper. To print the finished letter, follow these steps:

1. Press the **Alt** key and then the **P** key to access the **Print** menu.
2. Press the **M** (for Page Setup & **M**argins) key to change the left and right margins so that the document will fit on one page even after the chart is included. Notice that the **Page Setup & Margins** dialog box appears on the screen.
3. Hold down the **Alt** key and press the **E** (for L**e**ft margin) key to position the cursor in the **Left margin** box.
4. Type **.5** (for one-half inch) in the box, then press the **Tab** key to move the cursor to the **Right margin** box.
5. Type **.5** in the **Right margin** box, then press the **Enter** key to apply those settings. Your document should now fit on a single page.

The next step will be to preview the table on the screen before you print it on paper. To preview the database table, follow these steps:

1. Press the **Alt** key, then the **P** key to access the **Print** menu.
2. Press the **V** (for Pre**v**iew) key to preview the document on the screen. Notice that the **Print Preview** dialog box appears on the screen.
3. Hold down the **Alt** key and press the **P** (for **P**review) key to preview the document on the screen.
4. If the document appears as you wish, press the **P** (for **P**rint) key to print the document on paper.

If the previewed document will not fit on a single page, or if you want to make other changes before you print, press the **Esc** key to cancel the printing process and return to the word-processed document. Make the document changes that you wish, or use the **Print** menu commands to change the document's margins. When you have made the changes you want, repeat the previous steps to print the document.

Exiting Works

Now you can safely exit Works without losing the information in your file. To exit the program and shut down the computer, follow the same steps you have used in previous exercises. If you need additional help, consult the more detailed instructions presented in the **Exiting Works** section on pages 60–61.

Additional Activities

Educational Activities
Producing end-of-the-year reports that include tables and charts
Generating salary increase requests that include tables and charts
Creating student assignment sheets that include charts
Creating student assignment sheets that include data tables
Teaching students data integration techniques for reports

General Activities
Producing financial reports for clubs and groups that include tables
Creating demographic reports for professional organizations that include charts

11   Focusing on Communications

A communications program allows you to connect your computer with other computers in the same room or across the country. Communications programs serve as mediators that help make many other computers in the world accessible to you. If a charting program is like having a draftsman and a drawing program is like having an artist, then a communications program is similar to having a mediator who helps make many other computers accessible to you so that you can share ideas or information with others. The communications program lets you exchange data with other computers regardless of their type, model, or location. When you use communications software to connect distant computers via the telephone lines, then you are engaging in **telecommunications**.

Let's use another scenario to illustrate the utility of a communications program. Educators can use communications in many ways, but for the purposes of this discussion, we'll focus on a rather simple scenario. Let's imagine that you and three colleagues are engaged in a curriculum revision project. You all live in different areas of your city and have different commitments outside of work. It's difficult to find convenient times to meet for the project. Face-to-face meetings, whether they're scheduled after school, in the evenings, or on weekends, are always inconvenient for some group members. However, the project is important for your careers and has an impending deadline.

One possible solution is to communicate by telephones arranged to handle conference calls. Still, it's very difficult to carry on a four-party discussion under those circumstances, and, after long conversations, no one has all the notes and ideas recorded accurately. Further, after the calls are complete, each person must sit down and write up his or her part of the project. These sections must then be compiled later into a single, consistent document and then rewritten—a task that no one will welcome. The telephone conference approach, therefore, does not easily solve the problem.

Instead, you decide to adopt a communications solution, because everyone in the group already has a computer, a modem, and a telephone line. With this approach, all project members work on their parts of the project in their own homes, on their own computers. Periodically, perhaps twice a week, each member sends the full text of his or her part of the new curriculum proposal to all the other members. The text is transmitted from one member's computer to another's over the telephone lines—not through the mail. As a result, everyone can peruse the entire project on a continuing basis so that it remains consistent and cogent. Any suggestions or questions project members have about another individual's work can be added to the communicated text in a different font (easily discernable from the project font) and then returned to the original author for clarification or response.

This communications approach also lets the project team easily elicit comments and suggestions from the local administration, as well as district- and state level-curriculum coordinators who are also on-line (i.e., who have a computer, modem, and communications software). These expert opinions can be accessed and incorporated into the project design in a far more timely fashion than would be possible without telecommunications. Developing the curriculum in this manner helps ensure that when the project is complete, everyone involved in its adoption will have had an ample opportunity to help shape and respond to it.

When this simple scenario is expanded to include all the other benefits that communications programs can provide, the advantages of telecommunications will be clear. Communications programs allow educators to connect with each other and with vast databases of information, which can be helpful to themselves and their students.

An Introduction to Communications Programs

As we mentioned in the last section, using a communications program is like having a skilled interpreter available to you who can connect your computer with other computers around the world. Like the other productivity applications that we've studied, communications programs need some orientation. First, let's examine some of the general terminology associated with communications.

For telecommunications to be possible, you must have more equipment than just your computer and printer. We mentioned one new piece of equipment in the last section, a **modem**. A modem—short for **mo**dulator/**dem**odulator—is a device that allows you to connect your computer to the telephone lines and then send information from your machine to other computers that are similarly equipped. When you send a message, your modem modulates your computer's digital information into an analog form that the telephone lines can recognize. The modem on the other end of the telephone line (where you are sending the message) will demodulate the signal, changing it back from the analog form of the telephone to the digital form that the computer will recognize. Without a modem, you cannot communicate with other computers over standard telephone lines. Naturally, as well as having a modem, you must also have a telephone line available to connect to your computer.

Modems come in a wide range of prices and quality standards. The most important feature of a modem is its **baud rate**, the speed at which data can be transferred. Baud rates vary from a very slow 300 baud (you can read the text as it crosses the screen), to the common 1200 and 2400 baud, to a high-end figure (for general purposes) of 9600 baud. The higher the baud rate, the faster the data transfer and the shorter the amount of time on-line.

The time spent on-line is often an important consideration because you are charged by the phone company accordingly. Time is especially expensive in the case of long-distance telecommunications (connecting with computers in distant locations) and in the case of commercial network services such as Prodigy®, CompuServe®, and DIALOG℠. One other consideration about baud rate is worth noting: the modems at either end of the data transfer process must support the same baud rate. You can only transfer data at 2400 baud, for example, if both your modem and the modem at the other end of the line support that speed. Modem speed is an example of the need for compatibility between the computers involved in data transfer.

The issue of compatibility involves more than just baud rate, however. The computers involved in the communications process must establish a common set of rules so that the information sent between them can be translated. The compatibility rules (or protocol) include **parity**, **data size**, **stop bits**, and **handshake**. With these terms, users agree on a common language before communicating with each other; all the terms establish consistent settings for the transfer of data between distant computers.

Although these compatibility considerations can sound daunting to a novice telecommunicator, for the most part they need not concern you. Generally, the communications program that you use (Microsoft Works, in this instance) will establish a commonplace configuration, and you will use that setting to send and receive data. The exercises in this chapter all involve the transfer of files between two computers using Microsoft Works, so compatibility will not be an issue; the default configuration on each system will be identical. The point at which you purchase a modem and try unsuccessfully to transfer data is the appropriate time for you to make your communication settings consistent with the user to whom you are attempting to transfer data.

However, many individuals using this book do not have the necessary equipment to do the telecommunications exercise using actual telephone lines. Because of this, the communications exercise in the following section will simulate telecommunications, using a **null-modem** cable, one that connects two computers in the same room.

A null-modem cable connects two computers directly and bypasses the modulator-demodulator step necessary when sending data across telephone lines. Null-modem cables are available at most local electronics stores at a minimal expense. Use the cable to connect the serial ports of the two computers. If you do not have a modem and cannot locate a null-modem cable, you can still follow the exercises in this chapter. Although this will only be a simulated activity, the process you will follow is identical to the one you would use if you had a modem with telephone lines connected to your computer. However, you obviously will not be able to exchange files or text between computers without either a modem or a null-modem cable.

Well, that is enough on the theory of communications programs. Now it is time for you to master the Microsoft Works communicating powers. In the next section, you will learn to send and receive files in a classroom setting to simulate telecommunications. If you have the necessary equipment—a modem, a telephone line, and the telephone number of another computer user with the same equipment—the simulated steps that you'll follow in the upcoming exercises will work equally well in a real telecommunications situation.

Transferring Text and Files with Communications Programs

Orientation

We'll use the power of the Microsoft Works communications program to connect computers and exchange files. In this exercise, you will learn to transfer an existing word-processed file from one computer to another nearby computer. Before you can continue with the exercise, you'll need to connect two IBM-compatible computers with your null-modem cable. The following section provides instructions to guide you through this procedure. Consult the reference manual that came with your computer if you need additional assistance. Once you have the two computers connected, you'll use the Works communications program to transfer files from one computer to the other.

First, *make certain that both computers are turned off* before you proceed with this exercise. Connecting a null-modem cable to an operating computer does not present any danger to you, but you could damage the computers if they are not turned off. Better safer than poorer: turn off both computers before you continue.

Connecting the Two Computers

If you have a telephone line and a modem available to connect to your IBM-compatible, you can skip this part of the instructions. The instructions for installing your modem will be included in the reference manuals that accompany the modem. Use them to guide you through the installation procedures.

When your modem is hooked up, instead of linking two adjoining computers as instructed in this section, you should locate the telephone number of a friend with equivalent equipment (a modem, an IBM-compatible computer, and communications software such as Works), and complete the exercise over the telephone lines. Better still, you should try to locate the local telephone number for one of the many educational bulletin boards available across the country and begin exploring the world of telecommunications.

If you don't have a modem, you can still learn how to use the communications program in preparation for the time that you do purchase one. To complete this exercise, you need two IBM-compatibles (placed side by side) and a null-modem cable. Use the same port that connects an IBM-compatible to a serial printer. To hook up the null-modem cable, follow these steps:

1. From the back of the IBM-compatible, disconnect (unplug) the serial printer cable from the printer port (the small outlet where the printer cable connects the printer to the computer). If your printer cable is attached to the computer with small screws, you may need a screwdriver to complete this operation.
2. Now connect (plug in) the null-modem cable to the same serial port from which you removed the printer cable. (You can leave the other end of the printer cable connected to the printer so that reconnecting your printer will be easy when this communication exercise is complete.)
3. Next, connect the other end of the null-modem cable to the serial port of the other IBM-compatible. When you have finished, each computer should have an end of the cable connected to its serial port. If that is correct, you are ready to communicate through your two computers.

Getting Started

Use the same procedures to start Works that you have used in the preceding exercises. If you need additional help, consult the more detailed instructions presented in the **Getting Started** section on pages 55–56.

Opening a New Communications Document

When you see the opening Works screen, you will create a new communications document, so follow these steps:

1. Press the **Alt** key and then the **F** key to access the **File** menu.
2. Press the **N** (for Create **N**ew File) key to start a new document.
3. Press the **C** (for **C**ommunications) key to open a new communications document.

In a few moments, Works copies the communications program into memory and displays the opening screen of a new document. The blinking cursor indicates you can now begin using the communications application. Duplicate the preceding steps on the second computer so that both machines are running Works and have a new communications document open in both memories. When this has been accomplished, proceed to the next section.

Connecting and Establishing Consistent Settings

For the first step, you will use the **Connect** command to prepare the computers to communicate with each other. To do so, follow these steps on each computer:

1. Press the **Alt** key and then press the **C** key to access the **Connect** menu.
2. Press the **C** key again to select the **Connect** option and begin simulating an on-line experience.

Notice that the elapsed time clock on the bottom left-hand part of the screen displays the amount of time you have been connected—an important consideration when you must pay for time on commercial telecommunications services. In this simulation, you do not need to worry about the elapsed time.

To establish consistent communications settings for the computers, follow these steps:

1. Press the **Alt** key, then press the **O** key to access the **Options** menu.
2. Press the **M** (for Communication) key to access the **Communication** dialog box (see Figure 11.1).

This dialog box displays the default settings for the Microsoft Works communications program. You can change any of these you wish, but since both com-

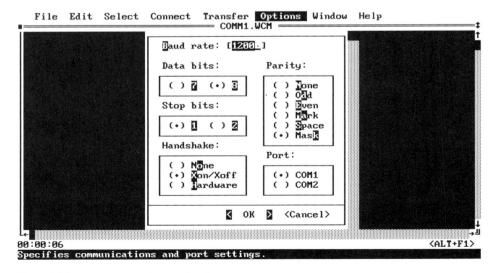

Figure 11.1 Communication dialog box

puters are using Works for this exercise, you won't need to make any alterations. If you have an opportunity to use telecommunications later, you will access this box to establish the settings to use with your on-line colleague or the bulletin board you explore. For this exercise, press the **Enter** key to indicate that the current settings are acceptable. Now you are ready to send text from one computer to the other.

Sending Text

To communicate text between computers, one IBM-compatible has to send the text, the other has to receive it. Let's select the option that allows you to witness the transfer of text on the screen as it occurs. On the *computer receiving the text,* follow these steps:

1. Press the **Alt** key, then press the **O** key to access the **Options** menu.
2. Press the **T** (for **T**erminal) key to access the **Terminal** dialog box.
3. Hold down the **Alt** key and press the **E** (for Local **e**cho) key to echo (or display) the transfers to the screen as well as to the disk. This command allows you to see the transfer process on the screen.
4. Press the **Enter** key to apply the **Local echo** command.

To prepare the computer to receive text, follow these steps:

1. Press the **Alt** key, then press the **T** (for **T**ransfer) key to access the **Transfer** menu.
2. Press the **C** (for **C**apture Text) key to access the **Capture text** dialog box.
3. Type **COM-TEXT** (**com**munications **text**) to name the incoming text, then press the **Enter** key to prepare to receive the text.

Now wait patiently for the other computer to send the text to the receiving computer.

On the *computer sending the text,* follow these steps to send the text file:

1. Press the **Alt** key, then press the **O** key to access the **Options** menu.
2. Press the **T** (for **T**erminal) key to access the **Terminal** dialog box.
3. Hold down the **Alt** key and press the **E** (for Local **e**cho) key to echo (or display) the transfer to the screen as well as to the disk.
4. Press the **Enter** key to apply the **Local echo** command.

To prepare the computer to send text, follow these steps:

1. Press the **Alt** key, then press the **T** (for **T**ransfer) key to access the **Transfer** menu.
2. Press the **T** (for Send **T**ext) key to access the **Send text** dialog box (see Figure 11.2).

Let's send a copy of the text in your first exercise, **LETTER.WPS**, to the other computer. To send the document, follow these steps:

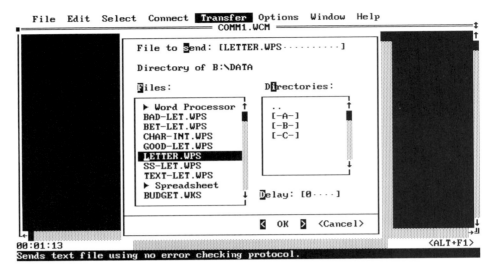

Figure 11.2 Send text dialog box

1. Hold down the **Alt** key and press the **F** (for **F**iles) key. When the blinking cursor appears in the **Files** dialog box, use the **down arrow** key to highlight **LETTER.WPS.**
2. Press the **Enter** key, and Works will send a copy to the computer.

On the screens of both computers, you should see the text of your first letter being transferred from one machine to the other. (Incidentally, the characters you see displayed on the screen are being transmitted at a speed of 1200 baud.) If some of the lines of text seem a bit strange, don't worry; that effect is produced by the different screen settings. You are only transmitting text—that is, the characters themselves—and not the formatting, such as the margin settings, boldface type, and fully justified paragraphs to enhance the appearance of a document.

Ending the Text Transfer

In a few moments, the text file will be transferred from one computer to the other. Your next procedure will signal the computers that the text transfer process is over. On the IBM-compatible that *received the text,* follow these steps to end the transfer process:

1. Press the **Alt** key, then press the **T** key to access the **Transfer** menu.
2. Press the **C** (for End **C**apture Text) key to end the text capturing process.

By the way, the text from the transfer is now stored on the Works **Data** disk in the drive of the receiving computer.

On the computer that *sent the text,* the transfer process automatically ends as soon as all of the text has been sent; therefore, you do not need to undertake any special procedures on that machine. Although the text you now see on the screen is distracting, the screen display is only an echo or record of the communications exercise (text transferring) that you just completed. If you wanted to remove the text you see displayed on the screen, you would have to close this communications document and then start the communications process all over. For the moment, rather than restart the communications procedures, you'll simply disregard the screen text and proceed to the next exercise.

Sending a File

This time, instead of just text, you'll send an entire file to the other computer. Just as before, one IBM-compatible must send the file and the other must receive it.

On the *computer receiving the file,* follow these steps:

1. Press the **Alt** key, then press the **T** key to access the **Transfer** menu.
2. Press the **R** (for **R**eceive File) key to access the **Receive File** dialog box.
3. Type **COM-FILE** (**com**munications **file**) to name the incoming file, then press the **Enter** key to prepare to receive the file.

A **Waiting** message box appears on the screen of the receiving computer to inform you that it is waiting for the other computer to send the file (see Figure 11.3). Notice that the number of **Retries** increases as the computer continues trying to receive a file. After nine attempts (which take place in two or three minutes), the computer will change the **Waiting** message to a **Transfer ended** message to inform you that the waiting period is over. Allow that to happen once, then press the **Enter** key to acknowledge the message. Now repeat the

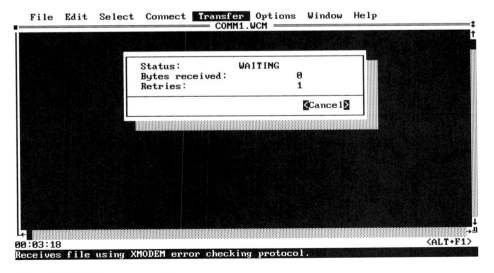

Figure 11.3 Waiting message box

same procedures, but this time send the file before the **Transfer ended** message appears. To repeat the process, follow these steps:

1. Press the **Alt** key, then press the **T** key to access the **Transfer** menu.
2. Press the **R** (for **R**eceive File) key to access the **Receive File** dialog box.
3. Type **COM-FILE** (**com**munications **file**) to name the incoming file, then press the **Enter** key to prepare the computer to receive the file.

On the *computer sending the file*, follow these steps:
1. Press the **Alt** key, then press the **T** key to access the **Transfer** menu.
2. Press the **S** (for **S**end File) key to access the **Send File** dialog box.

Let's send a copy of your spreadsheet file, **ETHNIC.WKS**, to the other computer. To send the file, follow these steps:

1. Hold down the **Alt** key and press the **F** key. When the blinking cursor appears in the **Files** dialog box, use the **down arrow** key to highlight **ETHNIC.WKS**.
2. Press the **Enter** key, and Works will temporarily display the **Waiting** message box and then will begin sending a copy of the file to the receiving computer.

In a few moments, you will see the message box change; the number to the right of the **Bytes sent** box steadily increases on the screen of the sending computer as the file transfer process continues. Correspondingly, the number to the right of the **Bytes received** box will continue to increase on the screen of the receiving computer.

In several minutes, the transfer will be complete and you will have sent files from one computer to another. You can use these same techniques to send programs and data files of all types between remote computers. After you quit the Works communications program, you can view the file that you just transferred by opening the files from the Works **Data** disk in the receiving computer.

Since you have already stored the files that you transferred between the computers, you don't need to save any files before you quit Works and shut down the system. Therefore, you are ready to exit Works in the usual manner. When you close the communications document that you used in the transfer process, the computer asks if you want to save the changes to **COMM1.WCM** (.**WCM** is the extension that Works uses to identify communications documents). Press the **right arrow** key to select **No** (you do not want to save the document), then press the **Enter** key. Next, the computer will ask, **OK to disconnect?** Press the **Enter** key to agree that it is okay to disconnect, then complete the exiting process.

Exiting Works

You can safely exit Works without losing any files. To exit the program and shut down the computer, use the same steps that you have used in previous exercises. If you need additional help, consult the more detailed instructions presented in the **Exiting Works** section on pages 60–61. When you have finished turning off your computer, remove the null-modem cable from the serial ports of the two computers and replace the printer cables that connect the computers with your printer.

Integrating Communications into the Instructional Process

Now that you are familiar with the Microsoft Works communications package, let's examine several approaches for using communications in the classroom. If you do not have the necessary communications hardware discussed in the chapter (that is, a modem connected to a standard telephone line), you will not be able to complete these activities as actual telecommunications exercises.

However, most of these activities can easily work, even if you do not have access to the communications hardware. For instance, your students can complete their computer-generated projects with traditional procedures. Instead of telecommunicating the completed work by modem, they can communicate it by mail. The success of some projects might suffer from the loss of motivating features such as the immediate response time provided by modem telecommunications. However, many of the activities can be completed successfully without the use of a modem.

Some of the telecommunications expenses—such as telephone line usage charges, network service joining fees, and monthly service charges—can be problematic. Therefore, you may want to begin your explorations of telecommunications with simple projects. Activities linking your class with another class of the same grade level at a distant school are especially effective. For instance, if you teach in an urban setting, connecting with a class from a rural community can offer students interesting contrasts in lifestyles and experiences. The physical distance separating the two classes is less important than the demographic contrast of the students.

Once your students gain experience with communications projects, you can introduce them to educational network services such as Prodigy, Tech Net®, or IRIS®. These educational services often have clearly delineated pricing structures that permit advanced budgeting so you can prevent unpleasant surprise expenses later. The options provided by these educational services vary from network to network, but they generally include on-line databases for student research projects, electronic mail capabilities, and extras like educational forums that allow your students to interact with famous authors or participate in national science projects.

When you decide to join a network service, try to find a friend or colleague who is an experienced network user. Ask your colleague to serve as your local "guru," helping you determine which service is best suited to your instructional objectives, equipment, and telecommunications budget. Having a knowledgeable support person available locally to assist your decision-making process and to explain confusing system elements will prove very useful.

The following suggestions can all be used effectively with a single computer in the classroom, although they could also be conducted in a computer lab. As always, a large monitor or an LCD with an overhead projector is helpful for introducing students to the use of the communications software, but the devices are not at all essential to any of these activities.

The Global Classroom

An excellent first project to introduce students to telecommunications involves linking students in your class with students in another class at a distant site. Educational researchers have observed that many of our students do not have an awareness of the world outside of their own immediate environment—home, classroom, and community. The Global Classroom activity introduces students to others of their age from different locations, backgrounds, and even nationalities. By establishing this linkage, you will open the world to your students, encouraging them to understand themselves more completely by comparing the experiences of other students their age to their own.

To make this activity most meaningful, try to establish personal contact with the teacher of the cooperating class before you undertake the project. Meeting together to discuss the objectives of the project is a key to its success. If you cannot meet face-to-face, telephone or mail communication is the next best choice. However, before you begin the project, make sure that both of you are committed to following through with the instructional activities planned. Agree on a tentative schedule for each portion of the project, one that accounts for the realities of the school year—such as time constraints at the start of the school year, holidays, meetings, and special events. Use several of the activities discussed in this section (or your own ideas) as a beginning, then expand the scope of the project later.

Once you have identified an appropriate site and an interested teacher, determine the type of activities in which your students will engage. The nature of the activity should match the type of learning outcomes that you want your students to achieve.

Related Activities

- Promote your project with the administration and parents by having your students use Works to create a newsletter or brochure detailing the project activities and your students' reactions to them.
- If your budget is too limited to permit communications projects, consider discussing your project ideas with local business and industry representatives. Often they are willing to sponsor technology-oriented projects of this type.
- If you have a limited budget and cannot arrange for support from local business and industry representatives, consider discussing your project ideas with your school's parent groups to see if they will sponsor it.

Interest Surveys

An interest survey that introduces two classes of students to each other is an excellent first communications project. At the start of the school year, have your students conduct an interest survey of favorites and least favorites similar to the one discussed in Chapter 6. When all students have completed the surveys, develop a database file containing student responses. When the database document is complete, use it as the first communications exchange file.

When you receive the database from the other class, let students explore the file to get acquainted with the students in the other class. Challenge your students to identify the characteristics that are similar for students from both classes (possibly favorite foods or movies) and characteristics that are different from the students in the other class (possibly pastimes or daily schedules).

To supplement this activity, instruct your students to create bar charts comparing their data with the results from the companion class. These charts could be telecommunicated within spreadsheet files. In this manner, each class could prepare charts on particular topics of interest and the two groups could share charts.

Electronic Pen Pals

Establishing electronic pen pals is a standard first communications project. Early in the school year, have your students telecommunicate letters of introduction to students from another school. Have your students explore a database compiled by the other class to match students with similar interests. Arrange for the letters to be sent on the same day so that each student in both classes sends and receives a letter. Ensure that every student receives a letter by asking for volunteers to write additional letters to cover absences or differences in class size. When the letters arrive, print them out so that each student can read his or her letter.

Throughout the school year, periodically assign your students to write additional letters—perhaps at the end of the first quarter, before or after vacations, at the first sign of spring (if climatically appropriate), and near the end of the school year. Students who develop strong relationships with their pen pals may wish to write more frequently. However, assign all students to write letters at specific intervals or the activity will prove frustrating for those students who write but receive no response.

Schoolwide Survey

After your students have completed the first interest surveys and have exchanged the resulting database files, ask students to conduct a similar survey of all the students in your school. When the surveys are completed and returned, have your class create a database file to hold that information. Next, have your students compare these data with the findings from their own class and their partner class. As an additional activity, you could instruct students to create bar charts to compare the four sets of data: the two sets of survey results from the classes and the two sets of survey results from the school populations. These charts could also be telecommunicated within spreadsheet files, so each class could prepare charts on topics of interest and share them with each other.

Related Activity

- Have the two classes of students survey their parents (modified as necessary for the survey population) to compare the generational differences between the groups. Assign the students to create bar charts of the data. Then ask the students to examine the charts to determine if their favorites and opinions are more similar to those of their peers or those of their parents.

Distant Peer Editing

Having students engage in process-writing with peer editing groups can be very effective for helping students write for an audience. However, often students have difficulty expressing open opinions when they are face-to-face with their peers. That discomfort is removed when peer editing can take place as part of a telecommunications project. Ask your students to complete their papers so they can be sent to members of the companion class for edits and comments. Because your students will want to impress their distant peer reviewers, they will be motivated to work especially hard on these writing projects.

Before you telecommunicate the files, assign peer editors based on writing ability or by random assignment so that the students will not be inhibited by being paired with their pen pals. Have the peer editors enter their comments in a different font (such as strikethrough) so students can easily distinguish the comments from the original text. When the files are returned, have students print them out, read the comments, and make editing changes based on the suggestions. After they complete the editing process, have the students delete the text in strikethrough characters supplied by their peer editor and then print out the completed paper (they might also telecommunicate a finished version of the paper to their peer editors for perusal).

Sharing Instructional Materials

Whenever you have your students create projects with Works (such as the **Planets** and the **Presidents** databases or graphs produced with **The Survey Charter** file discussed in preceding integration sections), save the files and exchange them with your companion class. In this manner, you can share the interesting instructional materials your class produces. In addition, you can ask the other class to work cooperatively with you on a more extensive project to share the workload. Alternatively, exchange files with the other class and challenge them to identify the same patterns in the data discovered by your class.

Price Comparisons

Assign all students in your class to gather data from the stores where their parents shop, such as the prices of selected items—staple goods, gasoline, movie admission prices, and record or CD costs. Discuss the differences in the prices that your students will discover. Next, have the students determine a class average price for each item, using a bar chart to illustrate the price ranges. Exchange these spreadsheet files with the companion school and have students build a composite chart comparing the price differences between the two geographic locations on an item-by-item basis. Ask students to determine probable causes for the price differences they discover (e.g., supply and demand, economy of scale, transportation costs, bulk purchasing in urban centers, etc.).

Scanning and Digitizing Projects

If you have either a scanner or a digitizer available, have your students create images of themselves, their school, or their local community to exchange with your companion class once you have captured the digitized images. In this manner, students in both classes will gain a better understanding of the people and places they will have read about in their pen pal letters.

Interactive Game Contests

As an academic motivational game, have your students challenge the students in the companion class to a contest in a selected content area. After you have conducted a contest among your students, have the champion in your class challenge the champion in the companion class to a Tournament of Champions. Using telecommunications, you can play the game interactively so that the classes at the two locations can be spectators of the event.

Related Activities

- Arrange the contest in a college bowl quiz game format in which each class creates questions beforehand in predetermined categories (emphasizing curricular topics). These questions are then randomly presented to students from the two classes. If students answer correctly, they receive a point for their class. If they miss the question, the other class has a chance to respond.
- Arrange a computer art contest in which the judges are a panel of students and faculty from the two schools.

Additional Activities

Educational Activities
Linking your class with other classes around the country or world
Connecting with other educators around the country or world
Joining electronic educational forums
Using electronic mail capabilities
Joining electronic bulletin boards for exchanging educational ideas
Joining electronic bulletin boards for acquiring useful files

General Activities
Communicating with friends and associates around the country
Conducting on-line database searches on research topics of interest
Accessing up-to-date information about the weather in your area
Checking airline schedules and fares
Accessing conference schedules or other events of interest
Booking your own airline flights at the best fares available
Accessing up-to-date information from national news services

12 Looking Ahead: Educational Technology in the 1990s

Now that you are an accomplished user of the many powers of Microsoft Works for enhancing your professional productivity and instruction, you are ready to explore some of the other exciting technological innovations available today. Recall the computer technology trends discussed in the first chapter—the next generation of computers will be smaller, faster, less expensive, more powerful, and more flexible than the machines we are using today. These same trends extend across all fields of technology that depend on computers, including the television and video industries.

Some of most exciting new applications, such as interactive video and CD-ROM applications, require additional and somewhat expensive equipment. However, powerful and interesting multimedia and hypermedia applications require little or no additional hardware or software. The following discussion is not intended as a "crystal ball" experience to foresee the wonders of the distant future. Instead, this chapter is designed to provide you with a brief introduction to several of the most interesting and *currently available* educational technologies—technologies that you may want to investigate independently.

Local Area Networks

LANs (local area networks) offer users a way to share scarce resources, such as printers or hard disk drives, among multiple computer terminals. LANs are not a particularly new technological innovation; some schools have used LANs since the mid-1980s. However, continued improvement in the performance of LAN technology has produced local area networks that operate much more reliably today than they did several years ago. As a result, LANs merit the careful consideration of educators.

Establishing a LAN to share resources requires the purchase of a **file server** (a hard disk drive dedicated to maintaining the network) and cables to connect the equipment together. Once the network is established—for instance, in a computer laboratory—teachers using the lab have better control of the computers than they would in a lab without networking. By operating as the file server, the hard disk drive removes most of the typical disk-handling chores that teachers normally have to manage, and students do not have to handle disks for routine tasks, such as loading programs into RAM or saving work files. With the network software, teachers have the power to control which users can access which files, and for what purposes—they can limit students to inspecting files only or inspecting and changing files. With these powers, teachers can regulate the use students make of their computer time without having to oversee the actual hands-on computer sessions.

As networks increase in sophistication, they will continue to become easier to use and to maintain. By removing the need for students to handle disks, the networks provide a major technology facilitation for many teachers. In addition, networks are certain to become continually more affordable in educational markets. These factors combine to make networks an area of technological advancement that merits present and future attention.

Hypermedia

Hypermedia is the combination of **hypertext** with media components such as sound, animation, film, video, and music. The term *hypertext* refers to written material that can be accessed in any sequence. The concept of hypertext is nearly fifty years old. It was originated in the 1940s by President Franklin D. Roosevelt's science advisor, Vanevar Bush. He visualized a device (the Memex) that could output data that was non-linear and non-sequential in nature. However, until the 1980s, educational hypermedia materials were not fully developed.

Trying to explain hypertext (or the even more complex concept, hypermedia) is a difficult task given the linear nature of this text. You must see the powers of hypermedia to understand what hypermedia instructional packages really are. Perhaps a simple example of how a hypermedia package might be used by students can help explain the concept.

Imagine, for example, that several students are instructed to explore some material on the life and works of Beethoven. If these were hypermedia materials, each student could examine them in a unique fashion. One student might progress from reading a chapter about Beethoven's childhood to reading a chapter about his adolescence; before reading about his life, another student might decide to listen to excerpts of the music Beethoven wrote as a youth; while reading about Beethoven's childhood, a third student might want to inspect political maps of Central Europe during the 1800s. Educational hypermedia products exist that would allow each of these students to pursue a learning path most meaningful to him or her.

Hypermedia software is available for many different computer systems. HyperCard® for the Macintosh is currently the most well-established hypermedia software. Similar programs are available for both IBM-compatibles (LinkWay®) and the Apple II family of computers (HyperStudio®). These programs can be thought of as visual database managers. All of the programs use **buttons** ("hot spots" on the screen you can point to with the mouse) as navigational tools for exploring the material. With HyperCard, each individual screen is called a **card**. Cards are linked together by buttons to create a program, called a **stack**.

Figure 12.1 shows a typical LinkWay screen display. Each of the icons that you see on this **page** represents a button linked to a **folder** designed for a specific purpose. For example, if you used the mouse to point to the **Graphics** icon and clicked the mouse button, you would be presented with potential graphic art selections to include in your folder. If you pointed instead to the **CD Rom** icon and clicked the mouse button, you would enter a folder designed to help you access the storage capacity of a CD-ROM disc with the processing speed of a microcomputer chip.

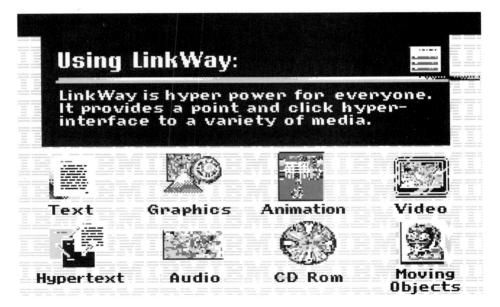

Figure 12.1 A sample LinkWay screen

LinkWay stacks can operate as stand-alone programs using only an IBM-compatible computer, or they can be used in combination with other devices such as videodisc players and CD-ROM players. When hypertext programs are used with these other media, exciting and powerful educational interactive materials can be developed. Videodisc players and CD-ROM players are discussed in the next two sections.

Videodisc Players

Videodisc players use laser discs capable of storing vast amounts of data. The discs resemble audio compact discs, but are roughly the size of a record album. A laser disc can store many forms of data: text, full-color slides, videotape, film, audio, or any combination of these media. If a videodisc is simply used for storing full-color slides, it can hold 54,000 slides on each side of the disc. Videodiscs are **read only**; the information stored on them is created only by the company producing them.

Videodisc technology is particularly exciting, not only because of the vast amounts of information that can be stored on the discs, but also because the data stored on videodiscs are randomly accessible in the same way as the data on your Works **Data** disk. Imagine that you are viewing the very first slide on a videodisc that stores 54,000 full-color slides, and you decide that you want to inspect the last slide. The videodisc player will display the slide you want to see in a few seconds. Contrast that feature with your serial videotape player: even when using the fast forward speed, the end of the tape will be a long time coming.

A videodisc player with remote control devices. *(Courtesy of Pioneer Video, Inc.)*

Videodisc players can be used with a video monitor in the same way that you use a videotape player to present material to your students. At a videodisc player's basic level of use, a computer is not necessary. You use the guide that comes with the videodisc to instantly locate the correct track for the material you wish to show. The freeze-frame capability allows you to display an individual slide on the monitor for as long as you wish. The quality of the pictures on videodiscs is excellent.

The difficulty with this most basic level of use is that the teacher must research the videodisc ahead of time to locate the appropriate slides or motion sequences to use in class. Even that difficulty can be overcome now, however, by using an additional device, a **bar code reader**. A hand-held bar code reader, much like the one used by the cashiers in supermarkets, can be connected to a videodisc player to automate the process of locating appropriate slides. Many textbook publishers are now cooperating with major videodisc developers by including bar codes in the teacher's manuals of their texts. With this system, the teacher has only to pass the bar code reader over the code in the teacher's manual, and the videodisc image corresponding to that section of the lecture notes is instantly displayed on the screen. Teachers can even print out their own bar codes if they wish to develop alternative lesson plans. This development places the power of videodisc technology in the hands of the novice—just pass the bar code reader over the code, and the technology will do the rest.

To experience the real power of videodiscs, however, you must add a computer to the system. When you connect a computer system with hypertext

When a videodisc player is attached to a computer, powerful multimedia instructional experiences can be created. *(Courtesy of International Business Machines Corporation)*

software to a videodisc player, you create **interactive video**. Interactive video refers to material in which the interactive characteristics of the computer are combined with the storage and display powers of videodiscs. The computer screen displays buttons, prompts, or questions as navigational tools. The speed and visual quality of the videodisc player, combined with a computer system, make interactive video very powerful indeed.

For example, In the Holy Lands™ is an interactive video program developed by Optical Data Corporation. Created in HyperCard, this product allows students to explore issues relating to life in the Middle East. If your students click on one icon, they can view video sequences of Israeli students discussing their points of view on a given topic. By clicking on a different icon, your students can watch Palestinian students discussing the same topic from their perspective. In addition, historical information related to the topic of interest can be perused, maps of the appropriate area inspected, and video footage of the actual Israeli countryside (filmed by professional photographers) examined. The combination of video, audio, and textual information produces a compelling product. Videodisc technology is an especially exciting area that all teachers will want to explore.

CD-ROM Drives

CD-ROM is an acronym for **C**ompact **D**isc–**R**ead **O**nly **M**emory. The discs are identical in appearance to audio compact discs and usually can be played in an audio compact disc drive if they contain sound or music. Like videodiscs, CD-ROM discs are read only; typically, information stored on CD-ROM discs is created by the company producing the discs. Also like videodiscs and your Works **Data** disk, the data stored on CD-ROM discs are randomly accessible.

CD-ROM drives use laser technology similar to that of the videodisc players, but with one significant difference—CD-ROM discs are not capable of storing motion video sequences. The data that a CD-ROM disc holds can be text, audio, music, computer graphics, and computer-generated animation. Although the discs lack some of the storage capabilities of videodiscs, one CD-ROM disc can still store an entire set of encyclopedias—including indices, maps, illustrations, speeches and many other features not available in a text version—with room on the disc to spare (Compton's *Multimedia Encyclopedia* is one example of a CD-ROM encyclopedia).

CD-ROM drives are attached to computers to create interactive capabilities similar to the interactive video applications discussed in the last section. In fact, the example of the three students exploring hypermedia material on the life and works of Beethoven actually exists as a CD-ROM application. The screen icons allow students to read text on Beethoven's life and times, inspect maps and illustrations of his world, listen to his music, read interpretations of his compositions, and even follow the musical scores of his music while listening to it.

Compton's *Multimedia Encyclopedia* used with a computer greatly facilitates and expedites the process of searching for information in the encyclopedia. The index is a computerized database into which students can enter topics to search.

A CD-ROM player with a CD-ROM disc. *(Courtesy of Toshiba America, Inc. Disk Products Division)*

As students enter their search word(s), the software gradually narrows the range of available topics alphabetically to assist in the process. When the student enters a search topic, the computer matches it with related encyclopedia topics and then displays the information on the screen.

In addition to the text entries, computer illustrations are available to complement the explanations and discussions. Some computer-generated animation sequences are included to graphically illustrate concepts, such as joint movements of the elbow. Finally, audio information permits students to listen to famous addresses such as Dr. Martin Luther King, Jr.'s, "I Have a Dream" speech. Interactive CD-ROM applications like Compton's *Multimedia Encyclopedia* offer students exciting tools for exploring information.

Multimedia

Multimedia is the term used for a combination of several different media in one educational package. Multimedia packages include powerful interactive video and CD-ROM applications together with materials created by students—projects that combine more widely available media, such as computer output with audio and videotapes. Projects of this nature permit students to explore the world of multimedia, even if they do not have extra equipment like videodisc players and CD-ROM drives.

As one example, students can use Scholastic's *Slide Shop* to generate a computer slide show illustrating the voyage of Christopher Columbus. The slide show might consist of a series of computer screen displays, including graphics and appropriate sounds (like the noise of the waves hitting the sides of the ships). Students can include important textual information in some of the slides, whereas they might choose to include only illustrations for others. When the slide show is complete, it could last five minutes to an hour, depending on the topic.

Next, the students connect the computer to a videotape player and record the computer slide show onto videotape. When the taping is complete, students play the slide show back and add important explanatory information as an extra audio track. When the project is complete and the tape played, the class can watch the project—viewing the computer illustrations, hearing the computer generated sounds, and listening to the explanatory comments of the students. While this project does not result in as compelling a final product as that of a commercial videodisc application, it is a project that an individual student—even an elementary student—can accomplish with teacher guidance. Projects like this one can introduce all students to the power of multimedia.

Distance Learning

Distance learning, as the term implies, involves facilitating learning in remote locations. Because of staffing problems, many small public schools in rural locations cannot offer their students a full range of courses. In small high schools, for instance, only one student may qualify for or be interested in taking a course such as physics or Advanced Placement American History. It seems unfair to deny the student the opportunity of taking a challenging course, but the expense of offering it for a single student is prohibitive for most small schools. One option is to transport the student to the nearest large school where the course is offered, but that necessitates considerable expense and inconvenience for the student and parents involved.

Distance learning offers another alternative. Instead of taking the student to the course, distance learning takes the course to the student. Advanced courses offered in large schools can be transmitted through satellite dishes to remote sites where qualified students can experience the classes at the same time as the students in the actual classroom. The remote student not only has the opportunity to see and hear everything offered to the regular students, but he or she can pose questions and respond to inquiries through two-way voice and data transmissions.

For distance learning to be effected, the participating sites must have the necessary transmitting and receiving equipment. Although this equipment is expensive, the federal government and many state governments believe the expense is warranted. Distance learning is currently on-going at many locations across the country, and many more projects are being initiated.

Distance learning has great potential beyond the small school situation. Many universities now offer graduate courses that students can take at locations more convenient for them than the central campus. In addition, distance learning for teacher inservice training has enormous potential. Teachers can receive the training in their own schools instead of having to go to a teacher's center, district training building, or local college for special programs. Inservice programs offered through distance learning would make far better use of teachers' time and should be just as valuable as on-site learning.

What Next?

The field of educational technology is exciting and ever-changing. All of the applications discussed here are having an impact on teachers and students today. Recall that technology continues to create products that are smaller, faster, more powerful, less expensive, and increasingly easy to use. These trends will influence the applications of educational technologies in the 1990s. Now that you can competently use a powerful integrated program such as Microsoft Works, select one of the topics discussed in this section as the next application to master. Remember the old Chinese saying: "A journey of many miles begins with just one step."

Appendix A

Microsoft Works Commands

Word-Processor Commands

■ File Menu

Create New File...	**Alt-F-N**
Open Existing File...	**Alt-F-O**
Save	**Alt-F-S**
Save As...	**Alt-F-A**
Close	**Alt-F-C**
File Management...	**Alt-F-F**
Run Other Programs...	**Alt-F-R**
Convert...	**Alt-F-C**
Exit Works	**Alt-F-X**

■ Edit Menu

Undo	**Alt-E-U**
Move	**Alt-E-M**

Copy	**Alt-E-C**
Copy Special...	**Alt-E-S**
Delete	**Alt-E-D**
Insert Special...	**Alt-E-P**
Insert Field...	**Alt-E-F**
Insert Chart...	**Alt-E-I**
Footnote...	**Alt-E-T**
Bookmark Name...	**Alt-E-N**

■ Print Menu

Print...	**Alt-P-P**
Page Setup & Margins...	**Alt-P-M**
Preview...	**Alt-P-V**
Print Form Letters...	**Alt-P-F**
Print Labels...	**Alt-P-L**
Insert Page Break	**Alt-P-I**
Headers & Footers...	**Alt-P-H**
Printer Setup...	**Alt-P-S**

■ Select Menu

Text	**Alt-S-E**
All	**Alt-S-A**
Go To...	**Alt-S-G**
Search...	**Alt-S-S**
Replace...	**Alt-S-R**

■ Format Menu

Plain Text	**Alt-T-P**
Bold	**Alt-T-B**
Underline	**Alt-T-U**
Italic	**Alt-T-I**
Font & Style...	**Alt-T-F**
Normal Paragraph	**Alt-T-N**
Left	**Alt-T-L**
Center	**Alt-T-C**
Right	**Alt-T-R**
Justified	**Alt-T-J**
Single Space	**Alt-T-S**
Double Space	**Alt-T-D**
Indents & Spacing...	**Alt-T-A**
Tabs...	**Alt-T-T**
Borders...	**Alt-T-O**

■ Options Menu

Works Settings...	**Alt-O-W**
Calculator...	**Alt-O-C**

Alarm Clock...	**Alt-O-A**
Dial This Number	**Alt-O-D**
Show Ruler	**Alt-O-R**
Show All Characters	**Alt-O-L**
Show Footnotes	**Alt-O-F**
Wrap for Screen	**Alt-O-P**
Typing Replaces Selection	**Alt-O-Y**
Check Spelling...	**Alt-O-S**
Thesaurus...	**Alt-O-T**
Paginate Now	**Alt-O-N**

■ Window Menu

Move	**Alt-W-M**
Size	**Alt-W-S**
Maximize	**Alt-W-X**
Arrange All	**Alt-W-A**
Split	**Alt-W-T**

■ Help Menu

Using Help	**Alt-H-U**
Help Index	**Alt-H-H**
Getting Started	**Alt-H-G**
Keyboard	**Alt-H-K**
Mouse	**Alt-H-M**
Works Tutorial	**Alt-H-W**

Word-Processor Keyboard Commands

Make text bold	**Control-B**
Center text	**Control-C**
Print current date	**Control-D**
Print current file name	**Control-F**
Remove hanging indent	**Control-G**
Create hanging indent	**Control-H**
Make text italic	**Control-I**
Justify paragraph	**Control-J**
Left-align text	**Control-L**
Remove nested indent	**Control-M**
Create nested indent	**Control-N**
Print page number	**Control-P**
Right-align text	**Control-R**
Make text strikethrough	**Control-S**
Print current time	**Control-T**
Make text underlined	**Control-U**
Normal paragraph	**Control-X**

Single space	**Control-1**
Double space	**Control-2**
1.5 space	**Control-5**
Superscript	**Control-+**
Subscript	**Control-=**
Normal text	**Control-Space bar**
Undo	**Alt-Backspace**

■ Function Keys

Help	**F1**
Tutorials	**Shift-F1**
Move selection	**F3**
Copy selection	**Shift-F3**
Go to page/bookmark	**F5**
Repeat search	**F7**
Repeat copy or format	**Shift-F7**
Select/extend selection	**F8**
Paginate now	**F9**

Database Commands

■ File Menu

Create New File...	**Alt-F-N**
Open Existing File...	**Alt-F-O**
Save	**Alt-F-S**
Save As...	**Alt-F-A**
Close	**Alt-F-C**
File Management...	**Alt-F-F**
Run Other Programs...	**Alt-F-R**
Convert...	**Alt-F-C**
Exit Works	**Alt-F-X**

■ Edit Menu

Move Field	**Alt-E-M**
Copy	**Alt-E-C**
Clear Field Contents	**Alt-E-E**
Delete Field	**Alt-E-D**
Insert Line	**Alt-E-I**
Move Record	**Alt-E-V**
Copy Record	**Alt-E-P**
Delete Record	**Alt-E-L**
Insert Record	**Alt-E-S**

■ Print Menu

Print...	**Alt-P-P**
Page Setup & Margins...	**Alt-P-M**

Preview...	**Alt-P-V**
Insert Page Break	**Alt-P-I**
Delete Page Break	**Alt-P-D**
Headers & Footers...	**Alt-P-H**
Printer Setup...	**Alt-P-S**

■ Select Menu

Go To	**Alt-S-G**
Search...	**Alt-S-S**
Apply Query	**Alt-S-Q**
Hide Record	**Alt-S-H**
Show All Records	**Alt-S-L**
Switch Hidden Records	**Alt-S-W**
Sort Records	**Alt-S-O**

■ Format Menu

General...	**Alt-T-G**
Fixed...	**Alt-T-X**
Currency...	**Alt-T-U**
Comma...	**Alt-T-C**
Percent...	**Alt-T-P**
Exponential...	**Alt-T-E**
True/False	**Alt-T-R**
Time/Date...	**Alt-T-T**
Font...	**Alt-T-F**
Style...	**Alt-T-S**
Field Size...	**Alt-T-Z**
Show Field Name	**Alt-T-N**

■ Options Menu

Works Settings...	**Alt-O-W**
Calculator...	**Alt-O-C**
Alarm Clock...	**Alt-O-A**
Dial This Number	**Alt-O-D**
Protect Data	**Alt-O-P**
Protect Form	**Alt-O-F**

■ View Menu

Form	**Alt-V-F**
List	**Alt-V-L**
Query	**Alt-V-Q**
New Report	**Alt-V-N**
Reports...	**Alt-V-R**

■ Window Menu

Move	**Alt-W-M**
Size	**Alt-W-S**

Maximize	**Alt-W-X**
Arrange All	**Alt-W-A**
Split	**Alt-W-T**

■ Help Menu

Using Help	**Alt-H-U**
Help Index	**Alt-H-H**
Getting Started	**Alt-H-G**
Keyboard	**Alt-H-K**
Mouse	**Alt-H-M**
Works Tutorial	**Alt-H-W**

Database Keyboard Commands

Copy cell above	**Control-'**
Enter current date	**Control-;**
Enter current time	**Control-:**

■ Function Keys

Help	**F1**
Tutorials	**Shift-F1**
Edit cell	**F2**
Move selection	**F3**
Copy selection	**Shift-F3**
Go to	**F5**
Repeat search	**F7**
Repeat copy or format	**Shift-F7**
Select/extend selection	**F8**
Select record	**Ctrl-F8**
Select field	**Shift-F8**
View form/list	**F9**
Leave report	**F10**
View report	**Shift-F10**

Spreadsheet Commands

■ File Menu

Create New File...	**Alt-F-N**
Open Existing File...	**Alt-F-O**
Save	**Alt-F-S**
Save As...	**Alt-F-A**
Close	**Alt-F-C**
File Management...	**Alt-F-F**
Run Other Programs...	**Alt-F-R**

Convert...   **Alt-F-C**
Exit Works   **Alt-F-X**

■ **Edit Menu**

Move   **Alt-E-M**
Copy   **Alt-E-C**
Copy Special...   **Alt-E-S**
Clear   **Alt-E-E**
Delete Row/Column   **Alt-E-D**
Insert Row/Column   **Alt-E-I**
Fill Right   **Alt-E-R**
Fill Down   **Alt-E-F**
Fill Series...   **Alt-E-L**
Range Name...   **Alt-E-N**

■ **Print Menu**

Print...   **Alt-P-P**
Page Setup & Margins...   **Alt-P-M**
Preview...   **Alt-P-V**
Set Print Area   **Alt-P-A**
Insert Page Break   **Alt-P-I**
Delete Page Break   **Alt-P-D**
Headers & Footers...   **Alt-P-H**
Printer Setup...   **Alt-P-S**

■ **Select Menu**

Cells   **Alt-S-E**
Row   **Alt-S-R**
Column   **Alt-S-C**
All   **Alt-S-A**
Go To   **Alt-S-G**
Search...   **Alt-S-S**
Sort Rows   **Alt-S-O**

■ **Format Menu**

General...   **Alt-T-G**
Fixed...   **Alt-T-X**
Currency...   **Alt-T-U**
Comma...   **Alt-T-C**
Percent...   **Alt-T-P**
Exponential...   **Alt-T-E**
True/False   **Alt-T-R**
Time/Date...   **Alt-T-T**
Font...   **Alt-T-F**
Style...   **Alt-T-S**
Column Width...   **Alt-T-W**

■ Options Menu

Works Settings...	**Alt-O-W**
Calculator...	**Alt-O-C**
Alarm Clock...	**Alt-O-A**
Dial This Number	**Alt-O-D**
Freeze Titles	**Alt-O-T**
Show Formulas	**Alt-O-F**
Protect Data	**Alt-O-P**
Manual Calculation	**Alt-O-M**
Calculate Now	**Alt-O-N**

■ View Menu

Spreadsheet	**Alt-V-S**
New Chart	**Alt-V-N**
Charts...	**Alt-V-C**

■ Window Menu

Move	**Alt-W-M**
Size	**Alt-W-S**
Maximize	**Alt-W-X**
Arrange All	**Alt-W-A**
Split	**Alt-W-T**

■ Help Menu

Using Help	**Alt-H-U**
Help Index	**Alt-H-H**
Getting Started	**Alt-H-G**
Keyboard	**Alt-H-K**
Mouse	**Alt-H-M**
Works Tutorial	**Alt-H-W**

Spreadsheet Keyboard Commands

Copy cell above	**Control-'**
Enter current date	**Control-;**
Enter current time	**Control-:**

■ Function Keys

Help	**F1**
Tutorials	**Shift-F1**
Edit cell	**F2**
Move selection	**F3**
Copy selection	**Shift-F3**
Go to	**F5**

Repeat search	**F7**
Repeat copy or format	**Shift-F7**
Select/extend selection	**F8**
Select row	**Ctrl-F8**
Select column	**Shift-F8**
Leave chart	**F10**
View chart	**Shift-F10**

Appendix B

Glossary of Important Terms

Alt key A key found on most IBM-compatible computer keyboards. The **Alt** key does nothing by itself, but is generally used in combination with other characters (similar to the use of the **Shift** key) to enter program commands. It is used extensively by Microsoft Works users who don't use a mouse.

application software These are productivity tools such as word processors, database managers, and spreadsheet programs. The term is also sometimes used to refer to computer programs written for a specific task such as creating schedules, tracking payrolls, maintaining attendance figures, and controlling inventories.

arrow keys The cursor movement keys on a keyboard. They are the keys that can be used instead of using a mouse.

auxiliary storage device (secondary storage) A device used for long-term storage of both programs and data. Necessary because of the short-term duration of RAM. Auxiliary storage devices include floppy disk, hard disk, and magnetic tape drives.

backspace key A special key on most computer keyboards that erases the character(s) to the left of the cursor's position.

BASIC One of the most popular programming languages available for microcomputers. BASIC is an acronym for **B**eginner's **A**ll-purpose **S**ymbolic **I**nstructional **C**ode.

baud A unit for measuring data transmission speed. The character per second transmission rate is calculated by dividing the baud rate by the number of bits required to send one character (typically eight to ten bits).

binary The base two number system. It uses only two digits—zero and one—to represent numbers. The binary number system is associated with computers because computers translate values in terms of switches being on (1) or off (0).

bit Acronym for **b**inary dig**it**; a single binary digit (either zero or one).

boot The process of turning on a computer and loading the operating system. The term is derived from the phrase, "to lift oneself up by one's bootstraps."

bug An error in a computer program. The removal of bugs from a computer program is known as program debugging. The term was reportedly coined by computer pioneer Grace Hopper (the developer of COBOL). The story goes that Hopper had a program that continued to fail for no apparent reason. When she looked into the computer system, she discovered that the reason her program failed was that there was a moth trapped in the computer's circuits. After that, whenever programs fail to function correctly, programmers say that there must be some "bug" in the program.

bulletin board system (or BBS) An electronic communication system that allows users to share information. A BBS is usually accessed via modem over the telephone network.

byte A basic unit of computer storage. One byte is the amount of computer storage necessary to store one character in computer memory (RAM) or on disk. Typically a byte is eight bits. Other units of storage include kilobytes (1 K=1024 bytes) and megabytes (1 meg=1024 kilobytes).

CAI **C**omputer-**A**ssisted **I**nstruction. The use of a computer to provide instruction to a learner. Several types of CAI include tutorials, drill and practice programs, and simulations.

cathode ray tube (CRT) The tube inside televisions and inside television-like display devices, such as video monitors, associated with most computer systems.

cell The intersection of a row and a column in a spreadsheet. A location for the storing of a number, formula, or text.

central processing unit (CPU) The hardware component of the computer system that actually performs all processing operations. The CPU controls all requests for input or output, interprets all machine instructions (programs), and manages the storage of data in primary memory.

CMI **C**omputer-**M**anaged **I**nstruction. The term refers to using a computer to coordinate and manage activities typically associated with teaching. Examples include maintaining grade books, creating tests, and keeping student records.

command A request to the computer to perform some function or operation.

command key Any key dedicated to performing a specific task, such as bringing up a user menu.

computer-assisted instruction See **CAI**.

computer-managed instruction See **CMI**.

computer program A set of instructions written in a language the computer can understand that commands the computer to carry out some function.

computer system The components that collectively comprise the computer. Typically a computer system is made up of a CPU, keyboard, video monitor, printer, and optional input devices (mouse, joy stick, light pen) and communication devices (modem).

computer users group A group of individuals who gather to share their acquired knowledge and the programs they have developed on a particular type of computer hardware.

Control key A key found on most computer keyboards. The control key does nothing by itself, but is generally used in combination with other characters (similar to the use of the **Shift** key) to enter program commands.

control unit The part of the central processing unit (CPU) of the computer that coordinates the processing of all information.

copy protection A procedure for preventing a disk from being copied—either physically or through software intervention—by normal disk copy procedures.

cursor A blinking line or rectangle on the screen that indicates where characters entered from the keyboard will be displayed.

database A large collection of related information. Typically manipulated by a database management system (DBMS) program.

database manager A software package used to create and maintain computer databases.

debugging The process of removing errors in computer programs.

default The command option selected automatically by pressing the **Enter** or **Return** key if no other option is chosen, or the disk drive accessed by a DOS command when no drive is specified.

Delete key (or Del key) A special key on most computer keyboards that erases the character(s) at the cursor's current position.

dialog box A message prompt displayed on the monitor within a computer application requesting the user to make a selection from available options.

disk drive A peripheral device that reads information from and writes information to a disk. See floppy disk and hard disk.

dot-matrix printer A printer device whose characters are actually composed of a series of adjacent dots.

drill and practice Software which allows the learner to repeat a process of steps over and over. Typically associated with practicing skills.

electronic mail A method of sending and receiving mail and messages on a computer through the telephone system.

Enter key A special key, typically named **Enter** or **Return**, which informs the computer of a pending request. Used by most word-processing programs to indicate the end of a paragraph or a short line of text.

Escape key A special key on the upper left side of most computer keyboards that is used to terminate (escape from) a command or to exit from a menu. Typically labelled **Esc**.

floppy disk A circular piece of mylar (with a flux-coated recording surface) that is used to store computer data and programs.

format As pertains to disk-handling, an initialization procedure to prepare a disk for storing data.

Function Keys (F1–F12) These keys are found on most computer keyboards. The function keys serve as shortcuts for issuing program commands. For instance, pressing the **F1** key accesses the Help layer, and the **F8** key initiates text selection.

GIGO Acronym for **G**arbage **I**n-**G**arbage **O**ut. If the quality of the input data to a computer system is poor (garbage), the output from the system will also be poor.

graph A diagram showing the relationship between two or more variable quantities; loosely, a chart.

graphics printer A printer device capable of printing both text and graphics.

hard copy Printed output from computer processing.

hard disk drive A non-removable (usually) data storage device with a capacity several times larger and faster than that of floppy disk drives.

hardware The physical components associated with a computer system. Typically composed of a system unit/CPU, keyboard, video monitor, and printer.

integrated package A software program with several modules that can easily exchange data with each other. Typically the packages contain a word processor, database, graphics, and spreadsheet components.

joystick An alternate input device typically used with computer games. It is used to control the direction of movement.

keyboard The main input device associated with most current computer systems. Similar in design to a typewriter keyboard, but with additional special keys.

kilobyte (or K) A unit of computer memory equal to 1024 bytes of information. Typically the unit of measure for RAM and floppy disk capacity.

LAN An acronym for **L**ocal **A**rea **N**etwork. A communications net connecting various hardware devices together by a cable or through the in-house telephone system.

laser printer A non-impact printing device that creates images on a rotating drum by using a laser. The drum picks up toner powder on the areas exposed by the laser, which is then fused to the paper to form the characters.

letter-quality printer A printing device that has fully shaped characters and has output quality comparable to a standard electronic typewriter. Examples of printers in this category are daisy wheel, ink jet, and laser printers.

light pen A computer input device that allows the user to select, move, or draw objects directly onto the computer video screen.

menu A list of commands available at a particular moment in a computer program.

microcomputer A small computer employing microprocessor technology. They are typically available in three general configurations: desktop, transportable, and portable. The smallest microcomputers (physically) are called laptops.

modem Acronym for **mo**dulator/**dem**odulator. A peripheral device used to connect a computer to other computers via the telephone system. Converts digital computer signals to analog signals for sending and receiving over telephone lines.

mouse A computer input device that controls the cursor's position by converting physical movement to electronic signals. Used as an alternate input device to the keyboard cursor keys.

off-line Pertains to peripheral devices. Equipment which is not currently in communication with the CPU, or a computer that is not linked to another computer with a communications package.

on-line Pertains to peripheral devices. Equipment which is currently in communication with the CPU, or a computer that is linked to another computer using a communications package.

operating system A set of computer programs which the computer needs to coordinate its own operations.

peripheral devices Any device connected to the computer system which expands the system's capabilities. Examples include printers, modems, and graphic tablets.

port An expansion location available on most computers through which a peripheral device can be connected.

printer An output device used to obtain printed output from computer processing. See also **hard copy**.

programmer A person who writes computer programs.

programming language A language that a computer can recognize either directly (such as machine language) or indirectly (such as Logo or BASIC). Languages include specific rules regarding syntax (construction of commands) and applications.

prompt A character or message displayed by the computer to indicate it is ready to accept keyboard input. Generally, the prompt informs the user what he/she is to do next.

random access memory (RAM) Computer memory whose contents can be read or written to directly. The contents of RAM are lost when power is turned off.

read-only memory (ROM) A solid-state silicon memory chip programmed at the time of manufacture and whose programming cannot be changed by the user. The contents of ROM are retained even when power is turned off.

Return key See **Enter key**.

select As it pertains to Microsoft Works, to select means to highlight a portion of a word-processed document, spreadsheet, or database for further manipulation.

selection As pertains to Microsoft Works, a selection is a highlighted section of a word-processed document, spreadsheet, or database on which you want to perform a block operation.

software Sets of computer programs that govern the operation of a computer system and give computers their flexibility.

spreadsheet A type of program that arranges data and formulas in a matrix of cells, allowing the user to pose "What if?" questions. Spreadsheets are also referred to as worksheets.

system software Programs that run the computer system and aid in applications program development. DOS is one common example of system software.

tutorial A piece of software that fills a teaching or training role.

user A person who utilizes a computer for data manipulation or problem solving.

video monitor The television-like display device associated with most computer systems.

word processor A computer program designed to aid in the creation of written documents. Allows for writing, inserting, deleting, changing, and moving text within a document.

Appendix C

Microsoft Works Accessories

The Alarm Clock

The **alarm clock** accessory functions just like any other alarm clock and can be set so that you do not get so involved in your work that you lose track of the time. When the alarm goes off, the computer beeps and a message appears on the screen reminding you of the time. When the message appears, you have the standard alarm clock options available—acknowledge the alarm, reset the alarm, or press a "snooze" feature so the alarm will beep again in ten minutes.

To set the alarm clock, follow these steps:

1. Press the **Alt** key and then press the **O** key to access the **Options** menu.
2. Press the **A** (for **A**larm Clock) key to select the **Alarm Clock** accessory.

In a few moments, the **Alarm Clock** dialog box will appear on the screen (see Figure C.1). The cursor is now on the **Message** line ready for you to type your message. Let's use the alarm clock to remind us when it is time to quit working for the day. To set a message, follow these steps:

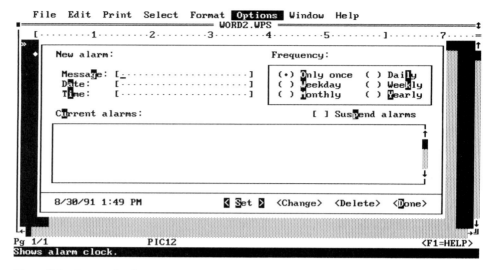

Figure C.1 **Alarm Clock** message box

1. Type Time to quit in the box, then press the **Tab** key to move the cursor to the **Date** line.
2. Enter the current date in the form shown at the bottom of the **Alarm Clock** dialog box, then press the **Tab** key to move the cursor to the **Time** line.
3. Enter a time several minutes after the current time in the form shown at the bottom of the **Alarm Clock** dialog box, then hold down the **Alt** key and press the **S** (for **S**et) key to establish that message. Notice that the alarm message appears in the **Current alarms** box. The **Frequency** box to the right of the **Message** line offers you options for controlling the frequency with which your message will appear—from **Only once** (the default setting) to **Yearly**. You have set your message, so you can now signal Works that you are done with the alarm clock accessory and ready to continue working until the message appears.
4. To return to your work, hold down the **Alt** key and press the **D** (for **D**one) key to exit the **Alarm Clock** dialog box.

In a few moments, the **Time to quit** message will appear on the screen. When the message appears, you have three options:

1. If you press the **Enter** key, you acknowledge the message.
2. If you press the **R** (for **R**eset) key, you can change the alarm time or message so that it will reappear at some later time.
3. If you press the **S** (for **S**nooze) key, you can tell the alarm clock to have the same message reappear in ten minutes.

You can access the **Alarm Clock** accessory from all the Works applications. It is a useful tool for helping you to remain punctual.

The Calculator

The **Calculator** accessory lets you perform simple calculations from any application. When the calculator appears on the screen, you can use the keyboard or the mouse to perform any basic operation (addition, subtraction, multiplication, or division) on rational numbers. When the calculations are complete, you can insert the result directly into your document at the cursor's current position.

To set the calculator, follow these steps:

1. Press the **Alt** key and then press the **O** key to access the **Options** menu.
2. Press the **C** (for **C**alculator) key to select the **Calculator** accessory.

In a few moments, the **Calculator** will appear on the screen (see Figure C.2).

Let's use the calculator to perform a simple computation. You know that there are sixty seconds in a minute, sixty minutes in an hour, and twenty-four hours in a day. So how many seconds are there in a day? To find out, follow these steps:

1. Use the keyboard to enter these numbers from the digits above the alphabetical keys. First, press the **6** key, then press the **0** key to enter 60.
2. Now hold down the **Shift** key and press the **asterisk** (*) key—the **8** key—to select multiplication.
3. Press the **6** key, then press the **0** key to enter 60 again.
4. Hold down the **Shift** key and press the **asterisk** (*) key again to select multiplication.
5. Press the **2** key, then press the **4** key to enter 24.
6. Now press the **equals** (=) key (*do not use* the **Shift** key) to request an answer.

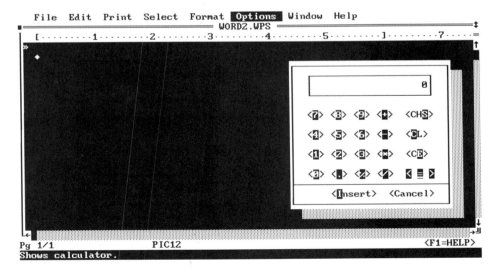

Figure C.2 Calculator

Notice that the answer, 86400, appears on the calculator's display line. You can insert this answer into your current document at the cursor's position by holding down the **Alt** key and pressing the **I** (for **I**nsert) key. The answer is quickly placed into your document.

The Automatic Telephone Dialer

The **Automatic Telephone Dialer** accessory dials telephone numbers for you. To use this accessory you must have a modem and a telephone line attached to your computer. In addition, you must have the number that you want the computer to dial highlighted on the screen before using the **Automatic Telephone Dialer**.

The obvious way to use the **Automatic Telephone Dialer** is to include a telephone number field in an address database. When you want to make a number of calls, you first open the address database. Once the document is open, you use the database **Search** command to find the record of the individual you want to call, then highlight his or her telephone number in the telephone field. Once the number is selected, follow these steps:

1. Press the **Alt** key and then press the **O** key to access the **Options** menu.
2. Press the **D** (for **D**ial this number) key to have the computer dial the selected telephone number.

When the computer has finished dialing the number, a message appears telling you to **Pick up the phone and press OK to answer**. If you pick up your telephone, then press the **Enter** key, you can complete your call.

Appendix D

Microsoft Works File Management Commands

Most of your routine file management can now be accomplished without having to learn the necessary operating system (DOS) commands to perform actions such as copying files, renaming files, or deleting files from your data disk. To have Works help you perform these file management tasks, follow these steps:

1. Press the **Alt** key and then press the **F** key to access the **File** menu.
2. When the **File** menu appears, press the **F** (for **F**ile Management) key to access the **File Management** menu.

In a few moments, the **File Management** options will appear on the screen (see Figure D.1).

The function of each of these commands is briefly explained in the following paragraphs. The Works screen displays will prompt you through the procedures you must follow to complete each file management task.

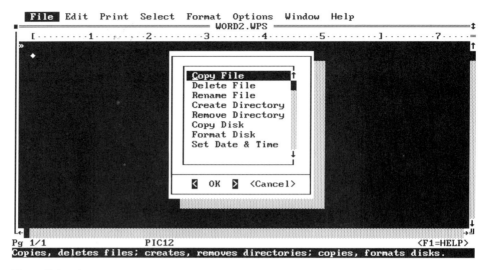

Figure D.1 **File Management** menu

Copy File permits you to copy the file you indicate. Use this command frequently to make backup copies of all of your important data files. Also use the command to copy files from your hard disk to floppy disks.

Delete File permits you to remove the file you indicate from your disk. Use this command very *carefully*. When you delete a file from a disk, it is lost unless you have made an additional copy of it on another disk. Use the command to remove unwanted or outdated files from your data disks.

Rename File lets you change the name of the file you indicate. Use this command when the original name you assigned to a data file is not appropriate to its current contents.

Create Directory lets you create a subdirectory to help you organize the files on your disks. This command is particularly useful for helping Works users with hard disks to keep their information easily accessible.

Remove Directory lets you remove a subdirectory from your disks. Use this command when an empty subdirectory (without files) is no longer useful.

Copy Disk lets you copy the disk you indicate—including all the data files stored on the disk. Use this command periodically to make backup copies of all of your data disks.

Format Disk lets you prepare the disk you indicate for use as a data disk. Recall that you cannot store information on a new disk until the disk has been formatted for use with that type of computer. Use this command each time you want to prepare a new disk as a data disk.

Set Date & Time lets you inform the computer of the current date and time. This is a useful procedure because Works will record the current date and time when you save data files. Many computers with hard disks have an internal clock so this command is not necessary.

Appendix E

Microsoft Works
Data Disk Files

BAD-LET.WPS is a word-processed document that includes a number of mis-spelled words placed in the letter for a practice exercise with the Microsoft Works spell checker.

CHARTER.WKS is a file designed to illustrate how a spreadsheet file can be used instructionally as a charting tool. Detailed instructions for using the file are discussed in the integration section of Chapter 9.

CLASSES.WDB is a database file containing information on forty-five stu-dents. It is used in Chapter 6 to illustrate the database report generator.

GLOSSARY.WDB is a database file containing the entries listed in this text's glossary. With the glossary in this form users can employ the powers of a com-puterized database when they seek clarification of terms. The glossary file allows users to search, sort, and print out the reports most suited to their interests.

GOOD-LET.WPS is a word-processed file, similar to the **BET-LET.WPS** file that users develop in Chapter 5. Although not discussed in the text, the letter includes examples of simple text-formatting techniques with styles, justification, and spacing for users who want a model to follow.

GRADES.WKS is a spreadsheet file included to demonstrate the use of spreadsheets to manage the calculation of grades. It is used in Chapter 8 to introduce formatting and copying techniques.

GUESS.WKS is a file illustrating the instructional use of a spreadsheet. The file is discussed in the integration section of Chapter 8.

HOLIDAYS.WDB is a file illustrating the use of a blank database. The file is discussed in the integration section of Chapter 6.

MAGIC.WKS is a file illustrating the use of a spreadsheet and is discussed in the integration section of Chapter 8.

MINERALS.WDB is a file illustrating the use of a blank database and is discussed in the integration section of Chapter 6.

MULTIPLY.WKS is a file illustrating the use of a spreadsheet and is discussed in the integration section of Chapter 8.

PLANETS.WDB is a file illustrating the use of a blank database and is discussed in the integration section of Chapter 6.

PRESIDES.WDB is a file illustrating the use of a blank database and is discussed in the integration section of Chapter 6.

SCHOOL.WDB is a database file that includes more extensive information on the twenty-five students that users enter into the file **STUDENT.WDB** in Chapter 6. The **SCHOOL.WDB** file is also used later in Chapter 7.

SPEND.WKS is a spreadsheet file illustrating how Works can be used for simple financial management. This file is discussed in the integration section of Chapter 8.

STATES.WDB is a file illustrating the use of a blank database and is discussed in the integration section of Chapter 6.

STATS.WKS is a spreadsheet file containing a simple illustration of baseball statistics and is discussed in the integration section of Chapter 8.

TEXT-LET.WPS is a word-processed file containing the same text that users enter and save as **LETTER.WPS** in the introductory exercise on word processing in Chapter 5. The file is placed on the data disk for users who are experienced with computers and do not need to enter the text of the letter themselves.

Index